A SPY ON THE BUS:

Memoir of a Company Rat

A Spy on the Bus: Memoir of a Company Rat
Margean Gladysz

© 2008 Margean Gladysz

Arbutus Press
Traverse City, Michigan
info@arbutuspress.com
www.Arbutuspress.com

LIBRARY OF CONGRESS CATALOGING–IN-PUBLICATION DATA

Gladysz, Margean.
 A spy on the bus : memoir of a company rat/ Margean Gladysz.
  p. cm.
 Includes bibliographic references.
  ISBN 978-1-933926-07-0
 1. Gladysz, Margean. 2. Transportation--United States--Biography. 3. Greyhound
  Corporation--History. 4. Business intelligence--United States--History. I Title.

HE151.5G53G53 2008
388.3'22092--dc22
[B]

                    2008001057

First Edition: May 2008

ISBN 978-1-933926-07-0

Printed in the United States of America

Contents

Acknowledgments

Overall, I must thank the patrons at the Kalamazoo Public Library from whom I learned that you can never have enough original source material—that someone, sometime, somewhere needs it! There is little available about the early days of the bus industry and nothing about the inspection function.

If my mother, Dorothy Worst, had not walked the half-mile to the mailbox and then saved all my letters, this book would not have been possible. I can never thank her and my father, John Worst, enough for the support they gave during my years on the road. They sent money, coats, prescriptions, cookies and letters that told me that home was truly where my heart was.

Chiefly responsible for this book, however, is Marsha Meyer to whom one Sunday I related the tale of unearthing these letters about my unusual youthful occupation. She told me they should be published. On the answering machine when I got home was her directive to call Michael Steinberg, professor at Michigan State University and editor of "Fourth Genre: Explorations in Non-Fiction." He told me not to procrastinate. Without their professional encouragement I would never have pursued this project.

Collecting themselves after learning about my "past," John Lohrstorfer and James Jasiak helped me resolve the problems of names and money.

Jacquie Heidamos, Carolyn Martin and Catherine Larson helped greatly with editorial eyes, suggestions, and comments.

Best of all, great friend Fred Peppel, who always suspected I had a "past", helped me with set-up concerns and provided subtle nagging. He was the last reader of the manuscript. I can never thank him enough.

I must thank former bus driver authors who helped me in my preparation to write and with publishing suggestions. Robert Beard gave much encouragement and laid out "homework" in the form of books written by pioneers in the field of bus transportation. Thus I was able to place my experiences within those of Russel A. Byrd, John W. Adams, Jim Lehrer, Howard Suttle and Bob's own book. John W. Adams was most generous with his advice and told me that the most fun would be in the writing. He was right. Thomas Jones of the Motor Bus Society was also helpful.

Most of all, heartfelt appreciation to Susan Bays and all those at Arbutus Press who brought the manuscript to life.

Of course, without my husband Edward's support (and listening ear when I would call him in to relate an adventure I was reliving again), I could never have tackled the project. He put up with late meals, skimpy meals, and meals out as these pages were produced. Now our two children, John and Margean Jr., will understand why we traveled the back roads so much

Dedication

To the bus drivers (and their successors) who drove their mechanical steeds with such *joie de vivre* and delivered me to my myriad destinations along the road of life.

Margean Worst 1942 on the farm

The Road Out There

It was 1946, I was 18, a college graduate, and about to become a spy. I was going to "hit the road". But what was it like—this road—when I had hardly been out of Kalamazoo?

When World War II ended in September of 1945, life started again in the country. No more rationing of automobiles, tires, coffee, meat and sugar. Companies ratcheted up to supply new products and replace those worn out. Along with booming business came major strikes—1946 was the high point of work stoppages—in the railroad, shipping and coal industries. Concern about Communist influence in unions engaged the country.

By 1947 the average family made $2,589 a year, with 81% making less than $3,000. Lawyers made an average of $7,437 and physicians, $10,500. The average one-family house cost $3,292 to build, exclusive of land; $1,198 would buy a Ford two-door sedan—which you would fill with 21 cents a gallon gasoline. Whiskey was $3.98 a fifth, Coca-Cola and Pepsi-Cola were 5 cents a bottle. Razor blades were 25 cents a dozen and cigarettes were $1.34 a carton. There were no birth control pills.

An overnight room at the Y was 75 cents. A room in a good hotel cost about $2.00. Most did not have a bathroom—you went down the hall for shared tub and toilet facilities. Rooms did have a small washbowl, raising suspicion that it had been used as a urinal! One was lucky to have a ceiling fan: usually opening a window and the transom over the door for cross-ventilation got you natural air conditioning. There was no radio in the room: there was no TV yet.

In 1946 there were 3,316,538 miles of road in the country—80% unpaved! Sometimes only one lane was paved and a car could drive on that lane until meeting an oncoming car when one would have to take to the dirt. There were some brick paved roads. Most often, paved roads ended at the city limits. There were no Interstates.

Downtown was the hub of activity: there were no suburbs, no shopping malls, no motels. There were tourist cabins here and there, but most travelers stayed in hotels or tourist homes.

In rural areas, many families still did not have cars and it was not unusual to see wagons on the road and hitching posts in villages.

But all this was shortly to change.

I Prepare For The Road

My first road was Worst Road, the mile-long dirt stretch between 33rd and 35th south of Galesburg in Kalamazoo County. Locally it stayed "Worst Road" long after the county named it "East M Avenue".

We had moved from Kalamazoo to the farm on the south side of that road in 1932. During those Depression times, my dad, John Worst, worked 6-hour shifts at Kalamazoo's Sutherland Paper Company which gave him time to deal with the farm. Eventually, he would be night superintendent at their East-side mill. My mother, Dorothy Weber Worst, a city girl, fell in love with country life and soon could milk a cow, plant a garden, and deal with chickens and pigs—as well as with myself and my brother Gordon.

I remember relatives visiting, kittens in the haymow, the outhouse, kerosene lamps, neighbors stopping, chores, hired men, picking potatoes, thrashers, mice in the corn shocks—all the things that made up life in the country during the '30s. The world came to us through the Kalamazoo Gazette, farming magazines, Liberty, Life, The Saturday Evening Post, and a battery radio. Finally, in 1937, electricity arrived and technology started to change our lives – a milking machine for one thing, a refrigerator for another.

Lessons were learned: self-reliance, responsibility, observation of the natural world, and family as the bedrock of life. My parents lived and taught these well.

My second road was down 33rd to where it meets Kilgore and where Comstock Fractional #1, the one-room, red brick schoolhouse built in 1868, still stands. It lacks the two outhouses and the long shed that could hold horses that it had then, but it does have electricity now. If you Google "kpl margean comstock" and open the 1933 citation you can find me in the front row wearing an apron. I had started Kindergarten the day after my fifth birthday on February 28, 1933. That mile-long dirt road was well worth walking: true to all the things said about one-room schools, its teachers gave me wonderful basic background and graduated me when I was eleven.

My third road was 35th, where, long before school buses, two-and-a-half miles of walking down Schram's Hill and across the Kalamazoo River, brought me to Galesburg High School. Here were "city kids" who didn't have to go home to do chores: here were afternoon football games because there were no lighted fields then: here were penny-a-spoonful suppers that brought city and country together. Along the side of the assembly room that seated all the students, a row of bookcases held books and encyclopedias that were my first exposure to lots of reading material and my favorite reading was about other countries. The teachers mentored and monitored us through 1939-1943 and when the eighteen of us graduated, all the boys went off to war and most of the girls went off to work or marriage. I was fifteen and I was going off to college.

US 12 went through Galesburg on its way to Kalamazoo and was my road for the next three years. Western Michigan College of Education had gone on a year round schedule and filled its dormitories with V-12 and V-5 marines and sailors so I lived at home and rode the Great Lakes Greyhound Lines through those years.

While I concentrated in history, political science, and social studies, my science requirement was filled by geography courses which became my favorite classes. I could visualize land, its features, its climates, and how these shaped the people that lived on it—my upbringing gave me background and empathy. This became the area that I wanted to specialize in. Dr. William Berry, head of the Geography Department, suggested the University of Chicago's Geography Department and contacted them for me. Indeed, they would accept me, but all scholarships and fellowships were going to returning veterans.

So this eighteen-year-old was going to have to take time to earn money for Graduate School. My thoughts turned to the Great Lakes Greyhound buses I had ridden for the past three years. I sent a letter requesting employment to its Inspection Department and was accepted. Although privately worrying, my parents never conveyed this to me—I was "sensible".

My Saga Begins

What was this hush-hush spying business I was about to begin? It promised travel, adventure and money to go on to graduate school—this job as Company Inspector or Company Spy with the Great Lakes Greyhound Company. It would be a dream job for a young woman when the average teacher's salary was $1,277.00 a year.

Just 22 years old in 1946, the bus industry had "officially" started in Hibbing, Minnesota, hauling iron miners. It swiftly grew, and early on Greyhound and Trailways became recognized travel names. Smaller companies became objects of takeover, merger, and rivalry.

Because this was long before everyone had a car, buses could be flagged down at roadside and corners, and people paid cash to ride. Drivers pocketing this cash and not issuing a cash-fare ticket was a concern of the bus companies. Another concern was road safety and handling of expensive equipment. To deal with these issues, companies hired or maintained personnel to "check" on honesty, safety, and equipment handling. This I was about to learn how to do.

So off to Detroit I went, straight from the farm near Galesburg, Michigan, to the big city. New people, new places, twenty-hour workdays, report writing, and homesickness were conveyed to my farm parents in almost daily letters.

It took almost four years to get the sand out of my shoes and return to a "normal" life. Eventually I married, had two children, received an MLS and became a professional librarian, but I never forgot what America looked like before there were Interstates, when roads were unpaved, when the population was only 139,928,000, and when buses picked up and left off travelers at the crossroads or in front of their homes.

In September of 2003, I was digging in my trunk and unearthed the forms, inspection training materials, report copies, and other memorabilia I had put there over 53 years before. Best of all, there was the thick notebook holding the typed copies of the hundreds of letters I had sent home. Deeply detailed, these kept my farm parents abreast of my life on the road—the work, the people, my adventures, and the country—in short, the bus transportation field, the inspection function, and the social conditions of the post-war era.

July 2, 1946
To John Prater
2503 David Stott Building
Detroit, Michigan

Dear Sir:

Having graduated and having spent a restful
vacation, I am now awaiting a call to begin
work. I am sending this reminder in order that
I may make definite arrangements in regards to
living space.

If a vacancy hasn't presented itself but is
still pending, might I suggest that it would be
timesaving if I were trained and ready to step
into the position the moment that a vacancy
occurred?

Very truly yours,

Margean Worst

14

July 8, 1946
To Margean Worst
From John Prater

Dear Miss Worst:

This will acknowledge receipt of your letter of July 2, concerning employment with this company. A vacancy does exist in this department and at such time as you are available for work in Detroit, I shall be ready to complete the necessary details for your employment. If your arrangements are completed by then, you may begin work on July 16, 1946.

Very truly yours,

John E. Prater
Great Lakes Greyhound Company

1946

I Begin

My Periods Stop

I Faint

I Move

My Roommate is a Prostitute

The Beginning of the
Drinking Affair

I Meet the President

July 15, 1946
From YWCA, Detroit, Michigan

Dear Ones: What a day: if I can only remember all that I'm supposed to remember. What with worrying about rooms, trying to read memoranda and the like, I nearly went crazy!

As you know, I've got my permanent room. Could anything be better than room and board with someone with whom I work and only twelve minutes from work? I'll tell you about her: she's evidently been married twice or else her alias is Mrs. Week, because they call her both Mrs. Bork and Mrs. Week. Ella has a three-year-old daughter, Katy. Her husband at one time was a cop, then an inspector, and is now working for the gas company. He goes to work at 7:30 and I can ride down with him when I wish. She is enthusiastic about the work: in fact, she doesn't think it work! No one in the office does.

Tomorrow first thing, I have my physical, then to the office to study some more (and get paid for it), then at 3:00 we're going to Bay City on a special assignment. On said run, the driver has been making out cash fare tickets for less distance than actually traveled and pocketing the difference. So, Mr. Prater has put four of us on checking for this. On the way back, we'll check an extra man [a driver working the "extra board", available for "second sections" when there were too many passengers for the first bus, or to fill in for an ill or vacationing regular driver, or to pull non-bid assignments].

All told, my day's pay starts at the doctor about 8:00 and finishes at 9:00, twelve hours. With the $8 I made today, that makes $20 for two day's "work". Not quite understanding it myself, I'll try to explain the pay system. We get $8 for each day we "work", regardless of whether we spend it in the office, making out reports, making out our itinerary, or on the road; and everyone pads that time generously to try to make a 12-hour day out of it. We buy tickets out of our own money and get paid back the next payday: thus, always running two weeks behind in road expenses. Ella says that everyone in the office is perpetually broke, borrowing from the "kitty" to tide over until payday. The office is very generous in this, asking whether you need money: Ella came in this morning with 40 cents and left with $5; Thurston Allen came in broke and left with $40. We need, said Mr. Prater, about $150 loose money for each two-week period: that's why I need all that money. Lord only knows how this will resolve itself and when I'll be running at a profit. Any expenses connected with the job—telegrams, reservations, taxis, phone calls, mail, meals, hotel rooms, anything—go on our "swindle sheet"; that is, "anything within reason" quoting the manual. The expense account goes into effect only when we're out of Detroit.

More about the people with whom I work.   Mrs. King, the office secretary, is an old hag (say the others) who thinks inspectors are dirt: she has charge of keeping all run [trip and driver] information current and runs the office routine. The other secretary is a singer, beautiful, and hates single girls: she is to be married in October, likes to have the male inspectors notice and make over her, but asks Mr. Prater to put up bulletins against anyone putting their arm around her (you know the type). Consequently, she makes cutting remarks about Miss McKay, the other single inspector, and, I'm warned, will start on me pronto. She has charge of writing up our "quick draft" reports, which then go to the Main Office. More Ella: she loves to sew, makes lots of her clothes, and has a charge account at Kerns, a big department store; she worked before for Mr. Jakeway, didn't like him at all, thinks there's no one like our boss, an ex-FBI man. They all say the same thing, worship the ground he walks on, and say that he spoils one for ever working for anyone else—he's so fair, generous, kind-hearted, etc.—the whole force has a bad case of hero-worship. Miss McKay: a girl of 21 who belongs to the Baptist Church, loves her job, lives about two blocks from Mrs. Bork and goes with....Ted Frye: a dapper young man with philosophical reading tastes and four aliases. Next is Thurston Allen: an unmarried young man who spent all afternoon figuring out a five-day assignment only to have it go up in smoke when he was assigned with us to this Bay City special report assignment. To date, this is all I know of our big, happy family.

I don't see how they get any work done in the office what with gossip, trade talk (which at the moment has me completely in the dark), trips to the "john" (which I now know means toilet), trips to get coffee, the boss coming in to chat, and mean looks from Mrs. King. By the way, Mr. Prater has told Ella my age...probably why she's taking such a motherly attitude towards me. More Ella—she's about 30, 5'8", auburn hair, built like a bean pole, laughs all the time, talks a mile-a-minute, has a swell sense of humor, and had me out with her on company time shopping for a gold kid belt.

Now, as to what my work consists of! My God! I'll never be able to remember everything. Forms for this; forms for that; forms for this company; forms for that company; forms for terminals; forms for drivers and other personnel; daily report forms; daily work-schedule forms; quick-freeze forms. Fares, cash fares, children, deadheads (*a non-driving driver riding on the bus*), employees—all to be kept track of; driver appearance and courtesy; operation of vehicle; safety, traffic, and rule violations; and so much else that there's no use putting it down. We cover Capital Greyhound,

Central Greyhound, Flint City Lines, Greyhound Detroit Suburban, Canadian Western, Great Lakes Greyhound and Valley Greyhound. This takes in all of Michigan, Ohio, Indiana, part of Illinois, Canada around the lakes, and Louisville, Kentucky, to Washington D.C. We are assigned drivers, and from this we map and route our itinerary. Our daily work schedule contains what we have done for that day, what we expect to do the next and where we may be reached. Then comes the fun: after making out this itinerary, it's usually our luck that the driver we're to check won't be on and our work's in vain. Over all of us hangs the awful fate of becoming "known" or being "turned up": we must feel like an ordinary passenger. So much for the business end.

It gives me a headache to even write about it. Still I'll make out. Everyone seems to have taken a liking to me and is helpful. They all love their work so I don't see why I can't do it and love it too. There is just so much to learn that right now I feel swamped. Don't worry. The room is settled. Ella will help me move. I'm working. It's 8:00 so must take a shower, do my exercises and go to bed. Love, Margean

---

July 16, 1946
From YWCA, Detroit, Michigan

Dear Ones: This morning I woke up at 5:00 wide-awake. It's now 6:45 and I'm waiting for the "Y" Coffee Shop to open. I've been studying my map to locate West Grand Boulevard where I must go for my physical. Lord knows how I shall get back. This morning I'm wearing my gray dress with blue accessories.

Ella said that our tickets today may be $6, Thursday, probably $14. The Western Union main office is just three blocks from work and I hope the money you're sending gets there soon.

More on work: Organized the first of the year, the aim of the office, never achieved, is to check each of its thousand-odd drivers four times a year. The first three months they hit about 50%, this last three months less because of all the special assignments. Ella rarely takes overnight runs: she has her daughter and husband to feed.

Now 8:20 at the West Detroit Clinic. Couldn't find the bus to take, so took a cab, 75 cents. I passed the physical: eyesight poor; blood pressure 112 (what does that mean?); a blood test and lots more. Back to town on a trolley.

20

At the office from 10:30 till 1:00 studying and learning from Ella: from 3:00 until 9:00 on the road; from 9:00 till 11:00 in my room writing reports. Ella left at 10:00 and I did one report all by myself; we will check and compare in the morning. A 14½-hour day, counting from the clinic until finishing reports!

As I said yesterday, there's so much to learn that I'm swamped, but things are gradually shifting into focus. Ella was very, very, very pleased with my work today. My watch isn't accurate or large enough and I really need a luminous dial. I will be getting a book of synonyms. Just try to think of half-a-dozen words that mean courteous, clean, smooth and other things that have so many variants of meaning and feeling.

Now if I can remember all the day's gossip. There are eight inspectors, and I've met them all with today's Mr. Cross and Mr. VanderWhy. All of us, except Cross, are under 30 and college grads except VanderWhy who is studying Police Administration at Michigan State. Mr. Cross and Ella are holdovers from Mr. Jakeway, who formerly ran the inspectors and was let go about the first of this year. There's a bulletin to the effect that anyone associating with him is to turn in a resignation.

You don't know the debate that went on about hiring me, an 18-year-old, and I've a sneaking suspicion that that is why I'm going to live at Ella's. Over and over I hear what a swell fellow Mr. Prater is. If I can only live up to the big hopes that Ella says he has for me.

Do you know, or can you guess, what my room and board will be? $7.00 a week! Isn't that marvelous for a separate room and meals when I'm home? Ella is simply marvelous! Her husband is a big six footer weighing a mere 280 lbs. Whenever you come over bring some beef or a chicken for my new family.

There was much more, but I'm so tired I can hardly see. Tomorrow it's more study and a run to Flint again. There are four of us on one run for four days to check cash fares. That means work from 10:00 a.m. (at office, on road, and on reports) till 11:00 p.m. at least. Letters will be short and sketchy, especially after filling out six report forms as I've just done. I'm dead! Love, Margean

———————

July 17, 1946
From YWCA, Detroit, Michigan

Dear Ones: Worked 9 hours today. Didn't go to Flint: McKay and Allen beat us and there was no double [*same as "second section", an additional bus when there are too many passengers for the first bus*]. Back

21

to the office and inside of half an hour we were out checking suburbans [*bus service to nearby suburbs*]: what a beating. We rode the Wyandotte Division from Gratiot Avenue to Ecorse. I won't attempt to put down all that went into the report, but it was a harrowing experience for which we "panned" the driver to the limit. The bus back was much better.

I've gone through everything in the office except the "blueprints" which show the location of every driver every minute of his time. From these we ascertain whom we are going to catch. Tomorrow morning I'm to make out an itinerary for Ella and myself. I want to do more interurbans [*bus service between cities*], as that will become my chief duty: I intensely dislike suburban work—the form is <u>hellish</u>!

Thanks so much, I received the money this morning. It came last night, but I forgot to check the desk when I came in with Ella. I had no trouble getting it cashed, and it reposes securely in my bra and girdle. It makes me feel easier. Payday falls on the 5th and 20th, so everyone is broke right now sticking around Detroit doing suburbans, six inspections costing only 60 cents.

You should see the information we have on drivers. Almost all of my old Kalamazoo to Detroit drivers are up for re-inspections. (That means that if a driver is inspected and rather serious violations are turned up, he is automatically re-inspected within 30 days: in the event that this inspection reveals the same fault, another inspection is given, after which severe disciplinary action is taken).

We have one driver on the Jackson to Kalamazoo run that I know. Every inspector, male and female, is actually afraid to ride with him. Because of these automatic re-inspections, he was suspended for three months, but I saw him on extra board just two weeks ago. Mentioning this to Ella, she surmised that he must have pull somewhere because his three months aren't up yet.

They throw the book at just about every driver I know. Having ridden with them for three years, I may be prejudiced in their favor. Saw an old copy of "Greyhound News" today, and who should stare out at me but one of my old drivers. Thinking back it would be hard to find anything to "throw at him", but that was before I knew about cash fares and issuing receipts and other stuff.

I move Sunday to Ella's and she is coming after me. Had some good meals today, but I'm just not hungry, rather from nervous strain or heat, I don't know. Well, I'm tired, but must press, wash out things, take a bath and do exercises. By 9:05 I should be in bed. Love, Margean

—·—

July 18, 1946
From YWCA, Detroit, Michigan

Dear Ones: Here it is 12:30 a.m. and I've just finished my reports. I put in fourteen hours. Today we were told that a new pay policy went into effect the 15th. We are now paid a flat rate of $1 an hour, plus tickets and an out-of-town per diem of $7. Figuring by that, I've already made nearly $50 this week.

I was over to Ella's for a delicious liver and bacon dinner today. Her little girl is at the stage where she keeps asking the same questions. Ella is a college grad who married at 25 and is now 30. Her husband is a huge man and does he eat! This shaded brick duplex should be cool. My room, tastefully furnished with twin bed, bookcase, dresser, table and rocker, is cozy. I believe this will work out fine. As I don't go to work until 3:00 tomorrow, I'll move one bag of clothing.

I've gotten my previous reports back from JP (John Prater, boss, that is). Two misspelled words! Very little checked wrong, just need fuller explanations. By the way, I made a special report on the Comstock congestion on the early morning run into Kalamazoo which results from the ticket agent's not opening when the drugstore does: the report is going through.

The men I'm working with are certainly a nice bunch. While in the office today, Allen, who is usually given the special assignments, gave me pointers on out-of-town travel and hotels. Ella says that I need never be afraid to inspect out with Frye, Cross, Allen, or any other for that matter. In fact, I'll have to.

By the way, before I can work any Canadian runs, I must have my birth certificate. Please send it.

It is 12:50 a.m.: I'm dead! This is a horrible scribble, but after all those reports in good penmanship, my fingers can hardly guide a pen. My first paycheck ought to be well over $100 and I shall be able to send back much of what I've borrowed. Love, Margean

---

July 20, 1946
From YWCA, Detroit, Michigan

Dear Ones: Just a line while I'm waiting for Ella to come and move my belongings. That is, she's coming if she doesn't have to sing at two weddings this morning. A college-trained contralto, she sings in Church and at weddings.

I'm going to Flint by myself today just to see what I can do. Then tonight, maybe, I'll do a suburban or two.

Yesterday we started out at 3:00 p.m. to do six Mt. Clemens and Birmingham suburbans. I can see right now that my daily capacity will be three or four: six I cannot keep separated in my mind. The last ride, from Royal Oak to Detroit, was terrible, a "cowboy"! Everything in the book he did wrong, weaving, crowding, cutting in, running lights. His multitude of sins caused me to spend 45 minutes writing him up.

Naturally I'm making plans on the how and when we can see each other. Anything you bring over in the line of meat and vegetables for us would be nice. We'll eat at Greenfields, a cafeteria, and absolutely the best place in Detroit to eat. What good stuff! What large helpings! What tasteful presentation!

I'm losing weight and my dresses are hanging. This isn't because I'm not eating but because I'm not getting enough sleep. I have been going to bed so late and then waking up at 6:00 unable to go back to sleep. One day I got 3½ hours, another 4, and last night the longest, 6 hours. I'm not tired though.

I hope everything is fine at home. I really miss the country, although I can't say that I'm really homesick for I'm too busy. I look forward to letters from you, especially one containing my birth certificate. Love, Margean

—•—

July 20, 1946
From Detroit, Michigan

Dear Ones: Two letters in one day is really too much, but I might as well relate my adventures.

After doing some work in the office, I caught my bus, alone, to Flint. I got along just swell with my "audit" (passenger count) and everything went fine. You should have seen me. We take our notes on easy-to-hide, little 2x3" spiral-bound notebooks and use pencils about 1¼ inch long. Anyway, I put this notebook in my white rain-hat on my lap, along with my raincoat, pocketbook, and a paper-bag filled with two small books, raincoat belt, map, schedule and gloves, and wrote my notes with my hand in the hat. There's a catch to it: I have to immediately decipher the notes after leaving the bus.

If I didn't look like an average passenger, I'll eat my hat. It was 98. There I was, carrying coat, pocketbook, bag and hat, sweat on my face, my hair down, chewing gum, and grumbling with everyone else. I waited in line for that 11:15 bus from 11:00 until 11:57, and finally got on the third section: my aching feet!

Coming home showed my good pre-work, bus-waiting tactics. There was a mob of us at the Flint terminal with everyone pushing to beat the dickens. When the driver pulled in, he stopped exactly in front of me. Now the next is mean and I'm ashamed to tell you: there were about five inches between me and the door, and this woman next to me literally fell into that five inches trying to beat me in. She "fell" in sideways, so I just took my elbow and gave a good, sharp, hard shove and back she went. The driver had seen her and wouldn't load her at all. Three people getting on the bus congratulated me on "getting the situation under control." I found it was easier to make this run alone, I could concentrate on all the things I had learned.

I believe I'll go north. I don't have it made out yet, but I think I'll go some morning to Flint and layover [*wait time between bus rides*] for the next Bay City bus. Stop there for the day and write reports; then the next day leave Bay City at 1:34 a.m., arrive at Mackinaw City at 7:00, stop over for the day and turn back. Something like this would give me light runs, practice and over-night pay.

Got your letter: you capitalists! And here I am in the hole for three months with what I've borrowed and a watch and prescription sunglasses to buy. This long trip will make a nice indentation. How about insurance, Dad? See what you can get for me and take the money out of our joint account (when we get it). With some of the drivers like the one last night, I'll need it. Love, Margean

—·—

July 21, 1946
From Detroit, Michigan

Dear Ones: Well, I've moved and everything is pressed and put away. Although meat is terribly scarce and terribly high, we had a great company dinner with Ella, her husband, her brother, Katy, myself, and co-worker Mary McKay. It's now 8:00 and they've gone on a picnic. I was too tired, and, besides, this is the first time all week I've been able to relax and listen to a radio.

It's always cool here with big shade trees all along the street. It's a good section of town, only twelve minutes to work by bus or twenty-eight by trolley. Just around the corner are stores, cleaning establishments, a movie theater and a lot of general shops; you can find anything you want.

When my birth certificate gets here, I've got only Windsor and Pontiac suburbans to train on. Probably by next Thursday I'll be my own boss. Starting tomorrow there's a new system inaugurated in the office: instead of having drivers assigned to us, we pick the ones we want, go after them, and if we don't get them, they go back into the unassigned section. This way it's easier to plan an itinerary: it's also much easier for me to stay off suburbans.

The way to make the real money is to get out of town and stay out: you make at least $15 a day that way. The trouble with everyone, except Mr. Cross, is that they don't keep enough money on hand so that they can go out and stay one to two weeks: they run out the first week and have to stick in town doing suburbans until payday. I hate suburbans, although they're really easier except for the forms. I'm going to try to keep $100-$150 running money for each two-week period.

The inspectors, collectively eight, draw about $2500 a month and the company figures that each report costs $10. That's a lot of money and a lot of responsibility resting upon an inspector's shoulders.

I hope to God I turn out well: if will to work makes competency, someday I ought to be a "crackerjack". I know right now it's the best thing for my personality that I could ever have done: it will develop self-reliance and self-assurance, neither of which I now have. I can't tell you how much I like the people I'm working with. They all have so much poise coming from being sure of themselves and their ability to handle a situation. I only have pseudo-poise from keeping my mouth shut, trying to appear sophisticated and not asking questions about everyday big city occurrences of which I am so appallingly ignorant. If I just open my mouth one knows I've never been around. I haven't a line of free and easy chatter or a snappy comeback. The office atmosphere is one of staccato wit, most of which passes over my head. I never was a good mixer and I'm more acutely aware of that than ever, now. What rambling! Still it's true, I feel out of place. But the work and the way it's organized are fascinating.

How about more letters, more news. Remember anything is news to me: even the most trivial thing, like the humming bird, calls up remembrances of a home that meant, and means, so much to me. Love, Margean

July 27, 1946
From Detroit, Michigan

Dear Ones: Arrived back last night safe and sound at 1:05 a.m. and took a taxi home ($1.15). I'm writing this in the office while Mrs. King is out to lunch, then I'm leaving for Toledo. Will probably make the same trip tomorrow afternoon. Good practice.

My room and board is settled. It's $10 a week; this is much to my liking since when I'm home I won't have to go out. Ella said that I was going to get bawled out at the office for working too much: it seems that JP doesn't want us to work over eight hours a day which adds up to six hours riding and two writing reports. Suits me.

Here I am in Toledo after a crowded ride, 97 total, and hot. Ella told me that the Lafayette Restaurant was the best, so here I sit with honeydew melon and coffee. Guess what I saw! The most beautiful four-team of huge Clydesdale horses drawing a beer wagon. Love, Margean

———

July 28, 1946
From Toledo, Ohio

Dear Ones: It's 3:15 p.m. and I have a layover until 5:00. I love layovers! We get paid for them and they give time to write reports.

You'd like the country between Detroit and Toledo. It was flat Great Lake bottom at one time, black and dark brown soil with not a stone. The crops are much better than at home, the corn is much higher, some tasseled out. They are combining clover and alfalfa for seed. I saw a twenty-acre field of cabbage.

Come over Sunday early and in the afternoon, Dad, we'll go to something you've always wanted to see, a theater that has all newsreels. Love, Margean

———

July 29, 1946
From Detroit, Michigan

Dear Ones: I went to Port Huron today and will again tomorrow. I'll stay about four days inspecting early morning runs to Detroit and the ones to Port Austin. It is a beautiful ride along the lake shore most of the way with lots of canals. Corn up there is simply marvelous! They're cutting wheat and oats with binders.

Tomorrow I'm getting my hair cut for economy of time and effort, so I'll look different when I see you Sunday. Love, Margean

----·----

July 30, 1946
From Hotel Harrington, Port Huron, Michigan

Dear Ones: Well, here I am! The shorn lamb. How does the photo look? He didn't cut any off in back, but all the rest is about two inches long.

I borrowed a "Monkey-Ward" catalog from the Montgomery-Ward store to "read" this evening. Love, Margean

----·----

July 31, 1946
From Port Austin, Michigan

Dear Ones: I'm here at Port Austin with a three-hour layover and no paper so I've cut the back leaves out of my book.

I could swear! I'm going to have the same driver back: in fact, he ran me out of the only hotel in town. Now I can't make out my reports or do anything, and it looks as if I'll have to think of a good excuse for going back with him because I'll probably be the only one leaving from this Podunk. As I said, I could swear, not only for the above reason, but also for making me write this standing up in the Post Office!

He's awful: I was never so shaken in my life. Most of the road is unpaved and we went down it in a cloud of dust (like some of our neighbors) at about 55 mph. To think I have to go through three more hours of that on the way back! He's such a good-looking redhead at that, but does he ever loiter at stops.

This little burg, which is right on the lake, has one restaurant at which I had dinner and started to do reports. Who should walk in but that driver! Then I went to the hotel where I got my audit put together, and who should walk in? One guess! So that's why I'm leaning over this post office desk, standing up, and writing!

After I get my reports written and count my layover time, I will have made $20 today. If it hadn't been for those run schedules not being right in the office, I wouldn't be in this mess—but $20 for two reports on the same man! It worries me about going back; my brain is doing somersaults trying to think of an excuse because I know I'll be the only through passenger. Damn!

My entire ride was along the beautiful lakeshore. But what heart-breaking country for farmers—just gravel, stones, sand, hills, and gullies—and still cold up here. Corn is about 15 inches high, they're thrashing rye, and they're "doodling" their second cutting. It's worse than around Cadillac.

You should see me today: gym-suit and sweater—I certainly don't look like what I am. Really like my haircut. Can hardly wait to see you. I ought to have my first pay check by then, but don't expect any payback until my second check.

The Harrington Hotel where I'm staying is ancient but the best in town. Two dollars without bath, my room has one of those 1880 marble washbowls. Nice. Port Huron looks like Cadillac. Port Huron smells of fish! Tonight I'm going to have a fish dinner. Love, Margean

—◦—

August 1, 1946
From Detroit, Michigan

Dear Ones: I carried paper along today so I wouldn't be caught again—besides, there are no more end leaves in my book. At 9:20 I started out for work, the bus being due at 9:35. There were two sections, so I took the second (as we have orders to do because they are always driven by hard-to-get extra men), and didn't leave till 10:00, arriving in Detroit at 11:35. Right now I'm in the library where I wrote my reports, having a layover till 3:30. Then back to good old Port Huron where tomorrow's work involves 12 hours.

About coming home yesterday. He didn't say a thing, just looked funny when I got on. When he picked up some people, I'd swear he told the man to sit across the aisle from me because the man looked around at me, then came back and sat right beside me. I did what Ella had told me to do—I moved right behind the driver where he couldn't see a thing I was doing. I looked innocent enough: I was cold and all hunched up in my seat with my arms folded, looking sleepy and bored, and writing my notes inside my sleeve. It took me a while to decipher those notes, but my peace of mind was worth it.

Because I was the only one on at Port Austin, I asked for protection [*that the report not be used because it would identify me*] on the report back. On the morning run there was a burly inspector-looking fellow who sat behind me, so that report is going through. It will be a week before the driver is called in and by that time he will have forgotten me, I hope.

After mailing the letter yesterday, I looked around the only General Store in Port Austin, a combination of Galesburg's Grants', a grocery and a meat market. I was looking through the dress section, all marked over $10, when my eye caught a $4.89 tag. It was navy blue with military buttons, white collar, and a military cape lined with red—my size. What could be wrong with it to be marked so low? Why was it with the expensive dresses? I checked it over—zipper, bound seams, all buttons accounted for—my size! I tried it on. I wanted it. The manager was called: there is a mistake, it should be $14.89 but, to appease me, I get it for the $4.89 plus tax. All of which made me feel wonderful and the manager sad I suppose. Anyway, it was too good to resist and I had made enough in layover pay to buy it.

It is 2:00 and I have an hour and a half before my bus leaves. I hate Detroit: it's so big, so smelly and so full of people. Love, Margean

---

August 2, 1946
From Hotel Harrington, Port Huron, Michigan

Dear Ones: I'm in the Medea Hotel where the bus loads, across from the Mt. Clemens bus station. It stinks of rotten eggs in here: there's a good reason, the hotel is noted for its sulfur mineral baths. The hotel is full of bathers and they seem to accept me in their number as they keep talking to me and keep me from concentrating.

I have a suggestion to make at the office. I believe it would save time spent in the office and insure "catching" more men if we inspectors were provided with carbons of the interurban run-bid sheets. We wouldn't have to keep running to the office to check where our men would be on a certain day and at a certain time. It will be worth suggesting.

Went to a show last night after a dinner of fried perch, potatoes, baked beans, Scotch broth and coffee. What an impressive list of calories for 65 cents!

I can't tell you how much the tension has let up since talking to JP: I really sleep now and have an appetite. Real perfection isn't our goal—just human powers of observation. Besides making rides more enjoyable, I find I do a better job with much less effort. Already, after just two weeks, I feel like a veteran. After getting back from home, I'm going to Washington and points south just for the heck of it—I think, really, to prove I can do it.

My bus is due in 12 minutes and from here, I'll be able to see its number and the driver to know whether I've had him before. If I have, I don't need to show my face: if I haven't, I'll be able to get the number while he's in the station, then pop out and ride back. Just like a soldier—or a spy —I've plotted my campaign.

Four-seventeen and back in Mt. Clemens from which I return to Port Huron if everything goes according to schedule. Those last two rides were awful with one having a 65 total, 15 cash fares and 10 children, the other with an 87 total, 7 cash fares and 8 children. I had little time to "relax." It's been 12½-hour days, without too much hard work and time to make out each report as I finished a ride. Carrying a detective story with me every trip, I'm on page 111 where they discovered the body, but haven't had time to read. All this suspense in my life made me hungry, so I bought a nickel bag of animal crackers. Love, Margean

---

August 7, 1946
From Windsor, Ontario, Canada

Dear Ones: With plenty of time to write, grab a bite and get my ticket, I'm in Windsor waiting for my coach to London where I shall stay for four or five days. Nice Canadian waitresses served me two chicken croquettes, mashed potatoes and hot beets for 25 cents.

As you can see, I got my check today, $180.90 before taxes, not bad for fourteen days' work: I can't get over how much it is! I went to the bank and turned it into Travelers Checks, the safest way to carry money in my business. Now I can carry it all on me and, if lost or stolen, I get my money back. Next payday I shall pay back some of the money I owe you.

Got back yesterday without catching a single man that I went after. In fact I got the Kalamazoo man again who drove me to Jackson last week when I was home. He said, "Did you have a good time in Detroit?" Drivers really remember. From Grand Rapids to Lansing I had a former Kalamazoo man, and from Lansing to Detroit I had a former Kalamazoo extra man. Three very ordinary rides, but the first guy was impressed by the coincidence. Why do such things happen to me? We need those carbon run-bid sheets. Love, Margean

---

August 8, 1946
From Hotel Belevedere, London, Ontario, Canada

Dear Ones: Gee, I hate to start out today. I leave here at 12:20 p.m., arrive in Toronto at 4:00, layover until 9:55, and arrive back in London at 1:30 a.m. That means 13 hours working and about 1½ hours of writing reports. On these run-bids you really catch your drivers. I got here last night at 10:00 but, after writing reports and doing exercises, it was 11:45 before I got to bed. Then I would wake up at 7:30.

Beautiful corn on the way here from Windsor: every farm has at least 10 acres—tall, clean, just starting to tassel out. All I saw were horses, very little machinery and grains were thrashed not combined. Level land, like that to Toledo, rich soil, lush crops: it certainly is a nice place to live. What wonders one could do here with our machinery.

London is an old city on the order of Cadillac, with about 80,000 people. All in all, it seems a pretty slow place, but they're building a store across the street from my window and were hard at work at 7:30. This morning I got a $2 bill as part of my change for a $5, and my pocketbook abounds in strange coinage including both copper and silver nickels. They use daylight saving time, but the buses run on slow time so there's no need to change my watch.

I wonder what our mailman thinks of all these addresses. I must get a map to see where I've been, and where I'm at and where I will be in the future. Love, Margean

———

August 9, 1946
From Hotel Belevedere, London, Ontario, Canada

Dear Ones: I lived through my 15-hour day on three cups of black coffee at night. There was only one adventure. When I got off the bus, I asked the driver where the bus would load to go home. "At Gate 4," he said, "Are you going right back? I'll be looking for you."

"Well," thought I, "You certainly will not. I had enough of that in Port Austin." So when 8:00 came along, I wandered out to Gate 4 and two buses pull in. "I told you so," said I, as I get in line. But my hopes are blasted as the driver of the first coach says, "All London bound passengers take the second section." Back I trot. I have to take it because it's the last coach for the day. It's him: he takes my ticket and says "I saved the seat back of me for you: just push my bag over. You can keep me awake tonight." So yours

32

truly obliged and had a ringside seat on the worst case of loitering and then burning up the road yet observed. We were nearly hit twice and had an accident in Hamilton, all his fault. It was the first time he'd ever been inspected. Anyway I finished my reports at 3:00 a.m., fell into bed and woke at 9:00 fit and refreshed. Today to Sarnia and back by 8:00 tonight, so shall get plenty of sleep. Tomorrow to Toronto again, but to stay overnight, 15 hours was too much!

Leaving London and all the way to Toronto, the land is extremely hilly, making a beautiful ride, especially along the lake. The road most of the way was one curve and hill after another, much worse than up north. What with the road as it was, and only two lanes wide, and his excessive speed, I filled up one of my little brown books. He scared me half to death with his crowding traffic, overtaking on curves: and I nearly had heart failure twice when we had to cut back in awfully sharp to avoid hitting, first an army truck, and then a school bus. My report could mean severe action for they are terribly hard here on the Canadian side. Most of these Eastern Canadian Greyhound drivers never need inspection: they are the epitome of perfection, but when a bad report does come in, they're doubly severe. He was the politest and most courteous driver one could want however, and I played that for all it was worth.

You should have seen the shocked look on the hotel clerk's face when I walked in at 1:45 a.m. "Good morning," he said in a reproving tone. "Good Morning," said I and went merrily up the stairs.

Guess where I'm writing this—under the dryer getting a shampoo and set for 50 cents. I'm wearing my gym suit because Sarnia is a resort town and I am a tourist.

I'm reading *Darkness at Noon* by Arthur Koestler. It's about the Moscow purge trials of 1933, a really superlative story which you, Dad, will especially like. Love, Margean

---

August 11, 1946
From Detroit, Michigan

Dear Ones: Back in Detroit after a trying week away. I was stranded overnight in Sarnia—the dumbest thing for I read the schedule wrong. Could have kicked myself after checking through my schedule and finding that I could have gone to Chatham and then back to London. Just plain dumbness! Saturday to make up for it, I worked seventeen hours and today eight catching all new men.

In Windsor last night I had soup, Salisbury steak with lots of mushroom sauce, mashed potatoes, beets, rolls and pineapple pie for 40 cents!

From Windsor to London, I sat next to an interesting man from Winnipeg. In the flour-milling business, he had sold his monthly quota and was visiting relatives. I was able to chat and still keep track of the 109 total and 14 children!

Coming through customs, I was the only one whose baggage wasn't searched, and was I glad for my forms were hidden down under. I had a wonderful time in Canada. Everyone was so nice: they all thought I was on my "holidays" as they call a vacation. Soon I'm going to take the whole 8-hour run from Windsor to Toronto, instead of getting off in London, for I found that was the only way to get on the first bus instead of a second section.

I shall go into the office tomorrow, but shall not work out, will rest, need it—only 4½ hours sleep to catch a 6:45 a.m. bus this morning. Love, Margean

———

August 12, 1946
From Detroit, Michigan

Dear Ones: This morning I feel wonderful after nine hours of sleep and a big breakfast. About noon I am going to the office with Ella and expect to plan out work to keep me in town for a Friday office conference.

After paying you $25 and paying this week's board, I still have $80 in Travelers' Checks and $9 in small bills. I have no idea how much my next check will be, but hope to pay back some more. What I have gives me plenty of money to work on this week and part of next.

Did I get a lecture from Ann at the office today because I got two drivers twice! I sent notes in with both reports explaining the circumstances, but she will probably make some remark at the conference.

Tomorrow, Ella and I are going to Flint for a double check on a driver whose cash fares are suspect. Then Wednesday to Bay City and back to Flint: Thursday, round trip, Flint to Port Huron; Friday back here with just 15 minutes to get to the office conference. You know how long it took me to get that figured out with drivers that had never been inspected? Six hours! Six hours of sitting and using almost a whole scratch pad. Six hours of trying to concentrate while everybody and his brother tramped through the office.

Lots of office gossip, my first conference, and no notes in my personal folder about things I'd forgotten or left out of my reports. A pat on the back from JP for catching so many men that I'd gone after. I needed that: my morale was low. JP hollered about the run-bid sheets not being reasonably up-to-date. How in hell could his inspectors do the work he wanted them to do? I'm afraid this was mostly the result of Ted and me griping about the impossibility of finding a man (one of the things I was going to bring up). So, Ted has been hauled off inspecting for a month to get our file and run-bid sheets in order and up-to-date: a victory for Ted. So, with all the above, is it any wonder it took me six hours to plan?

I looked real nice today in my beige dress with green accessories. I got compliments from everyone, and I'm afraid Ann is going to start "digging". Anyway, Ella says so.

Ella and her husband have gone to a movie separately. When she couldn't get ready fast enough he got real mad and went alone, the cad. I've found that he was married before; his boy was killed in a railroad accident and he also supports his daughter. He makes everybody so nervous. Love, Margean

---

August 14, 1946
From Detroit, Michigan

Dear Ones: Just a line while waiting on Grand Boulevard for the Bay City bus. What an adventure yesterday! We were supposed to catch this man on an express run. Ella got on and he locked the gate right in front of me and says, "Double." So I look at Ella and she motions that he isn't even the right guy so she's riding for nothing. I wait and wait for the "double" [second section] which turns out to be the 5:00 regular. Late getting out of the station, we arrive in Flint at 8:00 p.m. I have to catch the 8:09 back and I almost get lost in the toilet—a very trying day. Love, Margean

---

August 15, 1946
From the YWCA Flint, Michigan

Dear Ones: I'm in Flint staying at the YWCA. I had wired a reservation to the Flint Tavern Hotel, but when I got there, there was no room because of a convention. Arriving in a town at 8:00 p.m. is a bad thing! I tried every hotel–all with the same story, "No room." Not frantic but with two plenty sore feet, I inquired where the "Y" was, fully expecting it to be full also. It wasn't and I got half of a double room. Henceforth, when coming here I'll wire the "Y".

I have just returned from a round-trip to Port Huron. What dismal, sandy country! The corn looks good though and there's a lot of buckwheat around. Lots of rain, more than we have had.

I've good news: every legal holiday we get paid for an eight-hour day whether we work or not, plus whatever work we do. I'm going to work, be out of town and get that holiday pay all at once! Love, Margean

———

August 19, 1946
From Detroit, Michigan

Dear Ones: Got my paycheck $203.22, cashing it in the bank at Grand Boulevard on the way to Flint. The woman looked at me. "Is this yours?" she asked in an incredulous voice. I was looking very young and immature. "Yes," said I, and had to trot out every bit of identification I had. "You must have a very good job," she said. "I have," said I. $400 a month isn't to be sneezed at.

If I had had more experience, I would have been given a fifteen-day assignment for Capitol Greyhound on the Atlantic coast—so Ella tells me. Love, Margean

———

August 21, 1946
From Detroit, Michigan

Dear Ones: Well, this will be another scrawled letter for I just got up and my brain is full of cobwebs. I've a new desk in my room, a child's desk but it just fits me. Perfect for writing reports and letters.

Yesterday, without knowing it, I worked 13 hours. Report writing is so time-consuming and makes it hard to plan an eight-hour day. I expect to plan my northern trip for the next two days which will rest me and, checking schedules, it looks as though I could be gone almost two weeks. The way I have it planned, part of the time will be spent in Sudbury, Ontario, and part in Mackinaw City.

36

Last night Ella made a banana cake and wanted to top it with 7-minute frosting but was afraid to try. She put the ingredients together and I beat it. Turned out perfect so we were delighted (I miss cooking). We had stuffed flank steak, potatoes and string beans. The gravy, instead of having water added to the meat juices, had tomato juice. Her husband said, "I don't like it. I like a meat-base gravy." It had a meat-base and I noticed he had three helpings. Love, Margean

---

August 22, 1946
From Detroit, Michigan

Dear Ones: We've a new man in the office, another fledgling for Ella.

My round trip to London was enjoyable. On the way back I sat next to a tobacco farmer. Cigarettes are 35 cents a pack in Canada, but farmers get only 40 cents a pound and must pay federal tax out of that. Here the farmer gets at least 80 cents a pound and doesn't have to pay federal tax, the processor paying it instead. According to the farmer, there's a big government fight now—too much out of the farmer's pocket and nothing out of the processor's pocket. Cigarette papers are 13 cents a pack. All in all, I had a pleasant twelve-hour day and learned something.

Home from the office after meeting the new fellow: strictly a "floater" if you ask me. Have a "special" tomorrow at 6:00 a.m., then into the office for work on my trip. Love, Margean

---

August 27, 1946
From Hotel Coulson, Sudbury, Ontario, Canada

Dear Ones: 3:15 a.m. Had to ask for protection on the way up because I was the only passenger for the last hour. When I was alone on the coach, the driver asked me to come up and keep him company, so I went up and we talked. He was from Traverse City and knew Cadillac well. We saw lots of rabbits and three deer. Beautiful country around Higgins Lake— miles and miles through second growth forest. Lots of fires because of the drought.

Speaking of going up and talking, I find front seats best for inspection work, preferably the two by the door or the two in back of the driver. Next are the two seats behind the door seats, then the two aisle seats behind that.

The other inspectors don't care, but I like to be up front as close as possible and see what the driver sees.

7:54 a.m. On the Straits and onto the ferry boat deck. I don't find the vibration unpleasant—rather nice in fact. I'm not on the right coach and can get only to St. Ignace where I must transfer to a Soo bus—quite a bit of monkey-business. Hope I make the 10:45 coach out of Sault Ste Marie for Sudbury. I didn't want this driver at all but the two sections of Soo were loaded. He smoked and gabbed all the way from Petoskey to Mackinaw City. Another protection trip. Boy, do I need sleep!

All for now, need to walk around the deck because I'm beginning to dislike the vibration intensely. All my limbs feel as if they're asleep, an awkward sensation, and my heart is beating fast. My cheeks are flushed and I'm really sweating. I don't precisely feel sick, just not well. So this is what seasickness feels like.

12:00 p.m. Hour-and-a-half out of Canadian Sault Ste Marie in the roughest, most desolate and most beautiful country I've ever seen. It's like out-of-the-way sections near Cadillac and the fire tower; but instead of sand, down anywhere from six to ten inches is solid rock granite and shale supplying numerous quarries. Pasture and early wheat (I think) are the only crops I've seen so far, and where there are farms, there are wooden "snake" fences. There are magnificent herds of Guernsey cows producing for the many creameries and cheese co-ops I've seen.

About a half-hour out of Sault Ste Marie the road changed to gravel. We saw a bear meandering along going off into the trees as we came near. At the most unexpected times, one sees beautiful, wild lakes or maybe they are Great Lake inlets. What a horrible rough and bumpy road with the nastiest one-way suspension bridges over streams of awful depth, swiftness, and multitudes of feet below us! Leaving Thessalon the country cleared up.

Almost all the people are French Canadians, many of them without cars from the number of wagon-drawn families I've seen on the road.

2:00 and thirty minutes out of Blind River. The road snakes among hills and mountains of shale and basalt, with here and there a small pine clinging to a foot of dirt. The trees, other than pine, are just changing color.

4:15 and leaving Espanola. Guess what makes Espanola what it is? None other than Kalamazoo Vegetable Parchment Company! That's all it is—a road under construction, a huge mill and perhaps fifty houses. We had a flat tire in Massey and were held up 45 minutes.

Just before Sudbury is the town of Copperclift where an enormous copper and nickel smelting and refinery complex is located.

5:45 and in Sudbury at last. After a chicken potpie dinner, took two hours to write my reports—a 16-hour day. I love my room here. Love, Margean

—————

August 28, 1946
From Hotel Coulson, Sudbury Ontario, Canada

Dear Ones: I've been roaming over Sudbury, which is built on a series of hills, and have decided that it's about the size of Kalamazoo—and just about as old. It's crisscrossed with railroad tracks, and one can always hear a train bound to the mines, Espanola and KVP, or the coasts. For its size, it's the busiest train center I've seen. City transportation is by both bus and trolley—the latter like those in the "Toonerville" comic strip. More about Sudbury on Friday when I don't work, can ramble around to my heart's content and wash my hair.

It's raining very softly, very thoroughly, very soakingly—the all-day drizzle kind—and I have no protection, not even a headscarf. I bet it gets good and cold up here in the winter. I see by the *Times* that Calgary had a temperature of 33 and snow fell last week.

Had wheat-cakes for breakfast, and then went looking for embroidery floss finally finding some that matched. The girl thought my runner was beautiful, and told me that you can't get stamped cloth up here, although I've seen plenty in Windsor and London.

There are two long days ahead of me, 12 hours today and 17 tomorrow, with Friday off except for a terminal report. I hope my men are where I want them when they're supposed to be there.

My hotel, the best in Sudbury, is just a half block from the bus station. My $2 room, with its bed, desk, chest, leather chair, and lavatory, is nice.

6:00 p.m. Greetings from North Bay. Another beautiful ride among hills of solid rock, some having trees and some, where there have been fires, just rock. This is great mining county—copper, nickel, silver, and iron. Coniston, the first stop out of Sudbury, has a typical mining town appearance with board sidewalks and soil washes. It is surrounded by hills of slag left over from the mining.

I won't be going to Hagar tomorrow, it's only a gas station where I'd have a three-hour wait at night and I just know it would be closed.

There are many lumber camps, and every house burns wood, and every train has several cars loaded with logs. The trees aren't large because there isn't enough soil to hold up a large tree: therefore, after they reach a certain size, they are cut or eventually blow over. Forest fire signs are frequent, and after one has swept over an area, the forest doesn't spring back up—virtually no second growth. How odd it is to see trees, in crevices containing perhaps a foot of washed-down dirt, perched here and there on a mountain of solid rock-mountains of rock shaped so that no human could ever climb them.

In the few valleys interspersed among these mountain-rocks are farms, the houses of which wouldn't stable our cows. Where there is a level spot of dirt, one sees an acre or two of some bearded grain or clover in three-quarter bloom. Never exceeding three acres, the irregular fields are plowed in a grid-board fashion, the "deep-furrows" being small drainage ditches, for, with the rock subsoil, there is no seepage down. However, these deep-furrows are never over 10" deep, in great contrast to ours. There are small gardens of cabbage, turnips, and what we would call early potatoes, the only kind that could ripen here. Just a few cows and no tractors, naturally. One wonders how these isolated people make a living.

I neglected to mention that our drizzle this morning changed to snow! It's damp with a raw wind blowing, a combination for which I'm definitely not dressed.

Coming along North Bay's Lake Nipissing shore, one could not tell where the water ends and the sky begins, both the same leaden color. When, and if, I come up here in winter, I'll wear slacks plus every sweater, coat, scarf, and glove I own. Must shop for some fleece-lined shoe-boots, not clodhoppers, but those that are mid-calf high in which one wears wool socks. Not only would they be good here but on our night or northern winter runs. I suppose most of the winter northern runs will fall to me because none of our inspectors ride up here except Mr. Cross. Too, only lumberjacks and girls ride in the winter and none of our inspectors look like lumberjacks.

North Bay is strung out for about a half-mile along the shore, its lifeline being the Canadian Pacific and Canadian National. It is both a railroad center and a tourist center and abounds with hotels and restaurants, interspersed with drug stores, wholesale houses and some stores. Love, Margean

August 29, 1946
From Hotel Coulson Sudbury, Ontario, Canada

Dear Ones: After looking over my schedule, I must do some fast stepping not to double back with yesterday's driver. This unforeseen mix-up made me nervous and apprehensive, and caused me to lose some of the six hours devoted to sleep last night. I just had a brainstorm! I am going to Espanola and catch the 3:23 bus back—that way I double on no one. Mrs. King will howl at the long layover, but I'll send along a nice note.

Got home fine last night: a swell ride, but what loitering! He also smoked all the way. Some fresh drunk sat with me, but I moved. All in a day's work.

All one hears about is the Hamilton steel strike and there are many sympathy strikes, the largest at the Canadian Soo. People's reactions are about the same division of opinion on management and labor as in the states.

By the way, they're all baseball, basketball, bowling and hockey fans and participants up here.

I'm eating breakfast in a Chinese restaurant across from the terminal and from my seat I can see the coach when it arrives. Having a terminal report tomorrow, I don't want to be seen near it today. With no restroom, the report will only take five minutes while I get my ticket to St. Ignace.

5:00 p.m. Well, I've done my fast stepping, and landed up here in North Bay again. I don't know what made me decide to come here except that all the loose ends of the schedule clicked into place in my head, enabling me to catch regular drivers where I caught extra men yesterday. So, instead of a mere seven-hour day, it stretched into a nineteen-hour one. I'm going to do a general report tomorrow, a composite of all these Canadian runs for they all seem to have the same problems. It will show JP I'm on my toes. Love, Margean

———

August 30, 1946
From Hotel Coulson, Sudburg, Ontario, Canada

Dear Ones: 2:45 p.m. and I'm under the dryers having my hair done, a shampoo and wave for 75 cents. At the library this morning, I learned that Sudbury produces 80% of the world's copper and that it's doubled its population every census for the last 30 years, now having 32,000 plus.

Earlier this morning I finished a five page general report of which I am proud. I think we inspectors need to look at the large picture: this is our company and we need to look at all operations to see how they appear to passengers.

Was dead when I got in last night, having gotten up at 6:00 and not getting to bed until 1:30 a.m. A mediocre run: such loitering. Pretty northern lights were out but just the ordinary white variety. Getting anxious for that special South and to read all my accumulated mail. Payday is the 5th and I still have well over $100, probably $75 by the time I reach Detroit.

A woman told me that Kresge here puts out a better meal than any restaurant. Eating breakfast there, for 20 cents I got cream-o-wheat, four pieces of toast and grapefruit juice. For supper, 45 cents got me apple juice, rolls, macaroni and oodles of cheese, string beans, pumpkin pie and coffee. You ought to have seen the huge T-bone steaks they serve for 75 cents. Butter is 45 cents a pound. Item of interest—Canadian coins have a counterfeit sound which makes it easy to hear a cash fare transaction.

7:15 p.m. Man-o-man, will I ever be glad to get to some warm country. The weather here is like November at home, raw and chilly. It's foggy season and last night we ran into regular pools of it. No heat in my room so I have the bedspread wrapped around me for warmth. Still, I'd love to come up in the winter and get snowed in—what an adventure.

I believe I've caught every extra man up here. Same way out of Windsor: I caught every extra man and received a nice pat on the back from JP. I don't believe the others plan like I do.

By the way, Ella's husband is having landlady trouble again! Might have to move. If I do, it will be closer to town. Love, Margean

———

August 31, 1946
From Travelers Hotel, St.Ignace, Michigan

Dear Ones: Just a word to let you know I'm still safe. I had the absolutely best driver that I've ever seen from Sudbury to the Soo. Absolutely the best. Can you imagine anyone showing passengers how to operate their seats and footrests? and calling points of interest? Because there were three of us with connections to make at the Soo, and because he was over an hour late, he told us to stop worrying, that he would see that we got rooms. As it was, he was two minutes late for the ferry but he telephoned over and told them to hold the bus for us. So here I am, after spending an hour-and-a-half writing the best report ever.

I don't believe I've ever told you about doing reports. The first thing is to go through my little notebook and build the audit starting at the place where I got on. It's the number on, and then on and off at every station and point after that; here's where the good watch with a luminous dial comes in because the time helps indicate where the fare point is. You also keep track of children and other company employees (plus possible girlfriends). I take lots of notes and from them build the written part of the report. I like to have good things to say before I start on any bad and I try to explain circumstances that might account for the bad, all of which explains why it takes me so long to write my reports.

This is a very nice hotel—a good thing I had a reservation for the first thing that struck my eye was a card, "No Vacancies". Love, Margean

---

September 2, 1946
From Wenonah Hotel, Bay City, Michigan

Dear Ones: Just because I don't know for sure whether you went up North or not, I'm writing to tell you what happened if you didn't.

In the first place, I sent you a telegram, collect, to Dighton from St. Ignace, asking you to meet me at 3:10 p.m. in Lake City. This was idiotic, partly because I don't know whether you came up or not and partly because I don't know whether the telegram will ever reach you because it was sent on Sunday and had to be delivered on a holiday. So, at 3:10, I hope someone is waiting for me. If there isn't, I shall sit in a hotel lobby because the next bus through is the next morning. I can only hope that you are there.

Must tell of my trip yesterday and the mix-up I got into! I intended to go from Clare to Bay City, but when the time came to purchase my ticket, I was politely, but firmly, told that no passenger was allowed to ride between Clare and Bay City on Greyhound because Yellow Coach Lines had the franchise [*state license to operate in a specific territory*]. Well, that certainly hurt because I had a warm hotel room waiting in Bay City. But, most important, I had neglected to read the nice little "restricted" notice at the bottom of my schedule – a serious reflection on my presumed intelligence, one that I'll not tell at the office.

You can see I'm writing this from Bay City, so I got here. Did I hitchhike? I did not! Did I walk? I did not! I picked up my two-ton suitcase and walked two miles beyond the Clare City limits into the fare zone of Farwell, west of Clare, which isn't restricted. I flagged down the bus driver and at 9:00 p.m. got here. Now I have a sore throat!

This is a nice, old hotel. They serve good meals in their coffee shop, but most hotel dining rooms splurge on style and skimp on food. Because I probably won't be able to get anything in Lake City on a holiday, I had them put up their "Lunch Box". For 50 cents I have a meatloaf sandwich, two pieces of chicken, hardboiled egg, tomato, pickles, piece of cheese, banana, and a piece of cake. What a lunch! I just looked: it also has potato salad!

One can really smell fall in the air, especially taking the trip down from North Bay where one descends from late October to early September. I dread to see winter coming. To economize, I've decided to wear my gray coat another year although it is frightfully baggy in the seat.

I see by the paper that five Detroiters were lost at Algoma Falls in northern Ontario. Isn't it odd, I was in Algoma Falls just two days ago! Love, Margean

---

September 3, 1946
From Lake City, Michigan

Dear Ones: Well, you've left and wasn't it fun meeting! I toured through the stores afterwards and found sheet music for "I Get a Kick Out of You." Buying it, I went to the Doroty Hotel and inquired whether they had a piano. They had, so I spent the next two hours playing. Not only did I play my new piece but everything from musical comedy to cowboy songs that they could dig up. Never was I without someone to turn the pages—if it wasn't the day clerk, bellhop, or housekeeper, it was the cook or waitress. I don't know who had the best time, me or the staff or the villagers who dropped in. Love, Margean

---

September 4, 1946
From Detroit, Michigan

Dear Ones: When I got up this morning I found everyone sick. With my cold I was hardly able to drag myself about, but I did my washing and ironing and fed Katy. I went to the Doctor: she gave me a general examination and a shot which she said should be effective in two days, and if it wasn't, to come back and have another. She said my tonsils are a constant source of infection, sooner out, the better. When I got back home, Ella had had a relapse, a doctor, and a close shave with pneumonia.

Will be in the office for two days fixing up run-bid sheets—Mr. Prater said, "so I could get over my cold." Enclosed is the note from JP about the general report on the Canadian operation. He also told me how nice it was and said it was a thing no other inspector would have thought of. He also said there were going to be copies made—one for the inspectors, one for the Eastern Canadian supervisor, and one to read "as an example of what good inspection can find out" at the Department Head meeting. Don't think that didn't please me!

I told you about that Yellow Coach franchise between Clare and Bay City, the little restriction that caused me to walk two miles and catch cold? Well, I told JP about how I heard they were giving such poor service. Immediately he called and went into the possibilities of sending me up there to break the franchise, but no soap—we're trying to buy the company. But still it's another thing showing that I'm on my toes.

Checks should come in tomorrow. Looking at my accounts today, they figure up to $247 of which $133 is my hourly salary. If that were all I got, that would be $66 a week. Love, Margean

———

September 3, 1946
To me from John Prater

Miss Worst:

I liked your August 30 Summary from your Canadian trip. Such constructive summaries might well be prepared on other divisions for their value to supervision.

JEP

———

September 5, 1946
From Detroit, Michigan

Dear Ones: Got my check this morning, $247.99 before taxes. Pretty good? What is more, due to slow mails, three days of my Canadian trip aren't on this. Got schedules filled out, a Saginaw trip, one to Toronto, and sent my telegrams for hotel reservations. Mrs. King and I are getting along swimmingly, I'm doing some work for her.

Don't worry, I'll be home for the Kalamazoo Fair next week. Got your letter and clippings. Everyone is getting married. Love, Margean

---

September 6, 1946
From Detroit, Michigan

Dear Ones: A beautiful day, just right for traveling, but I'm condemned to sitting in the office. Suppose I should be thankful for this opportunity to rid myself of this cold, but find myself with itchy feet already.

Had another shot and a prescription for thyroid extract tablets. I don't know why my periods have stopped: I know I'm not pregnant! The bend of my arm, where she has twice injected that shot, really hurts!

Cashed my check today and had to trot out every bit of identification and then he wouldn't believe "that a girl your age could draw so much." Love, Margean

---

September 8, 1946
From Ludington, Michigan

Dear Ones: Last night got scolded for working too hard. But if this job has a future in it, it's going to be my future. Wasn't that note from JP nice!

All set to catch a couple of drivers for cash fare re-inspections. This evening in Clare while waiting for the bus had escalloped potatoes, pork chop and mince pie, 41 cents because I didn't get an entire dinner.

Frost hit hard up here, a combination of that and no rain have made the corn stop growing and wither. Saw truck gardening on good black dirt.

Shot still doing no good. Doctor said those pills would keep me awake but they don't. I fall into bed! Love, Margean

September 9, 1946
From Doroty Hotel Lake City, Michigan

Dear Ones: Lake City greets you! This is the hotel where I cooled my heels and played piano Labor Day. It is absolutely the best hotel I've ever stayed in for $2.00 and would have cost much more in any large city.

All the trouble I went to yesterday traveling on North Star Lines, was to no avail for my driver wasn't on the coach at 7:00. The trip from Charlevoix to Lake City is mostly through deep forest where any moment one expects to see deer.

Tomorrow back to the doctor for a checkup on that thyroid extract. It's given me lots of pep, but isn't doing anything else as yet. I don't for the life of me, know what's wrong because I feel well and I know there's no longer any nervous strain nor am I working too hard, for who could call this work. Love, Margean

September 14, 1946
From Detroit, Michigan

Dear Ones: Into Detroit at 11:30 p.m., good driver and arrived right on time. Real pleasant this morning—no one here, just me and the radio.

Saginaw and back today, by way of Atlas, Goodrich, Ortonville, Clarkston, a very good farming area with prosperous homes and barns. Arrived there at 3:14 and wrote reports, then looked around for hotels to stay at in the future. A fairish-sized burg with the most beautiful terminal, excepting St. Ignace, I've yet seen. Built of logs, it has a huge fireplace and I'm to do a terminal report.

Had an old Kazoo-Detroit driver on the double up, but don't think he remembered me. The only trouble is that I might not get on the first section tonight, and he might be driving the second section, in which case I'll have to do some plain and fancy dodging.

10:45 p.m. Home and a thirteen-hour day after writing reports. Had a re-inspection back—still very bad which means he'll have to be re-inspected by someone else within 15 days.

Sunday morning: Woke up with my sore throat back. Am dressed in my high school graduation dress for Toronto. Haven't seen anyone since getting back—suits me. All I need is a room and a radio, and I never get lonesome. Love, Margean

September 15, 1946
From Ford Hotel, Toronto, Ontario, Canada

Dear Ones: A good driver gave me plenty of time to look around. Noticed that most of the cattle are Red Angus, Brown Swiss, and Herefords, some good, some poor. Most of the section I came through is untouched by frost with corn and hay still growing. Tobacco is being harvested between Windsor and London, and one can see it being cured in barns with open-air circulation. All these barns have chimneys—all smoking away! Truck garden farms, of which there were plenty, are in the full swing of harvest: I understand that many of the Hamilton strikers tried to get work on these truck farms.

Was looking over rooms for rent in the Detroit paper this morning. If I ever need to move there are plenty, some cheaper, too. The only thing that would bother would be transporting my multitude of belongings. I'm in no hurry, but it would be pleasant where there's no tension in the household.

Very conveniently I'm at the Ford Hotel right across the street from the bus terminal. Only $1.50 for a double bed, desk, easy chair, closet, and lavatory: nothing fancy, but clean and neat. While waiting for my room, in walks my driver and goes up in the elevator: evidently he stays here too.

Well, must close, do my exercises and go to bed. My sore throat has moderated. Made $18 today, of which $2 has gone in expenses. Love, Margean

———

September 17, 1946
From Detroit, Michigan

Dear Ones: It's the end of a long day in the office. I found two new men and two new office girls when I got back. The new men are both young, 25, one serious, the other not. I had a deuce of a time trying to plan because of the noise and confusion. Will be glad to get away.

JP is now head of the Personnel Department and we won't be seeing much of him. As soon as possible our office is being moved to the Book Towers where the Personnel Office is located. In front of the others, JP congratulated me on my Canadian report that he had read at the Department Heads' meeting. He should not do this, I know people don't like it. Love, Margean

September 18, 1946
From Detroit, Michigan

Dear Ones: Little Katy is ill again with another cold keeping Ella up all night. They are looking at something in Ypsilanti and didn't get back till 8:00 p.m.

Allen and Lawson are on a swell special. In a company car, they are making speed checks on northern and Ohio runs, driving about 400 miles a day. Allen was telling me that some of our men are doing 70 mph on the curves between Saginaw and Bay City.

It's been heck to work the last few days, what with everyone in the office getting in each other's way. Yesterday JP told me that we're taking over another line in Ohio, the C&LE with about 275 men.

Have on my beige raw-silk dress with green and gold accessories. Have my hair tied in a George Washington pigtail with the sides curled up high. Look pert and older. Have just been to the doctor and had two shots. Friday two more, then a checkup on the 30th. Love, Margean

---

September 19, 1946
From Detroit, Michigan

Dear Ones: Did I have a scare this morning! I was deciding what to put in my bag for my trip and wondered where I had put my forms having spent part of yesterday putting the right number into envelopes and so forth. Looked all around, couldn't find the manila envelope, was getting frantic! Having purchased some shampoo in Cunningham's yesterday, that was the only place I could think where I might have left them, so dressing on the double I rushed down to their Lost and Found. They were there.

Am in Mt. Clemens right now and in thirty minutes must catch a bus for Detroit. Had a hamburger for lunch, which reminds me, a lot of restaurants are closing because of the meat shortage here. In fact, for dinner last night we had a can of the beef you folks brought over.

Will be glad to leave again for the North Country. The Alpena run will be new territory and two days of my itinerary are all-night work that I like. Passengers are different at night and the driving is too.

Would I like a time-consuming special like the guys are getting! Would like to be teamed up with Allen: he's the nicest of the men in the office. Treats me like a lady, while Ted calls me "the infant" or "the juvenile." He should talk—I'm making more money than he is! According to the charts for last month's work, Allen and I are tops as far as getting numbers of drivers. Love, Margean

—•—

September 20,
1946 From Detroit, Michigan

Dear Ones: Ella's husband was on a bender last night and brought home a friend. Tomorrow, he is going to see about "the deal" in Ypsilanti. He makes everyone so nervous. He needs a good beating: I bet he gave plenty while in the police force. Poor little Katy still isn't over her cold and coughs all night.

Packed for my trip to Sault Ste Marie. Slacks, sweaters, and blouses: if it's as snappy up there as it is here, I'll need them. Checks should be in today. Hope so or must borrow from the "kitty" because I have only $50.

In just six minutes, I have to catch the bus to Birmingham. Here go two now, mine will be next.

1:00 p.m. Back in Detroit waiting for the Doctor to come in. Probably more shots. I believe I told you before that she said not to worry, it was a glandular disturbance.

3:45 p.m. Well, I don't know just how to write this, but here goes. Had one shot and passed out cold while she was giving me the second. Came to five minutes later with the aid of smelling salts and wet towels. Don't know what happened, just keeled over. So, while I was lying down, she and I had a long talk during which she advised me: (1) to quit my job, go home and raise chickens because my work was taxing my health; (2) I was anemic which was causing most of my glandular trouble, the remedy – iron tablets, go home, and eat meat; (3) I wasn't getting the fun out of life that a girl my age should, the remedy – go home or move to the YWCA. Another appointment the 30th. I've paid out about $30 in doctor bills now.

6:30 p.m. I have put my application in at the YWCA Residence even though the woman said it wouldn't do much good. Will close. All tired out. Have to be up early and catch an 8:25 bus to Sault Ste Marie. Lots of love, Margean

—•—

50

September 21, 1946
From St. Ignace, Michigan

Dear Ones: In Bay City with some time to spare. Am feeling average with just a slight headache, probably the aftermath of my shots. The iron capsules I now take are large enough to choke a horse. Speaking of horses, you should see the ones the Detroit police ride: beautiful bays with white feet.

Gossip from the office. Yesterday morning Ella was talking with JP and they were discussing all of us. He said that I was the most conscientious and most able to concentrate of all his inspectors. What a great compliment! Ted Frye and Mary McKay are going to announce their engagement even if he hasn't his final divorce papers yet. What a life.

7:30 p.m. On the ferry boat, City of Cheboygan, ready to pull out. An uneventful trip up sitting right behind the driver who chatted all the way: I remember him when he trained on the Kalamazoo-Detroit division, only he doesn't know me. Will stop and walk around before the boat gets to me. Had a swell trip, sitting first at the stern and then the prow—feeling better each minute of the Strait crossing. Love, Margean

———

September 22, 1946
From St. Ignace, Michigan

Dear Ones: 9:00 and back on the ferry. A beautiful, cool morning with the Straits looking like glass. I had a frightful time yesterday and this morning dodging drivers I had ridden with before. All I do is look dumb, easy for me. My work comes so easy now that I can't understand how there could be any nervous strain.

I've been thinking about what the doctor said and the whole question of work. Have decided to stick it out to Christmas at least, and by then I'll probably have made up my mind to stick longer. I've always lived up to what people have expected of me, and I can't see a good reason to quit now. If I stopped, I would consider myself a failure. So long as I sleep and eat well, to hell with the glandular disturbance and all the rest!

I would have liked to go to church this morning—would like to sing or hear some good music. Must be losing weight again: my slacks, which I had fixed so neatly by setting the buttons just right, are too slack around the waist.

1:30 and waiting for dinner. Hamburg steak, mashed sweet potatoes, mixed vegetables, salad, tomato juice, drink and desert for 85 cents, inexpensive for a resort-town and huge portions too.

9:00 and back in St. Ignace with reports written. Nice ride with a good driver—had a deadhead driver on. Three employees, only they don't know it. Did a lot of embroidery today. Love, Margean

———•——

September 23, 1946
From YWCA, Lansing, Michigan

Dear Ones: It is a beautiful day, sun shining and warm, the bay slick. Makes one feel like singing but instead I listen to the clock tick and other sounds of hotel life. On my embroidery I've finished all greens, browns and yellows, quite a bit of a red-rust plus two daisies. Only a million cross-stitches to go.

Guess who I'm going down with today? A driver I rode with for about six months back and forth to college. He is a big, jolly Scotsman, one of our oldest. I can see that he is trying to place me, but I don't think he will with my hair cut. I look about 12, if that. Nine hours of dead sleep last night.

I know now what filled my mind when I fainted. I was trying to put through a phone call and couldn't, and I kept repeating "I don't like this. I don't like this." I don't think I told you just how it happened. I had just received a shot in my left arm and had swung around so she could get at my right when I got an awful cramp or spasm in my left arm. "Put it up on the headrest," the doctor said, so I did. She poked the needle in and I remember thinking, "Gee, my heart is beating awfully fast," and then blackout, the telephone call, and "I don't like this." My left hand was all dirt where I hit the floor, and I still have a big black and blue spot on my left knee. From the angle I was sitting, I can't figure out how I could possibly have hit the floor in such a manner.

My driver just walked down. "See you beat me up," said he. "Yes," said I, "An early bird. Even had breakfast." We have a date at 8:50.

Heavy dew last night left the sidewalks wet. Everything smells good. Must close and get to work

9:00 a.m. On the ferry. He did recognize me. Asked if I wasn't the little girl that rode from Galesburg to Kalamazoo, said he couldn't place me last night but knew that he knew me. Damn! He isn't even supposed to be on this run.

4:00 p.m. It has turned to rain after the lovely sunrise this morning. Called you and wrote my report. Neglected to say that my cold's back. Love, Margean

---

October 2, 1946
To me from John E. Prater
Great Lakes Greyhound Lines

My dear Miss Worst: I was very sorry to learn that your health had declined to the point where you found it necessary to return to your home for a rest and possible treatment.

I know you have been working very hard and I have been pleased with the results you have been getting. It would seem unnecessary to remind you that we have suggested in the past that this business of working long hours can be easily overdone; however, this is not intended for a lecture but merely a message to let you know we all wish you a satisfactory recovery and a good time catching up on your reading during the interim.

With very best wishes from the entire office.

Sincerely yours, John E. Prater

October 4, 1946
From YWCA Residence, Detroit, Michigan

Dear Ones: Moving. On my way back from the second trip with one more to go. What a job! I have plenty of space in this temporary room for my stuff , a four-drawer dresser, a cabinet, a cot. We have two maids. I have a special key for getting in for my odd hours. Rent and two meals a day will be $30.38 a month. Even though that is $8.50 a week and I won't be here all the time, I feel that it is cheaper than at Ella's where my meals were a dollar a day. In fact, I never paid less than $10 a week even when my room was reduced to $7.

Ella and her husband have bought a restaurant at Algonac near Port Huron, and Ella will continue working while he runs it. From the description, the restaurant is a fairly large one and a four-room house goes with it. He sold the car for $1,050 and for $450 bought a Ford which he painted gray. It wasn't dry yet so he couldn't move me.

Ella said that everyone was worried sick over me. JP told her I was the <u>only</u> inspector who saw the work in relation to company operations as a whole and that I knew the fields of operation the best.

Will go to the office late this afternoon where it will be question after question about how I feel. The two new men aren't out of training yet but one of them is on probation for not doing good work. Ella feels that both he and Cross will be given their walking papers.

5:25 p.m. Just as I was preparing to leave the office, JP said, "What have you got worked out?" "Just a trip to Bay City," I said. "Well, I don't want you knocking yourself out, we need you," he said. Have three easy runs. Pampering myself. Love, Margean

---

October 5, 1946
From YWCA Residence, Detroit, Michigan

Dear Ones: I shall never get thin on the meals they serve here. Dinner last night was fried whitefish, baked potato, Waldorf salad, melon and a cookie, well prepared and attractively served, a pleasure to eat.

I'm about a half block off Fort St. and two blocks from Grand Boulevard and the 24th Street Greyhound garage. Served by Lafayette-Green, and West Jefferson buses and Fort trolley, it's about ten minutes uptown with no transfers—much better time than at Ella's. The neighborhood is not as nice, however. My street is all right, but Fort isn't—I'll have to walk in the middle of the street late at night. Still, it's only half a block from the stops.

I'm going to expect you on the 19th and take you to dinner in Windsor. When you come, please bring my black winter coat and my music book "Torch Songs." We have a nice piano here.

By the way, I forgot to mention that JP said yesterday that I ought to make some trips to Louisville and compare the Greyhounds in another report.

Recorded my change of address at the Post office and went shopping. I was extravagant but they were the first I've ever seen. I got two pair of the sheerest black nylons for $1.13 a pair. A truly beautiful luxury! I wore a pair to Church today and before I left the house, three girls stopped me to ask where I got them. I also bought a lock-box for my work papers and jewelry.

Am sitting on a bench down by the river with a girl from the Y writing this. Flies are eating us alive—a welcome answer, no doubt, to the meat shortage. Love, Margean

October 7, 1946
From Hotel Bancroft, Saginaw, Michigan

Dear Ones: In Saginaw after I thought I would never get here. Didn't catch my special, his double, or the first section of the next run, and then I had to stand to Flint: I have my troubles.

5:00 p.m. Detroit: Just out of the office and the nicest compliment. I went in to tell JP about my address change and brought up a transfer to Kalamazoo for terminal work. "Miss Worst," he said, "please don't ask me to do it until I quit here. Then, I'll see what I can do, but while I'm here, I'm not going to lose you to any other department."

Guess what, I'm not legally hired! No one in the company is supposed to be under 21, but my company records are doctored!

And, more good news! Since this morning my glands and I are on speaking terms again. Love, Margean

———

October 8, 1946
From YWCA Residence, Detroit, Michigan

Dear Ones: Have some days planned ahead including a trip to new territory, Cincinnati. After you come, I'm heading South for a long time. I will need a lot of money on hand so don't know when I'll pay back some more.

At the office today, Allen wasn't feeling well and was crabby. We have a new man, Mr. Glatz, who is definitely superior and has done work of this nature all his life. He told me that JP said I was one of his best—he doesn't say that about the new men.

My permanent room has been assigned and I move in tomorrow—a triple with plenty of light. You don't know how much I like having the girls around. Love, Margean

———

October 9, 1946
From YWCA Residence, Detroit, Michigan

Dear Ones: Back from Saginaw where I took great pains to get on the double. Two miles out we broke an airline and I (the only passenger) was transferred to the first section, Cross's man.

Relaxing before my Cincinnati trip. Anxious to make a southern trip to Washington, D.C., but all the northern men are up and no one else dares take them.

Have just called you. It eats up the profit, but I love to hear your voices. Am so glad you're coming over. We'll go to Greenfield's Saturday night and then Sunday to Windsor for dinner unless you'd like to eat here at the Residence. Love, Margean

---

October 10, 1946
From Metropole Hotel, Cincinnati, Ohio

Dear Ones: A lovely trip making me doubly anxious to get to Louisville and Washington D.C.—the one through Kentucky hill country, the other mostly through mountains. That will take planning and I'll do it after you visit. The runs are easy because Great Lakes of Indiana is restricted to interstate passengers, meaning that no one can board after Toledo unless leaving Ohio. This makes an audit comparatively simple and allows concentration on driving

After getting off the bus, I was hurrying to find this hotel when a curiously familiar voice says, "Hey, how do you suppose anybody can catch up with you? I've been trying for a block." I looked around and there was Ted Frye! "Well," he said, "the whole office is down here today." Anyway, four of us are—Ted, Allen, Lawson, and me. We chatted and I got tips about Capital lines.

By the way, Greyhound has purchased C&LE which gives me marvelous connections—Cincinnati, Columbus, Dayton, and other points.

We have orders to stay off Michigan lines until the new run-bids come in changing for winter schedules. Now, I don't know whether I want to go North or South. I know that in December I want to go to northern Canada: I'll plan it in November and grab the men. Love, Margean

---

October 11, 1946
From Metropole Hotel, Cincinnati, Ohio

Dear Ones: Got up about 45 minutes ago and it's now 9:00 and raining, an all-day drizzle, and me without any rain protection. I had intended doing and seeing so much. Life is perverse.

56

Allen told me to stay at this hotel, the second this week where I've had a room and bath for $2. This is also where the drivers, who have about a twelve-hour layover, stay in a company block of six rooms.

Last night my chief impression of Cincinnati was all downhill and all curves: going out, in the nature of things, it will seem all uphill. Cincinnati reminds me of Grand Rapids in its hillyness. They have trolleys and very narrow streets like Toronto. Terminals here and at Dayton are much better than in Detroit.

Have been studying my Capital Greyhound schedule. So many states or parts of states to see.

Schedules are fascinating things—all the stops and their leaving and arrival times. The time between is the driving time that paces the bus. Fighting the schedule are the loading and leaving emergencies, the unknown number of stops along the way, the need to chat and catch up on news at small stations where no one is getting on and, of course, the weather and road conditions. Drivers handle this in all sorts of ways—speeding to catch up, getting out to tap tires, never driving slowly to kill time—always challenging their horses to perform. I handle this by coming up with the run's drive time vs. the driver's run time and usually give reasons leaning to his side. Passengers get antsy though when there's loitering—it reminds them that they need to use a bathroom. Love, Margean

----

October 12, 1946
From YWCA Residence, Detroit, Michigan

Dear Ones: Here at the Y Residence, I am now in my permanent, well-lighted, comfortable room, a triple. It has a large bay with a table in it, plus a French-type window with panes that open in. We have three cots, three bureaus, four chairs, and a lavatory. One roommate is a plump, pleasant girl, the other a good-looking blond who is not quite unmarried. She has a baby boy and is divorcing her husband who is in prison.

About 47 girls live here. You don't know how much I enjoy being here. I can relax! Sunday two girls and I went to a Church of God: they don't believe in instrumental music so we sang without.

4:00 p.m. Awake after a long nap preparing for tonight. Had a swell run yesterday with a nice young fellow who let me off at the Boulevard only a half block from here. After writing my report, I tumbled into bed at 2:00 a.m.

You mentioned that I must feel very secure in my job. I do: I know I'm doing something that I'm good at and I know that I've got a future. What more could one ask?

Chill wind and cold drizzle for my run to Canada. Love, Margean

---

October 12, 1946
From YWCA Residence, Detroit, Michigan

Dear Ones: Unthinkable to write two letters the same day, but if I'm too tired to write tomorrow, this will do. It's 9:45, just two hours before I leave for Toronto. The rain has stopped, the moon is very full, and it's very cold. This will be the last trip there until November because most have been inspected—by me!

I'm sitting on the mezzanine of the Book Cadillac watching the people in the lounge below: what a well-dressed and buzzing crowd. I wonder who the woman in blue-green satin is—haughty mannerisms and her striking attire make her stand out from all others. She looks like a queen should look.

My good looking, blond roommate used to be a Greyhound suburban driver. Her husband problems remind me that I'm reading "The Great Mouthpiece" a biography of William Fallon, the criminal lawyer. Do you remember this famous figure from your "roaring twenties." Love, Margean

---

October 13, 1946
From Ford Hotel, Toronto, Canada

Dear Ones: I never thought I could sleep in the daytime, but I put in ten hours today so probably will be unable to sleep tonight. This room has a radio, a thingamajig on the wall, so maybe I've had one before and didn't know it. It was on all afternoon and I didn't hear a thing! All Canadian electric lights flicker making it difficult to read. This hotel is conveniently across the street from the terminal. "Sorry, No Vacancies" was on the counter making me glad I had telegraphed.

A swell trip up and, except for loitering, he got an A-1 report. Love, Margean

58

October 14, 1946
From Toronto, Ontario, Canada

Dear Ones: I sent off the last letter and decided I was tired enough to go back to bed, which made about eighteen hours of sleep. Had breakfast and a sandwich put up to go (egg salad, 10 cents) because we don't stop till late this afternoon. It's an hour before bus time, but I want to be out there early to get his check-in time.

Tomorrow I must fix my week's schedule, always a lengthy and formidable undertaking. If they aren't made out the way I do them, I don't get my men. The haphazard methods the others use don't work for me—or them. Love, Margean

—·—

October 15, 1946
From YWCA Residence, Detroit, Michigan

Dear Ones: I have your room reserved, a $4 double at the Fort-Shelby on Lafayette and First. You can't miss it. I hope you have kept track of the things to bring. I've forgotten half of them. Please bring my electric popcorn popper, I've gotten special permission to use it in my room.

Had a lovely trip in yesterday then up to the office. We have a new duty: we investigate applicants for employment. Mr. Glatz was out yesterday for a ticket agent at Royal Oak. The report was excellent: 26, unmarried, attends church, highest praise by neighborhood gossips and former employers—all of which adds up to the office believing I should make his acquaintance. Well, I might go to church!

Had to call up the dispatcher and find out when my extra men go. Finding out was pleasant. Mr. McIndoo chased everyone out of his office and gave me all the information—one will double out at 12:01 and then, because of Canadian Thanksgiving yesterday, there'll be doubles on everything back. So it's off to Chatham. Love, Margean

—·—

October 16, 1946
From YWCA Residence, Detroit, Michigan

Dear Ones: Made a round-trip to Belle River in Ontario for the extra men. With a three-hour layover, I headed for one of the three hotels. They have no waiting rooms, just "Beverage Rooms." Being dressed fit to kill,

I must have made an impression on the waitress, the woman cook and the bartender, for one by one they came to where I was sitting (trying to write my reports) and wanted to know what I was doing in town, etc. By the time the bartender got around to my table, they were agog with curiosity. He asked whether I'd like a drink of beer. No, I don't drink. Wine? I almost weakened, but, "No" (and this was on the house too). Love, Margean

———

October 23, 1946
From YWCA Residence, Detroit, Michigan

Dear Ones: The trip I've looked forward to has finally materialized: Detroit, Columbus, Athens, Ohio; Athens, Clarksburg, West Virginia; Clarksburg, Washington D.C., Annapolis, Maryland; Annapolis, Washington D.C., Clarksburg; Clarksburg, Athens, Columbus; Columbus to Detroit. All day work except the last and five hours free in D.C. Then, about November 5th, it's off to northern Canada and then suburbans till Thanksgiving.

Had a run home with a student driver—he'll make a good addition. Got to thinking how time passes so quickly! How one is always waiting! How one must always be on time or, preferably, early. Love, Margean

———

October 24, 1946
From YWCA Residence, Detroit, Michigan

Dear Ones: All packed and ready to go, but you know what fate can do. My envelopes are stuffed and I have a big collection of my little notebooks. My wardrobe consists of two black dresses, lots of scarves and my travel iron, the latter necessary with such a limited wardrobe. Two books, "Elements of Geography" and "Dark Street", and some embroidery constitute my amusement when there is no opportunity for movies. One or two days have sightseeing time. I'll be seeing the Washington Monument and maybe the White House. Shall I give Mr. Truman your regards?

One of my suburban reports came back with a note from the supervisor. He said that when he talked the report over with the driver, he was careful to mention first all the good points (of which I had a great number), but when he mentioned the bad ones—speed, safety zones, crashing gears, over-riding a passenger—the fellow blew up. Derogatory remarks about our department and me in particular led to docking two weeks' bonus pay.

The supervisor asked for more reports like mine. The report is tacked on the bulletin board—"green eyes" from the others.

On one of my Saginaw trips last week, the fellow neglected to put down my cash fare. Instead, two children were listed—$2.56 in his pocket. JP said that maybe the driver thought I was a child—I love his humor. The girls hadn't caught the cash fare discrepancy, so henceforth I'm going over my audited reports to see whether they miss anything more like that.

Docker, one of our newer men, has a special on the 24th St. garage roof. He has a periscope and binoculars and is checking on some employee suspected of stealing equipment. Don't we do the oddest things? My "special," according to JP's form of humor, is keeping Docker supplied with coffee! Gave Docker my list of Windsor "extras", as we are the only ones that ever work over there. Rutare got turned up on Birmingham while writing notes on the bus: that's twice!

I've looked and do not have Joss's [*a Swiss, graduate student friend from my Western Michigan College days*] address here. Could you send it. One of the letters you sent was from a college chum now engaged and wanting to see me next time I'm home. Have my mailbox full when I get back: I'm the envy of the other girls—their parents don't write, but then they don't either. Love, Margean

------

October 25, 1946
From Columbus, Ohio

Dear Ones: Stuck in Columbus without a room, so I'm cooling my heels in the lobby until something shows up or doesn't. The YWCA is full with cots in the halls. Let me tell you how it happened for, by rights, I should be in Athens.

Catching my bus to Columbus at 9:30 a.m., I sat in the second seat right, the other half of which was occupied by a very presentable young man. After a laugh when I dropped my purse and everything spilled out, we got to talking. It developed that he was going to Athens to the College Homecoming. My room? Didn't you know hotels have been booked solid since August for this weekend? NO! To be certain, upon arrival in Columbus I phoned. Sure enough, no room. Remember what I said about schedules and fate? Instead of cooling my heels two days in their lobby, I decided to stay in Columbus—it's larger.

To resume about the presentable young man: a college grad of '40, a CPA for Capitol Airlines. He explained some of the forms he had with him, so that checked (don't I make a good spy). During the war he was a Captain in the Navy. We had lunch together at the Fostoria stop. Talked of schools, politics, foreign affairs, farming, economics, depressions, raising sheep, candy making, China, India, the Golden Gate Bridge, the Navy, the Army, the rain, growing seasons, etc. We parted with neither knowing the other's name.

Due to the all-day rain, it was impossible to get a good impression of the land. However, most of the way down to Bucyrus was flat, black, stoneless, good-looking dirt with corn husked and winter wheat not as tall as ours. Many feeder cattle, sheep, hogs and little piglets—many more of these than in our area where dairy cattle meet the eye first. After Bucyrus the land became undulating, gently rolling and inclined to wash, but still without sharp hills. Large red apples still hang in the orchards. One is taken by the prosperous appearance of the towns and farms—it is a rich land.

Marion, Ohio was President Harding's birthplace, and my presentable young man pointed out the beautiful Memorial where the President and his wife are buried. This town is near the farm of Louis Bromfield, the author of "Pleasant Valley" which you liked so much, Dad.

Keeping track of 110 people, 15 children, and 9 cash fares, besides keeping my end of the conversation going, really kept me busy.

The lobby chair is comfortable and someone may fail to come in. Don't worry, it's part of my job. Remember schedules and fate. Love, Margean

———

October 26, 1946
From Warner Hotel, Chillicothe, Ohio

Dear Ones: Just ten minutes after mailing my letter, I had a room, a lovely one too. See, things do turn out for the best, don't they. Because it was no use going to Athens, I came to Chillicothe instead landing in this ancient, sprawling hotel. Haven't I had the most marvelous luck in getting rooms?

The only bad thing about hotels is their lonesomeness, the one in Toronto with its radio wasn't bad. However, with books and embroidery, the time passes, and there is always the daily letter with its accumulation of thoughts—sort of ink and think. How's that for poetry?

An old town with stone-fronted buildings and brick sidewalks, Chillicothe is the county seat and large enough for Kresge and Woolworth stores. Next week it celebrates 150 years. Just think, in 1796 some adventurous soul first came to these foothills! A sign of progress, Chillicothe has a nice Atlantic Greyhound bus terminal and lunch stop—with which I shall attempt to find fault tomorrow.

My trip took me into the beginning of foothills—nice, rounded, forest-covered hills that, from a distance, seem hazy and eternal. Dapple and roan horses, well-fed, lazy looking creatures, along with feeder cattle, and big and little pigs, browse the pastures. On hills sloping down to the road, picture-perfect houses fronted by white-fenced fields are about a fifth of a mile off the highway. Only worked three hours today so I had plenty of time for a show—Danny Kaye in "The Kid from Brooklyn"—real funny and asinine!

Not feeling in the mood for dinner, I bought some apples and grapes and should have gotten enough for tomorrow. I imagine that you are having steak or roast for Sunday dinner.

Two months from yesterday and Christmas will be here! Then, two more months and I'll have a birthday. How ancient I'm getting. Love, Margean

---

October 27, 1946
From Waldo Hotel, Clarksburg, West Virginia

Dear Ones: Hills! Hills! Hills! Nothing but hills all day. Not nice ones like we have at home or even up North, but real mean, steep, rocky, tree-covered, mountain hills up straight for 927, 943, 987, and finally 1,243 feet according to the markers. Imagine inching up by hairpin, U and V curves to 1,243 feet. I thought the hills of northern Ontario were something but we have bigger and better right here. For seven hours I was either going up, down, or around or just about to. This Highway 50 (George Washington Highway because he surveyed most of it) from Cincinnati to Washington D.C. is the devil's dream, in places so narrow even the Canadians would be ashamed of it. I didn't think much about those "Beware of Falling Rocks" signs until a boulder splattered to nothing 75 feet ahead: we stopped! If I ever make this run with a bad driver or in the winter, I'll die. As it was, to make some of the grades, he had to downshift three times.

The hills are so high that by 1:30 the south side is in shade, probably the reason the houses are on the south-facing slope. But it's beautiful: I never dreamed such grandeur existed. Quilting the hills are pines and trees with leaves of brick red, burnt brick, gold, and yellow. And what do you think keeps pace with us the entire route? The "Big Inch": anyway, an oil pipe with "pumping up" stations ever so far.

I've seen some of the longest towns on record today: only one street, one-quarter, one-half, one, or a mile-and-a-half along the highway. Imagine Galesburg stretched along U.S. 12. Clarksburg is on four hills with no downhill—all uphill—suspension bridges crossing from one hill to another. At Parkersville, we crossed the Ohio River, on a mile-long suspension toll bridge about a half-mile high that gives you that funny feeling in your stomach!

Everywhere there are oil wells, natural gas flares, coal seams, sawmills, and glass factories, mostly extractive industries where people earn their living. West Virginia is noted for its superior coal and low sulfur oil. Some of the sawmills are in the few remaining U.S. virgin lumber stands.

My run of hotel luck didn't hold. Upon applying for my room tonight, I learned that I couldn't have one on my return trip because a nursing convention has every hotel, tourist home and cabin filled. I scurried around and finally got one in the Methodist minister's house—maybe I'm lucky after all.

Have you a map to follow my journey? It was Highway 23 down to Columbus, then Highway 50 from Chillicothe to Washington D.C. Because I have to get up at 5:30 a.m. to catch a 6:30 coach for Washington D.C., I'm going to bed. It's 8:00 and pitch black. Love, Margean

———

October 28, 1946
From Carvel Hotel, Annapolis, Maryland

Dear Ones: "By the Sea, By the Sea, By the Beautiful Sea"—only it's Chesapeake Bay! To celebrate being near to a world center of production, I must have oysters.

At 3,095 feet on Back Bone Mountain, I hit the top of eastern United States. Today was even more terrifying than yesterday in its heights, hills, mountains and curves. Most of the roadbed had been blasted in or built up so the road hugs the side of the mountain protected from nothingness by cable and white posts. Rivaling Michigan, this is great apple country with great big Rome Beauties, and Golden Delicious. No machinery. Grazing instead of farming. Shacks and privies along the road. It's a rare tourist camp with inside toilets—in fact, tourist camps are rare.

Favorable, fog, favorable, mist, rain so ran my weather. Part of the time we were above the rain, part of the time the mountains hid in clouds or in fog, sometimes the sun shone. My unlucky day. I had my "bad" driver. He drove so fast he made the 400 minute run in 306 minutes! I nearly died as we negotiated hairpin turns, 87-degree turns, "straight-ups" and "straight-downs" on the wet pavement! Once, when stopping for a flagee, we skidded. What would have happened if there had been nothing but space on the side of the road! I used three extra sheets to write up the report: I had plenty to say.

Here the bus station is in the back yard of my hotel about three blocks from Main Street in a residential area. Established in 1793, it is one of the oldest hotels in the U.S. still doing business. There are no elevators and the door to every room is finished with an extra slatted door, like a shutter, so one can have good ventilation and still lock oneself in. My room is large and airy–real nice.

In just twenty-five minutes I'm on my way to Washington D.C. Had milk toast for breakfast. Tonight I promise myself seafood. Love, Margean

———

October 29, 1946
From Carvel Hall, Annapolis, Maryland

Dear Ones: Washington D.C., the city of Presidents and politicians. I walked and walked and walked, so now my feet hurt. The people shove and push worse than Detroit. But such chic! Such style! Such glamour! These Washington babes pile on the makeup and I look drab beside them. And I'm melting, simply melting: in fact, I haven't had to wear my coat once, late October or not.

I had my seafood at a cafeteria. In fact, Washington is full of cafeterias. One specialty is spoon bread, sort of a cross between Johnnycake and fried mush, topped with butter. Delicious! Unexpectedly, many of the prices are cheaper than at home.

This is the first time the Annapolis boys have been inspected. After my Canadian trip is over, I'm coming back, get them all and write a divisional report. So far, the only terminal I've come across with separate rooms for Negroes and whites was in Winchester, Virginia.

Tomorrow back over the mountains starting at 3:30 that means it'll be dark during the worse half. What if I have a bad one! Love, Margean

October 30, 1946
From Washington D.C.

Dear Ones: How this month has flown! I've inspected 23 fellows in 22 days. I neglected to tell you that Annapolis is the only state capitol without a railroad—no station—no nothing. So you can understand why my little hound dog has such a lucrative bone here—rich enough to make the run every half-hour.

Heavens! I must get dressed and make a terminal inspection. Tonight I sleep in a Clarksburg Methodist haven.

Later: For the first time I've missed a bus through a dumb misreading of the schedule, missed it by twelve minutes and can't get out till 6:00 tonight. I've had the damndest luck this trip. This means I have to keep awake all night! I'll get into Athens at 5:30 a.m. and am not due out till 3:45 p.m.—my poor minister and his wife will wait in vain for me. Had oyster pie for supper. Love, Margean

October 31, 1946
To parents from Athens, Ohio

Dear Ones: Here I am in Athens without a room so, as I'll be in Columbus at 6:30 p.m., I'm going to stay up. Have been up since 8:00 a.m. yesterday, but will sleep from 8:00 tonight until 1:00 tomorrow afternoon. And I bet I'll sleep all that time!

Contrary to my expectations, I had a good trip with two excellent drivers. My first driver told me that on one curve you can "shake hands with yourself" or "meet yourself coming back"—it's around a big rock U with a 35 degree curve. He told me that another hill-mountain has 36 hairpin turns down and that another is six miles long from the top down. On one mountain there's a three-quarter mile drop straight down—thank God it was dark. He put the spotlight on two deer: "They graze there every night," he said. That wasn't all the animals, two rabbits, a cat, an opossum, a dead collie and two skunks completed the zoo. So, he kept me awake and I kept him awake—company employees should stick together. $61 for two days' work, but it's not worth it—I'm tired! But I like this Cincinnati-Washington run the best of anything yet.

12:10 p.m. Spent my morning in the University of Ohio's Library, the first really good chance I've had to read catching up on magazines and the like. It makes me kind of homesick for the quiet of college study hall—but I'm not weakening. Love, Margean

November 1, 1946
From Southern Hotel, Columbus, Ohio

Dear Ones: Just up from a refreshing 16-hour sleep, and how I did sleep! At 4:45 p.m. I leave for home, arriving about 11:30 and expecting many letters. Speaking of letters reminds me, have you sent my letter to Joss? I have the beginning of another one telling of our "mountains," laughable considering his in Switzerland.

Looking back over the trip, we can be thankful that we don't live in the hill country through which I passed. The lack of conveniences impressed me the most. Electricity went through during the war but still one sees innumerable homes without it. Lack also shows up in another familiar landscape feature—the outhouse. It is a rare home without one, and even the tourist camps are almost exclusively equipped with this relic. In coal country one sees the "company town" and "company house," two rooms down and two up with the inevitable privy in back. This journey may be broken into several parts: Chillicothe to Parkersburg, hills; Parkersburg to Clarksburg, much higher hills; Clarksburg to Romney, mountains; Romney to Winchester, higher hills; Winchester to Annapolis, hills.

It's now 3:00. I must pack, fix myself up, pay my bill and get over to the terminal in plenty of time to get a front seat, a front seat being almost essential at night. To the office tomorrow. Love, Margean

---

November 2, 1946
From YWCA Residence, Detroit, Michigan

Dear Ones: What a lovely bunch of letters including a nice one from you, Dad. Tell more about your plans on the Red Dane cattle, are you changing from Holsteins for good?

Real good to be home. Have washed my clothes and hair. Had a nice chat with the housemother. Church tomorrow and an evening run to Lansing. Love, Margean

---

November 3, 1946
From YWCA Residence, Detroit, Michigan

Dear Ones: In about an hour-and-a-half, your daughter will be rolling to Lansing where a YWCA bed awaits. It's been a full day: church, dinner (roast veal with dressing), reading, and, in 15 minutes, tea (ice cream and cookies).

I neglected to mention that Mrs. King left. Our new office manager is a snappy-looking, ageless Italian woman, Miss Santini. Shall see that I stay on her good side. She lives on this side of town and has asked me over to meet her brother when he gets here from Chicago. Love, Margean

---

November 4, 1946
From YWCA Residence, Detroit, Michigan

Dear ones: Was I mad last night! I got to my corner at 5:55 in plenty of time for the 6:10, but it passed me at 6:52 motioning that there would be a double. It came at 7:14. I thought my feet would drop off from all that standing, but they got a second wind and stood all the way to Lansing too!

Have just finished my reports—three men and a terminal. Tomorrow is our office conference: I hope I haven't done anything to be called down for and, too, I hope I don't get any praise—inspectors might not like it.

From weather reports forecasting a cold wave, I'll wear slacks up North. I've looked forward to this trip ever since August when I went for the first time. Love, Margean

---

November 5, 1946
From YWCA Residence, Detroit, Michigan

Dear Ones: Is this a surprise? Take out what I owe you and bank the rest. Dad, please do some shopping for me for an endowment policy —$5000.

We're going on a "closed payroll" salary basis—no one knowing what the other makes. Next week I'm to go in and talk with JP to decide what I'm worth. We're enlarging. Five more are to be hired. McKay is leaving to marry Ted. Rutare is quitting. Love, Margean

---

November 7, 1946
From Hotel Ojibway, Sault Ste Marie, Michigan

Dear Ones: My re-inspection yesterday was awfully tame and monotonous. Anyway, he carried on a most interesting conversation with the woman behind him about their respective children, his ten and her four.

For the last day-and-a-half I've been pondering over the interesting question of how much I'm worth. JP said that we'd probably be surprised how much he thinks we're worth. From the way the wind has blown, I think that's good news for me. Anyway, I bet it'll be a raise.

By the way, we have orders to "change our jobs." "Some have been running into difficulty," he said, "and I think it would be a good thing if you all held the same job." He continued that he had one that didn't have a lie in it—just the whole truth! We are assistants to an attorney. "They damn well don't have to know I'm not practicing." He went on that this would give us our excuse for travel, etc. As this is an order, please tell my relatives and friends that I am no longer in "social work" because I could get more pay as an "attorney's assistant."

Must close and catch my ferry to Canadian Sault Ste Marie. Love, Margean

---

November 8 1946
From Hotel Coulson, Sudbury, Ontario, Canada

Dear All: Because scheduling has been tight, I haven't written. So, although deep in a murder story, I'm quitting right at the psychologically exciting moment to write this. Ever since St. Ignace, there has been cold rain that makes today's six-hour layover dreary. If the wind shifted, it could turn to snow. Men have on their red mackinaws, children their long black hose, and women their fur collars.

Passed "Old Agony" this morning, that being the popular name for the North Bay-Sault Ste Marie train, puffing away living up to her reputation. A local, she makes the run in twelve hours, the bus takes ten. Last time up here, I forgot to mention that around the copper and nickel smelters and refineries of Copperclift and Connister no vegetation grows. Fumes poison the ground. They are dismal places.

Evening: this is turning into a regular diary! We broke down tonight— a perfect night for it—blinding, pouring rain. Water got into the distributor and it stalled. It was very cozy with flares lighting up the gloom. He called into the terminal and then waited a half-hour: when he tried the motor again—it started.

More about the conference! JP said that either the last of this month or the first of next, we start work on C&LE. First I'm going to work on Valley—lots of short 3-4 hour runs and practically virgin territory—so JP asked me to remedy the situation.

For supper tonight I had "fish and chips," a heaping plate of fried fish and French fries for 25 cents. The rest of the full course meals were T-bone and tenderloin, 75 cents; pork chops, 40 cents; ham and eggs, 35 cents; liver and onions, 30 cents.

Incidentally, in passing, I might as well mention that me and my glands are on the warpath again! Love, Margean

———

November 9, 1946
From Sault Ste. Marie, Michigan

Dear Ones: Back in civilization. A nice trip down, 77 total: he did the 380-minute run in 240 minutes but was late all the way, having to handle tons of luggage and freight.

Guess what I saw tonight! Red northern lights with snaky tentacles fan-spread across the sky. It was an awesome sight!

On the ferry tonight were two cars bearing deer. The man next to me said a lot of bear have been coming through.

You'd be surprised how much good the war did this section of Canada. It helped kill some of the provincialism typical of poor, isolated communities, at least in the draft-age group. Ideas are drifting in: the hot-dog stand, that sign of progress, is springing up.

When I get back to Detroit I shall have been out seven nights—$49. Now that I'm in the clear it's really piling up, another $50 to bank on payday, my room paid until December 2, and no visible necessities except Christmas.

I wonder what you did today. It's always an interesting thing to ponder. When I look at a clock I know what you should be doing. Do you realize that I haven't been home in a long time? Love, Margean

———

November 10, 1946
From Wenonah Hotel, Bay City, Michigan

Dear Ones: Church today at the Soo, in fact, Sunday School and Church in the Methodist corner of the fold. A good sermon, some singing, and the gathering of people made the morning pass quickly—if someone had only asked me to dinner it would have been a perfect day! As no one was so kind, I walked back through the rain and slush to my hotel room overlooking the locks and watched the ships going through. Taking about 25 minutes, there wasn't a time when there were not at least two ships somewhere in the locks. I'm not sure, but I believe it's a 16-foot rise or drop depending on which way you're going.

Rain, rain—by the time I left Church there was no snow left and the rain cut and the wind was raw—a good day to be inside. Winter is here!

Am working on my embroidery. Love, Margean

November 11, 1946
From YWCA Residence, Detroit, Michigan

Dear Ones: Greetings at 5:15 a.m. Due out at 5:45. Bus schedules have no regard for men or sleep, and, like the mail, must go through. So, the driver and I have a date, and I hope I'm not the only one on at this ungodly hour. No place is open, naturally, and our first stop is 10:10. I wonder how many miles I've traveled since being left on the corner for the Cheboygan man last week? It doesn't seem as though this trip is almost over. Must close and catch my man.

More greetings at 11:15 p.m. The end of a long day—with a driver with a hangover. As I sat behind him, I got a recital of his woes, aches, and pains plus a complete description of how he acquired them. Not only that, but at Bay City I got an invite for dinner and drinks! The first time any Greyhound wolf has tried to pick me up!

It's a doozy of a report—drinking activities at St. Ignace, non-sleep at St. Ignace, drinking in uniform and the inside dope on a threatened drivers' strike in December. It took over two hours to write. Naturally, I asked that it not go through—felt that I needed something more than protection and that JP must send some of our men there for a special look-see. Between the driver's woes and those of a woman sitting beside me part time, I had my hands full with turning a sympathetic ear and keeping track of my audit!

Went to a movie here tonight, the first since that news film I saw with you.

"Two Guys from Milwaukee!" with Dennis Morgan and Jack Carson was a lot of fun. I shouldn't have gone: I'm low on funds since paying you back and hadn't anticipated that JP would want me on that new assignment so soon. Only $82 until payday: well, $82 is enough to spend time on Valley. To give you an idea of how much it costs on the road, my entire eight-day trip, including the tickets, rooms, meals, and everything came to $59.66. You can see why we need money on hand. I made $49 overnight pay, had $22.62 expenses, and cleared $26.38. I worked, including my report time, 70 hours—so I cleared $96 (less taxes) this week. The bookkeeping I do lets me know where I stand.

Must wash, do my exercises and get ready for bed. Bet I will have a flock of letters waiting in the. How I've enjoyed this trip! Love, Margean

——•——

November 13, 1946
From YWCA Residence, Detroit, Michigan

Dear Ones: How can you expect a coherent letter after what's happened to me? I'm so jumpy I can't eat or sit still, much less write. My cup runneth over or some such thing. Now to see if I can give you a picture of what happened.

I spent all morning working out my travels. After lunch JP came in to dictate some material after which he seemed free, so in I go and he waves me to a chair. "I've been here four months now," I said, "what can I do to improve, what are the gripes and what have I done that I shouldn't?"—or words to that effect. "Wrong!" he said, "if they were all like you, this company would be the envy of the U.S. I've never been associated with anyone with so much interest, so much ambition and so much concern for the work. The only thing," he said, "is your use of superlatives: everything is very good or very bad—no between, but," he went on, "that's no fault."

Then we talked about my special. I have done two re-inspections on him, and I'm to go after him again: the driver is saying he has turned me up [*identified me*]—a man inspector, but it was me sitting right behind him. JP got awfully mad about it: so he is sending me on him again.

Then we talked about company operations. I asked again what my chances were of ever getting into terminal work. Good, wonderful were the adjectives he used. "In fact," he said, "I almost told Radcliff about you last week but I wanted to talk to you again. You'll get in, if I can possibly get you in, but you'd be the only woman working into such a

72

position in the Greyhound Corporation. We're going to have to break down some prejudices and push you into the limelight. This will be our first move," he went on, "I want you to practically memorize the method of applicant investigations and I'll send you out on some. Your inspection reports already cause a lot of favorable comment. Applicant investigations will be right up your alley, and I know your reports will be better than anything done so far. I'll use you on ticket agents only and also send one of my regular applicant inspectors on them, and then I'll turn the reports in together so Radcliff can see the difference. You know, he sent back a note telling us how much he appreciated your telling us about the commuter-ticket situation. I'll also put you into the training program so you can inject a little of your enthusiasm into our new people. In fact, I think you should meet Radcliff. One of these days I'll fix up a luncheon for us, and I'll embarrass you by telling what a wonderful employee you are and the background you have: then, we'll see what happens!" I've never heard so many nice things. So that's how matters stand, except they're even better because I can't put down everything—I wasn't taking notes.

So I got a raise, and a promise preparing for a job that I've always wanted. I'm riding on top of the world. I can't believe it. And, oh yes, to keep me out of danger of being turned up [identified], I'm to juggle my destinations and origins to "Put the finger on some other person: I want you clear."

Gee, am I keyed up. I am sitting on top of the world. Love, Margean

———

November 14, 1946
From YWCA Residence, Detroit, Michigan

Dear Ones: I'm going to have company on my special run down South. I'm to start right out in this new training mode with Mrs. Farr on out-of-town trips. All of which means that JP is serious about expanding my range of activities: "See if you can impart some of your pep and interest," he said. So I spent most of today getting her acquainted with "road work" and sent a double reservation to a Columbus hotel for our trip there. She used to be our secretary, but JP said she was too smart for the kind of money she was making.

Everyone was in the office today: what a hubbub! A new man started in, a nice 22-year-old kid from Seattle who seems to be on the ball, an eager beaver. Now that Rutare was fired, Mr. Cross quit, and Miss McKay resigned, the staff is down to working dimensions with only the better ones left. Well, as soon as Lawson is fired or turned up again, everything will be perfect. I spent a couple of hours poring over the instructions on applicant investigations to master the essentials and hoping that my first "case" wouldn't involve too much foot work. I also read over some of Mr. Glatz's completed reports. He is real good.

It's a wonderful day—crisp, cool, and delightfully fall—or maybe the world just looks awfully bright to me. A perfect night to ride, leaving at 6:40 p.m. for Lake City. In celebration of all that has happened to me, I will get all dressed up for my run tonight: I have an outfit lined up in black.

Still, I'm not going off half-cocked on this future. I know it depends upon hard work on my part, work so good that it has to stand out, work that has to break down prejudices. That's a tough assignment. Maybe it'll be a year or two or three before there's an opening, or JP thinks I'm ready and I feel prepared. This personnel and training experience will be good start. Love, Margean

---

November 15, 1946
From YWCA Residence, Detroit, Michigan

Dear Ones: What an adventure last night. Guess who I rode with, one of my old Kalamazoo drivers and what a nice conversation we had. He, too, now lives in Detroit and works the Traverse City night run. He's still as handsome, as polite and as much a gentleman as ever, but, more to the point, from an inspection viewpoint, he's a good driver. His is the first familiar face I've seen to talk to in Detroit. It relieved my mind to see him cut and issue cash-fare receipts; at least he's not stealing money from the company. My report is written in a way to put the "finger" on a hunter riding from Detroit to Standish.

We broke down in Bay City and had to change coaches: then we had to jog along to West Branch to wait for the second section: here we looked into the Onemaw Hotel Bar, where the ticket office is located, and saw hunters growing drunker and louder by the glassful. Then we decided that because he had a cold and I had cold feet, that we needed some coffee. Well, what with the breakdown and the wait in West Branch, we finally arrived in Lake City an hour-and-a-half late at 3:00 a.m. "Hope I see you again," he said, "you're the first familiar face I've seen in Detroit." Echoing my sentiments. "You might," I answered.

Well, to get on with my adventure. Here I am in Lake City at 3:00 a.m. and naturally there's no room. No room! An understatement! Hunters are sleeping dormitory fashion upstairs, on the four sofas and four easy chairs downstairs, and, if it had been large enough, would have slept in the chandelier next to the ceiling. So Mr. O'Neil, who remembered me from my visit last summer when I did all the piano playing, gave me a pack of cards and I played solitaire—I won $27.35 according to my score. About 4:00 a.m. the hunters began waking up: by 6:30 they'd all cleared out and I grabbed a couch for two hours. A lesson was drawn from this: Never come to Lake City during hunting season!

In 45 minutes I'm due out. Tomorrow Mrs. Farr and I have a date with my special, an unknown gentleman, and a regular driver. I'm hoping that the money I called about came today or comes tomorrow because I have to finance the fund-less Mrs. Farr down South. According to my figures, I'll draw over $200 this pay period including part of my eastern and all my northern trips: and I've enjoyed every minute of it. Love, Margean

---

November 16, 1946
From YWCA Residence, Detroit, Michigan

Dear Ones: Am I mad! Boiling over! Angry! I get up at 6:00 a.m. to take an 8:10 bus to keep my re-inspection and special company, get down to the terminal early to get on the first section and who should be on but the same fellow I had down yesterday! My special has gone hunting! I swore! I had an eighteen-hour day planned, all predicated upon getting up to Charlevoix or Lake City, ruined!

Well, guess what I did. I took Mr. Hobb under my wing for training and we went up to Mt. Pleasant where he knew some people. We got back at 10:25, a whale of a lot different then 5:36 if I'd caught my special. I'm undecided how Mr. Hobb will turn out, I don't believe he'll kill himself working. He spent so much time trying to wrangle a date with me that he didn't pay much attention to all the valuable information I was giving him. Lord, he almost turned us up being so conspicuous in what he was doing. But guess what: he bought my dinner, the first time in Detroit history. I much prefer Mr. Docker. Love, Margean

---

November 17, 1946
From YWCA Residence, Detroit, Michigan

Dear Ones: Got your most welcome letter. It makes me feel good to know you're standing up for me. There will be two openings that I know of next spring, one in Battle Creek and one in Mackinaw City, both where new terminals are going up; however, I know that's too soon to think about a change.

An applicant investigation consists of a lot of footwork. First you contact the police department most likely to have a record of the applicant: if it is a criminal record, we stop right there. Next we contact the applicant's school to ascertain the truth of his name, address, date and place of birth, his education with grades, diligence, and general aptitude. Most important, we contact people in his neighborhood who know him, the gossip, the butcher, the neighbors, the bank: we find out who his associates are, what his reputation for honesty, industry, and integrity is, who he had quarreled with and why, whether he fights with his wife (domestic troubles being a cause for many accidents), and try to fill in gaps in his employment record: then, and this is the test, we try to see the applicant. Next we contact his employers getting the dates of employment, what his job consisted of, what his salaries were, and the employer's opinion: we talk to his supervisors and fellow workers trying to determine his actual character, industry and ability. Finally, we contact the people he has given as references, always finding out the relationship between the reference and the applicant to discount bias. Lastly—and this is where genius counts—we write it up! Whether he is hired or fired depends upon what we write down: is that, or is that not, responsibility? I wonder who, if anyone, did me!

The way I'm to do it is this: first JP will assign me an investigation and he and I will go over what I'm to do step by step. Then I do it and write it up. Then back to the office, close the door, and he'll pick it to pieces. Then another investigation and critique until I get to the point that I'm better than any other in my reports. I think it a good idea that I make mine best to begin with and skip the intervening phases.

I've planned what I'll wear when that all-important luncheon comes up, business-like but distinctive, the way I always try to look.

Leave for Columbus tonight with Mrs. Farr under my wing. Because she worked in the office, she knows the ropes and we'll have fun. Love, Margean

---

November 19, 1946
From YWCA Residence, Detroit, Michigan

Dear Ones: What fun on the trip. We raised Cain. Going down, we sat across from each other—so we could lean across the aisle and chatter—she next to a middle-aged man. Naturally he was talkative and considerate, even to the point of offering us a "nip" from his bottle. The driver had a girlfriend along, and you should have heard the sour grapes comments from the middle-aged men. Passenger reaction can take off on anything which is one of the things that make me love this work.

We had a "little boy" on his first run. So sweet: you could tell that everything in driver school was sticking behind his wet ears. Was Connie impressed: we named him Johnny and gave him a girlfriend and all the trimmings. It gave me a chance to point out how always getting as many good things as possible into a report can influence the way a person feels about their job.

Got your long letter telling of the wedding. You haven't received any from me because I've been busy with Connie and not getting enough sleep since we left Sunday. She's from Kentucky and at 18 married a man 32. They moved to Detroit where he was regional sales manager for Chrysler and went all over the country. When the war came along, he enlisted and was killed in a plane. She's now 30 and looks about 24-25. She's pretty with a kittenish face and contagious grin. We get along famously having many interests in common. By the way, when I'm training, I get 10 cents an hour more. Love, Margean

———

November 20, 1946
From YWCA Residence, Detroit, Michigan

Dear Ones: At the office training, then working up my trip. My agenda: Canada and then runs around Kalamazoo when I'm there for Thanksgiving. By the way, when I'm home, I have a run where one of you can go with me.

I forgot to tell something funny that happened when Connie and I came back from Columbus. I'd just paid the hotel bill and bent down to pick up my suitcase when—wham—there went my garter-belt. I clutched my middle. "What's the matter?" said Connie, "Appendicitis?" "No," I gasped as my stockings started to dangle, "something else." No woman's room was in sight so I headed for a phone booth. While Connie stood nonchalantly in front busting with laughter, I repaired damages with a pin.

This morning I corrected my trainee's "papers" and helped her plan an overnight trip, so it was late before I started on my own schedule. I had notes in my file and was clearing them up with Miss Santini, our new office manager, who told me that she thinks my reports are the best in the office and that she has been told to give me all the local ticket agent investigations. She and JP are certainly pulling for me. No one likes her

—an Italian ex-teacher with "snap" in every movement. This antagonizes the rest, but we get along well.

Look at the paycheck I got! Please bank the $50. Am simply floating in spondulix. Love, Margean

---

November 21, 1946
From YWCA Residence, Detroit, Michigan

Dear Ones: Travels start tomorrow and I will not be in the office until December 1st, when investigations will probably start to fill my time. Don't expect any letters, I'm working God awful hours.

Celebrating, I got a new dress today—$18.90 reduced to $7.90—but looks like a million. It's a simple black dress made out of heavy silk shantung with small gold buttons down the front. Then I spent time mending and the little incidentals that take time and effort. I keep my wardrobe right up to snuff: there's never anything in it I can't wear. As soon as I get in from a trip, I wash and iron everything that needs it. On the road it's sometimes difficult to look spruce, which is why I like dark, heavy dresses.

Later today my roommate, Beverly, and I walked to the Railway Salvage to find out if any pineapple was in. The blocks rolled by and we got two miles of fast exercise. Starting out foggy, the day has warmed up fast, the sun bright, and everyone said it was too good to last. Then I went down and played piano.

I have had a wonderful rest. After fourteen days of war, my glands and I have declared a truce. Just so I feel well, I don't mind this continual battle. Love, Margean

---

November 22, 1946
From Lake City, Michigan

Dear Ones: For the office part of my day I wore my new dress. Did I ever get compliments! JP asked me who the lucky man was. "Two unsuspecting fellows," said I. On my round trip to Chatham, Ontario, the wind and snow almost blew us from the road. What a change from yesterday! 15 forecast for tonight! When I got home I changed to slacks, gray coat, and headscarf—from the sophisticate to the schoolgirl!

At present, I'm sitting in a White Tower hamburger place right by the railroad track where the driver will have to stop and he's due in ten minutes. Charlevoix, here Worst comes! Let's hope there's a place to make a four-hour stopover! It's 6:10 p.m., he's out of the station and in about 15 minutes he'll be here. Love, Margean

—◆—

November 23, 1946
From Lake City, Michigan

Dear Ones: 3:30 a.m. We've broken down just out of Lake City: it's snowing and blowing and there are just eight of us on. Are we having fun! "Matilda" is temperamental, especially when she was left with her motor idling 59 minutes and when she's two hours late.

4:40 a.m. Have just hiked back into Lake City with the driver in hopes that the bus will be fixed in time for me to catch the morning driver back, or that I can get a room here until the Bay City-bound Detroit from Traverse City comes through. I really want the latter, because I found that my old hunting special driver is going to be on it tonight instead of on Charlevoix as per the run-bid sheet. Am cold (my feet) and sleepy and can't do my reports because the driver is standing by the stove. What luck: this will have to go in as protection [*the report not used because it would identify me*].

Guess I might as well write and write. First, about the "joys" of a triple room. Both roommates have blues because of employment difficulties. Beverly, the quiet one, is genuinely in a mess: laid off, the company contesting her unemployment compensation and she has had to dip into her considerable bank reserve. Betty, my good-for-nothing roommate, gets her compensation via a date with the right party. Ever since I've been here, she has been without a job. She has to pay $8.50 for her room and board and $8.00 for her baby's room and board which means she needs approximately $20 a week to live on. That little fact, plus observing that she rarely gets in before 3:00 a.m., if at all, adds up to one thing in my mind. And soon it'll add up to one thing in the minds of the proper authorities. In fact, every time I come home from an extended trip, I expect to see a new roommate!

Thursday night the YMCA gave a dinner and party for our girls. I didn't go because I had to get sleep for this trip. Because Beverly keeps too much to herself, I dragged her downstairs to see who else was left behind and found six kindred souls, including Mrs. Tolsin, our housemother. Although novice players, we found cards to play Five Hundred. After playing a game, I dealt out and hauled down my electric popper amidst "ohs" and "ahs". So we had popcorn along with Mrs. Tolsin's apples and peanuts, a regular feast! What fun!

What luck that I changed to slacks and wool sweater: I'd have been frozen. It is about 10 above and the snow crackles under foot!

7:00 a.m. Just finished my reports and guess who walked in? Driver and the bus load: this time they broke down seven miles out and rode back in the rear of a pickup. I'm glad I didn't go this time. Love, Margean

———

November 24, 1946
From YWCA Residence, Detroit, Michigan

Dear Ones: This finds me at the end of a very long day. I got in at 4:30 a.m. from the special re-inspection, losing money on the deal. How? Well, like this: a man boarding at Alger bound for Pinconning, handed the driver a dollar for a 63 cent fare. The driver had no change and asked the passengers if they had any: as luck would have it, I had the needed 37 cents which was taken and not returned. No cash fare ticket was issued! It's so sad, because with this third inspection that is enough to fire him.

Coming into Detroit a lot of trolleys were lined up and a huge crowd drew our attention—all two of us. Upon being stopped we found that the trolley had run over a drunk or suicide, which the police hadn't decided. I saw the body carted away on a stretcher.

Let me tell you what happened after the ending of my Lake City adventures. After breaking down the second time, the driver sent to Bay City for a new coach. Bad luck was his lot, for the new extra driver got lost and arrived in Lake City at 10:15 a.m. My old driver finally got underway, none too happy because he had planned to go hunting. What did I do? I got the 10:38 coach and went to Houghton Lake where I got a hotel room.

I slept from 11:30 a.m. to 8:15 p.m. then kept my date with my special, his only passenger most of the way into Detroit. I slapped protection all over the report which took me 2½ hours to write because of all the things besides the cash fare—smoking, dress, loitering, safety stops, intersections, and other driving violations.

This is the third time he and I have had a date. "Gee, you look awfully familiar," he said, "What do you do?" "I work for a lawyer," I said. "Work in the David Stott Building," he asked. "No, Empire Building," I said, not even sure there was one in Detroit. "Where are you from?" "Kalamazoo," I said, glad to tell the truth for a change. He established to his satisfaction, I hope, that he'd seen me at the Hollywood Club. I'm glad he worked out his own solution.

I reported the above in detail to JP because of the suspicions and implications therein—namely David Stott Building and my familiar face.

Lord knows what'll become of the driver. I don't think I should have been assigned to him three times! Do you remember when I had to walk out to Clare City limits? It was this same driver I had been sent to ride. I believe that the cash fare (and my consequent thinner pocketbook) will be sufficient to fire him if he doesn't report it. If the union protests, it will turn me up [*identify me*] for good, especially if I have to testify. They can't use the report without turning me up like a red flag!

Anyway, I got home at 4:30 a.m., wrote that four-page report and crawled into bed. Then I couldn't get to sleep: the trip, the details of my report, its implications and possible consequences kept me awake. So at 8:00 I got up, did my washing and ironing and washed my hair. By then Beverly was back from church and the dinner bell rang. The rest of the afternoon and evening was filled with a gossip session, sewing and tea, with radio interspersed between.

At present, my chief worry is my report. I had on my gray coat, slacks, and headscarf: he would probably never recognize me dressed up. I hope never to see him again, but in this business, one never knows <u>who</u> will turn up on a bus.

My white gloves were stolen, so I've locked my safety-box and other stuff in my large suitcase. Betty, my wayward roommate, was not in when I arrived this morning, hasn't showed up today, and it's doubtful if she'll roll in tonight. I am suspicious. I can hardly wait until she's kicked out! Love, Margean

---

December 2, 1946
From YWCA Residence, Detroit, Michigan

Dear Ones: What a day! What an office shake-up! What changes in the offing!

I've been turned up so cold it isn't funny! And was it my fault? No! They used the special memorandum I wrote back in November on that St. Ignace driver to fire him. The union is fighting it, and I have to sign a deposition that it is true. Is JP mad! Not at me, but at himself, for he overrode my objections to sending it through. You may remember that I suggested sending the men inspectors up to look into what was going on up there. The driver even remembered what I looked like and what my occupation was (worked for a lawyer), as well he should from the details in the report.

I can't work Bay City north or Bay City at all any more! There go my northern Canadian trips, my Sault Ste Marie trips, my Traverse City and Ludington trips, practically everything. So: what's being done?

I'm to have exclusive possession of the Flint Trolley Coach inspections, and Monday I'm to go up with Allen to learn the layout. I get $25 a day for my time up there because this is the President's personal company. Allen, with all his special investigations, can no longer handle it (Allen is the one that should have been sent to St. Ignace to check on that situation). I also have all extra men, not only for myself, but to assign to other inspectors who have such problems figuring out how to catch them. Tomorrow I start gathering the information on them a better way, a job I've been itching to do. Next, Allen has been made head of the Training Department and I'm the trainer on all interurban lines! Last, all ticket agent investigations are to be routed through me and I'm to redouble my efforts in keeping my ears open to learn all I can about the company. So my former fields of operation have been cut but I now move into different responsibilities.

JP, Miss Santini, Allen and I were closeted trying to clear out the confusion of dumb new inspectors, reorganization, poor training and my future. Allen and I are IT: "the only ones with any brains or sense of responsibility." I have to pare the "college education" off my reports: "no fault" but when I teach new trainees they could never live up to mine. (I don't know how I'm going to do that).

There's to be an office conference the 5th. Except Allen and me, everyone is mad: Ella, because she is no longer the trainer except on suburbans; Frye, because he got hell for having 36 men behind his name for three weeks without retiring any; Hobb, because he wasn't paid for some long, unnecessary layover; Farr, because she's lost in a fog; Lawson, because he was docked for long rides with poor reports; Prater, because one of his best has been turned up by his own hand, because training under Ella has accomplished nothing, because the new people are dumb. The only happy ones are Allen because he has new responsibility; Worst, because she's starting up the ladder; Glatz (who wasn't in), because he's swell; and Docker, who is doing all right! And I'm really ready, but scared to death that that driver will take a shot at me!

If at all possible I'll come home this weekend: the conference will be over, people will hate my guts and Lord knows what will happen. JP was going to do an override of my cash fare special report, but the same thing will happen. My head aches from all the planning and plotting the four of us did today.

By the way, there is a notice on our bulletin board that hereafter all Grand Rapids bound coaches are to approach all intersections in the curb lane and to stop, regardless of whether or no there are passengers at Grand Boulevard, Livernoise, and Oakland Boulevard. All my doing for being left behind that time.

This is the Report that Turned Me Up

"I noticed while loading that the driver looked very sleepy and yawned a lot. So, as is my practice on night and early morning runs, I seated myself as close to the front as possible—right behind him—and got the information in the paragraphs below.

"While making the ferry crossing, I took some embroidery and went up to the cabin, all the other passengers staying below sleeping. After getting myself situated and to work, the driver entered, wandered around, and then sat down beside me bemoaning the fact that his head hurt. 'Not enough sleep or too much night life?' I asked. 'Both,' he replied, going on to say that he was working extra board and, this being the first time since October 10 that he's been to St. Ignace, he'd been renewing old acquaintances at the Nicolet Hotel Bar. One of the deckhands, who subsequently walked in, confirmed this, and said, 'You certainly looked silly last night in that Alpine hat'—hats, it seemed, everyone entering the bar had to buy. Anyway, the driver rambled on that he'd got to bed at 12:30 and got up at 4:30: 'What a head! That's what you get for drinking 'boiler makers.' I furthered my education by learning that "boiler makers" are whisky with chasers of beer.

"About this time we docked and went below: I resumed my seat behind him. Between Mackinaw City and Gaylord I catnapped, surreptitiously watching him yawn and yawn and yawn. At Gaylord, where he announced a 15-minute rest stop, the following conversation took place. 'Asleep?' he asked. 'Almost,' I replied. 'Me too,' he said, 'between Indian River and Wolverine I dropped off twice for a second.' (I know he did for twice his head dropped and he snapped it back and shook it to clear the fog away). 'Better have some coffee,' I said. 'I will,' he answered and proceeded to drink two cups of black coffee.

"From Gaylord into Bay City he was very talkative, mostly about his drinking capacity. The following is quoted: 'Lots of times I've got up to St. Ignace about 12 at night and never went to bed before starting back. Of course, you're not supposed to drink in uniform, but I always put on a jacket. I like whiskey best, whiskey and 7-Up, beer gives me a terrible hangover, like today.' Then I learned about his travels—tall tales about this and that, this bar and that, this dame and that—rambling at such length I don't know whether he was trying to impress me or keep awake. Probably both. There was a comment that the company didn't care about its drivers, 'But wait till our contract expires.'

"At Bay City there was some delay before I could get my luggage during which he checked in. When he came out, with a checked overcoat over his uniform, he asked me to go over to the Republic Hotel Bar across the street for a couple of drinks. I said no, that I had an appointment. When I started for the Wenonah Hotel he walked across the street with me and entered the Bar door while I walked on."

You can see he would have been a moron not to remember me! Love Margean

—•—

December 3, 1946
From YWCA Residence, Detroit, Michigan

Dear Ones: Did I work today getting my extra men into some semblance of order. Then in the afternoon Allen came in and we went into consultation over Flint Trolley Company, drawing a map of the city bus routes, learning to read their schedules, finding that I contact a Mr. Geise. After we'd finished the map, I told Allen I didn't think it necessary for the two of us to go up there and he agrees. We talked over the training program and pooled ideas. I went over some of his special investigations with him, getting the drift and being impressed: he certainly should have been sent to St. Ignace.

Can hardly wait for the conference. Hobb doesn't know it yet but he told JP he was 24, had four years in the Navy, and was a claims adjuster for an insurance firm: investigations turn him up as 20, two years in the Navy and no such job. Allen told me he would probably be fired this week, as all he wants to do is sit next to some pretty girl on a coach.

Allen and I have always gotten along fine: we will have fun. Love, Margean

—•—

December 5, 1946
From YWCA Residence, Detroit, Michigan

Dear Ones: Conference! Did JP hit the ceiling, chiefly over the new inspectors—Hobb and Farr—being in a daze after five weeks in the business. "Dreamy-eyed inspectors," he called them: "Everyone in this office is over 21 except one," he said, "all you need to get along in this office are interest in your work and a little consideration for others: if you haven't got it, you need your walking papers!" And on and on, with Miss

Santini winking at me every once in a while. He mentioned things that I do in making out reports, daily reports, and specials which the others now have to do: "It saves a damn lot of office work."

Worst-Santini relations. Tonight was the second night that Miss Santini and I went home together, she living further down the line than I. We have discussed the work of the office, improvements that would make inspectors and office staff more efficient. I guess we are two schoolteacher types. This not going to go over with the rest of the inspectors.

Worst now can request an automatic re-inspection on a driver if she thinks he warrants it. Here is how that came about. While checking through reports back from audit, I found several that I thought should have had a re-inspection. So I am to attach a note requesting one where I felt it was needed.

Worst has been busy on extra men for the past three days finally getting them into working condition and collecting the necessary telephone numbers needed to find out when and where these men are being sent. We have never had this capability before for efficient trip planning. A proper commendation was given at the conference. Others probably hate Worst.

Worst goes out on the road tomorrow, home and points South. Worst got paid today! Will deposit some when home. Worst is tired, but happy. Love, Margean

---

December 9, 1946
From YWCA Residence, Detroit, Michigan

Dear Ones: No double today so didn't go to Chatham: instead I had three teeth filled, finished Christmas shopping and packed for tonight. Not much drilling to be done, not enough to hurt much anyway so for $9 my teeth are set. What crowds downtown! I had to battle through the mob with a strategic retreat here and a planned advance there.

Off in a half-hour for Columbus. The driver and I have a date: in fact, I slept two hours this afternoon so I'd feel in the mood. He and I have an extra special date for he's suspected of stealing cash fares. Consequently, I'll flag him down and pay him about $6.00. Love, Margean

---

December 10, 1946
From Southern Hotel, Columbus, Ohio

Dear All: A routine day. Slept until 12:30 p.m. and left at 1:30 for Chillicothe. During my three-hour layover I went to the library to read the latest magazines and newspapers.

What a day where weather was concerned—poured—splattered—showered. People plunged through it for Christmas shopping. Imagine the dreary landscape-bedraggled cows, pigs and horses looking terribly hurt by fate. Great pig country—red, white, and black with white stripe—big ones with good curls in their tails! Love, Margean

December 12, 1946
From Southern Hotel, Columbus, Ohio

Dear Ones: And still it rains—steady—drenching—a downpour. Nevertheless, I ventured out to watch the wet, frantic Christmas shoppers with less than twelve shopping days. What a mob: their feet hurt—their tempers are short—they are all wet. At present I'm resting my feet in the book department. The one that intrigues me most is Van Loon's "Lives" —but then, they all do. I could spend years looking and reading through them.

Right now I'm wondering what the New Year holds in store for us. All things good I hope. Love, Margean

December 13, 1946
From YWCA Residence, Detroit, Michigan

Dear Ones: Back from my jaunt—tired! The funniest thing happened coming back. We had a deadhead [*a non-driving driver*] and he and the driver talked all the way. At Brush Ridge the driver said he was positive he had a speed-check car tailing, so for about five miles they anxiously watched this car speculating on the ifs and buts. Finally it turned off and we once more high-tailed it for Detroit. It was a conversation full of gossip by 100% company men. Stuff like "If they ever get rid of me, it's because I'm fired!" Love, Margean

December 14, 1946
From YWCA Residence, Detroit, Michigan

Dear Ones: I wasn't going to work today. I promised myself! I shouldn't have! I was dead when I woke up this morning, just absolutely dead! I figured on going to the office, calling up to find if any extra men were going out, and sending some of our people out on them. I shouldn't have!

I got there at 9:00: sure enough, there was a swell rundown with two extra men driving. I didn't want to take it because I was planning on leaving Sunday for some special work in Columbus. Docker wandered in, he didn't have the $4.76 to go; Hobb wandered in, he wanted to work suburbans; Lawson wandered in, he didn't want to work! I went.

Before leaving I had lunch with Miss Santini and she was mad—here, she said, I had worked out this wonderful ten hour rundown and all they had to do was get on and go. Two-bits she mentions it to JP! So I made the round-trip to Findley, working thirteen hours when I had planned to work four—I stay philosophical.

The 23rd we get our turkeys and darned if I know how to get it home! Right now Lord knows when I'll be home. JP wants me to keep the inspectors at those extra men during the holidays.

All tomorrow free until 8:50 p.m. Free? Wash hair, wash clothes, take bath, iron, send Christmas cards, pack, and in between eat and play piano. Which reminds me: Betty, my wayward roommate, is out! Good riddance! The Y got fed up with her gallivanting around. Love, Margean

———

December 16, 1946
From Southern Hotel, Columbus, Ohio

Dear Ones: We hit a blinding snowstorm, the kind with huge flakes, all the way from Findley to Marion. Pavement conditions were terrible! Saw two accidents involving trucks but had two exceptionally good drivers.

Something happened last night that restored my faith in humanity. Leaving the coach in Marion at 1:30 a.m., I went over to the hotel and wrote reports until 2:30. Then the problem confronted me: just how was I going to stay awake until 6:45 when I was due out. I got out my embroidery and prepared to lay siege against the arms of Morpheus. But I didn't need to. The kindly desk clerk told me that a man had checked out of a room that had twin beds and that, if I'd care to, I could go up and sleep for my three hours because the room had been paid for. I didn't hesitate—I went to bed! Once that man must have been a Boy Scout, anyway, his good deed for the day was done.

Just five months ago today I started work. I wonder what I'll be doing five months from now. Love, Margean

—◦—

December 17, 1946
From YWCA Residence, Detroit, Michigan

Dear Ones: A funny incident: I was riding early this morning with my eyes closed when suddenly we swerved. What met my opening eyes was a road sign, "Pray! Prepare to meet God!" What a shock!

A meeting with JP this week relative to our new salaries, I suppose. Miss Santini said that Mr. Glatz and I would get the highest, not Allen as I expected. This is something I hadn't counted on because I think Allen is best. Love, Margean

—◦—

December 18, 1946
From YWCA Residence, Detroit, Michigan

Dear Ones: Well, I can't make it to Cadillac with you which disappoints me. I was asked to keep on the job because no one else was going to. So, I'm stuck.

I shall probably be late getting in Xmas Eve. Shall we have presents then? I hope so! How I'm looking forward to it! And turkey for Xmas! It's times like this that make me homesick! Lord only knows, though, what the conference has in store for me. Love, Margean

—◦—

December 20, 1946
From YWCA Residence, Detroit, Michigan

Dear Ones: This is to let you know the good news from my talk with JP. I am now on the "closed-payroll" plan, a member of the administrative department of Greyhound Corporation and, as such, have company insurance, pension plan, vacations with pay, sick leave with pay and numerous other benefits.

My salary, for a 40-hour week, is $250 a month plus whatever I make on my overnight expenses. JP told me that 235 hours was the most I'd worked in one month so this is a substantial increase. I forgot to ask whether this was inclusive or exclusive of my Flint special which pays $25 a day. Do you suppose that for my birthday I could buy myself a fur coat to celebrate making $3000 a year?

A typical incident: Frye was in the office this morning. "Going to catch a lot of extra men this weekend?" I asked. "No, think I'll stick around here," was his reply. No money, I bet. This is why JP wanted me to work. The Christmas bus rush started yesterday: yesterday I caught three extra men; today, two; tomorrow, two; Sunday, one; Monday, two; Tuesday, one.

Got a lovely new roommate, an orphan. Is she ever clean and neat, a welcome relief from the last character.

Gee, I feel so good today. Christmas is coming. Love, Margean

---

December 21, 1946
From Hotel Gibbons, Dayton, Ohio

Dear Ones: I hit Dayton right in the middle of a snow and sleet storm. Little attention was paid to the schedule that said we were to arrive at 10:02 p.m.: we arrived at 11:21. Of course, pavement conditions were not wholly responsible for our tardiness, a traffic jam in Toledo—three blocks in 27 minutes—had a great deal to do with it. Why am I complaining? My Dayton hotel room was going to be held until 11:30—hence my worry whether the hotel was a block or a mile from the station. From the letterhead you can see I slipped under the deadline—risking life and limb on the slippery streets in the fastest six blocks I've ever walked!

What a seat companion I had! She was the best-preserved 45 year-old I've ever seen. A believer in astrology, she told me what sign I should marry under and that yesterday, December 20, was favorable for a long trip and for increasing my business career—both, incidentally being true. Then I heard her family troubles—two husbands, two grown children, depression days, etc. But the old gal certainly enjoyed living, relating incidents and sidelights until I felt I knew David, Bob and Louise. Assuming that I'd never been in this territory before, she undertook to show me the sights. What a lark!

To use a favored sentence construction—what a lot of drinking was going on! I could see it in three different seats around me and when a sherry bottle rolled along the aisle, I knew there was some in back. The fellow behind us got gay, singing and praying. The slightly inebriated passengers got a great kick from the lordly "Amens" which sent them into gales of laughter. Later, the hilarity died and only lordly snores reverberated against our four small walls.

A turkey and I will be on the first section, if possible, of the 9:15 p.m., pulling into Galesburg. Prepare to welcome your lady of leisure home with double blankets. Love, Margean

———

December 27, 1946
From YWCA Residence, Detroit, Michigan

Dear Ones: What do I find in my mailbox when I get here at 4:00 p.m. but a message that it's urgent to get in touch with Mr. Prater immediately! As a result, I meet tomorrow with the Mr. Manferd Burleigh, President, on the St. Ignace incident of last November. The driver has denied everything and tomorrow afternoon brings his grievance before the President, and the President wants to see me before it takes place.

JP tried to get in touch with me at home for this conference was supposed to take place today but, because I couldn't be reached, it was postponed. Tomorrow morning JP is coming for me. He's happy because it will give him a chance to confront higher-ups about the "protection" I had splashed across my report and wasn't given. He's happy because it's my chance to impress officials. I'm to dress as old as possible. Me? I'm scared to death!

Coming home the bus had an accident. A car swung from the curb lane in front of our coach in the second lane to turn left. A neat way to commit suicide! No one was hurt—only damage, one badly crumpled fender.

Nice dinner tonight, but I have no appetite. Love, Margean

———

December 28, 1946
From YWCA Residence, Detroit, Michigan

Dear Ones: Be careful how you handle this letter—it was written with the hand that had a hearty handshake from both Mr. Manferd Burleigh and Mr. Merle Morrow.

90

JP picked me up promptly at 11:00 and we carefully went over my report. Driving up to the terminal, we parked and went up the baggage-room steps, down a corridor and were admitted to Mr. B's outer office. Here I was introduced to Mr. Morrow and Miss Wilson, Mr. B's secretary, a refined looking lady. About forty-five and dressed in a brown suit, Mr. Morrow was a nice looking man, nothing outstanding, just a pleasant looking man. Cooling our heels, we discussed the unseasonably warm weather.

Right at 11:30, JP and I were ushered into the inner room where a short, stocky, white-haired, intelligent-looking man was introduced to me, Mr. Manferd Burleigh, President of Great Lakes Greyhound! Me, with my miserable cold, could only manage a throaty "How nice to meet you."

Instantly we got down to business and I learned the tale the driver had told—that the whole thing was a frame-up. That because the company knew there was drinking going on at St. Ignace, and because the company had a grievance against him for poor driving, that he was deliberately framed. Such a thing was furthest from the truth for, you recall, I wasn't even after him that day—that he was on instead of the regular driver. I reaffirmed everything in my report suggesting that verification could be obtained from the deckhand, but if it went that far I didn't know if I could identify him, beyond that fact that he was called "Red".

In my mind and in JP's, I believe, Mr. Burleigh just wanted to see what JP's "watchdogs" looked like and to check my general appearance. JP then proceeded to fill Mr. B's ears full of my background: my education; my eagerness to become an inspector as evidenced by my contacts over a year ago with Jakeway, mentioned that Jakeway had given me a long list of "qualifications" to "brush me off," but that I had overcome them all; mentioning the close scrutiny given before I was hired; said that I was intensely interested in my work, little interested in men, and his best inspector. My work was excellent, marred only by my superlatives, whereupon Mr. B. said that was a woman's prerogative.

Mr. B. asked me whether I'd been over all the lines, to which I replied everything but Indianapolis-Evansville and C&LE, but that I was correcting the latter soon. Here JP mentioned that I had been given the Flint area to handle: Mr. B. immediately pricked up his ears because he just got back from there.

Did I get my ears filled with the imminent Flint trolley strike—that it had been instigated and agitated by four men in the Union, all of whom hold Communist Party membership cards. In fact, for a while, I do believe I was forgotten as the assistance given by the FBI was discussed. JP then discussed Communism as he, when in the FBI, had found it. I was amazed and am now actually scared at the insidious ways in which Communist members and Communist dominated people hold such positions of trust and are kowtowed to by our government. This went on until 1:30 p.m. when it was time for the hearing to start.

Of course, I haven't heard the end of this yet: but the last word was that the firing of the driver would stick. You could see that Mr. B. had every confidence in my integrity and was truly impressed by my ability, thanks to JP. On the way down the corridor to the backstairs, I thanked JP for the gold stars and buildup.

It was my big moment today. I hope I made an impression. I looked older in my black dress and shoes, and I looked nice, dignified, refined and cultured. Even my voice did everything I wanted it to.

By 2:00 everything was over—something of a letdown—and I went to see about a coat at Hudson's. Just the thing: I got a black coat reduced from $65 to $45 with a zipper fur lining, much better than my gray one. It looks like a million on me. I was lucky to get it, last one in black and my size.

Home at 3:00 to recuperate and get rid of my cold. I leave tomorrow night. Till then I rest. Love, Margean

—•—

December 31, 1946
From YWCA Residence, Detroit, Michigan

Dear Ones: I got Joss's book today and shall bring it when I come home. It's beautiful, the Swiss mountain photography magnificent, the prints and paper so rich.

Into the office today with everyone wanting to know what happened? Miss Santini said, "You, in a bar with him? (for that's what the driver had said). He sure picked on the wrong kind of an inspector." All day long I was teased about being a barfly and asked what my capacity was. Love, Margean

—•—

1947

Changes

The End of the Drinking Affair

I am the Only Woman

Roses from Across the Sea

I Turn 19

Snowbound in Canada

Change in the Air

I Move

Gang War?

I Choose Mr. Burleigh, or Mr. B. Chooses Me

I Start the Big Time with American Burlington

They Might Shoot at Me

The Senator's Wife

January 2, 1947
From YWCA, Dayton, Ohio

Dear Ones: How difficult to write "47" instead of "46". I wonder what "47" holds in store for all of us—it always piques my imagination to think ahead.

What weather. Leaving Detroit with about five inches of fresh snow, we ran into first snow, then sleet, then rain. Not a nice little sprinkle but a steady, dreary soaking downpour. Why must it always rain when I go south?

I got into Dayton at 6:00 a.m. and, because I was due out at 3:00 p.m., I was darned if I'd pay a hotel $2 for a room. I headed for the YWCA, where I shall stay after this, and got a nice room for 75 cents.

At 4:00 I step foot on C&LE. As yet the men have no badge numbers or nameplates, so I "fly blind". Counting all the divisions, there are 137 regular drivers and 100 extra men. Love, Margean

---

January 3, 1947
From Hotel Shawnee, Springfield, Ohio

Dear Ones: My weather comments yesterday were understatements. Oh, it rained on all right, but I put in three of the blindest rides because of fog. My drivers upon coming to a railroad crossing would not only stop and open the door but would actually get out and walk on the tracks just to be sure. Because of the fog I saw little except the eternal swish-swish of the windshield wiper.

I hope it's a sign that they're all good drivers for I had three fine ones yesterday with just minor technicalities wrong. But Lord, the audit! In an hour and a half ride between Dayton and Hamilton, I had 115 passengers, 34 cash fares and 14 children! One usually gets an audit of over a hundred in a 4½-hour ride like between Kalamazoo and Detroit. We left Dayton city limits with 76 on board, and there wasn't a time when there weren't standees.

If luck is with me, I'll be able to get out tomorrow afternoon on a double [*second section driven by an "extra" man*] instead of waiting until night. Because it's Saturday, there should be doubles and triples. There are always weekend doubles on Cincinnati runs. Cincinnati is the collecting point of runs from Washington D.C., all southern U.S. and southwest U.S. People going north—Toledo, Cleveland, Detroit and Chicago—must

94

all take our bus to either Lima for Chicago destination or to Toledo for a Cleveland or Detroit destination. We have a gold mine, especially on weekends! However, our franchise does not permit the carrying of local (or intrastate) passengers, which makes an audit for the nine hours fairly simple: this new C&LE has the local (or intrastate) franchise, so we get the trade coming and going now.

You should see the C&LE terminal and garage in Dayton—modern design and beautiful. According to JP a combined C&LE and Greyhound terminal will be erected. It will have to be a huge one to handle the combined operations because each terminal now is about the size of our Detroit terminal and has eight loading docks each. Love, Margean

---

January 3, 1947
From Secor Hotel, Toledo, Ohio

Dear Ones: What weather! According to newspapers, however, I should be thankful I'm not in Michigan where half the bus lines are out. How hard did it hit you, the sleet storm I mean? Here ice coats everything. I've had three rides today over solid glare ice, and it's a wonder I have fingernails left. Outside of West Liberty, Ohio, there's a hill to put our Schram's Hill to shame: I inched up and slid down it twice today. Wonderful drivers. Love, Margean

---

January 5, 1947
From YWCA Residence, Detroit, Michigan

Dear Ones: Home again, arriving last night at 10:00. I didn't realize how bad the storm was until we reached Bowling Green—ice one to two inches thick coated everything. Telephone and electric wires down; telephone poles across the road; orchards devastated; trees with whole sides ripped off; stubble and corn stalks, all with a coat of ice. A cruel sort of beauty, but it does remind one of "Winter Wonderland".

The queerest thing happened on the bus last night—queer because it was the second time it's happened. From Toledo to Detroit there was a deadhead on, and he kept looking at me and then talking to the driver. I knew I hadn't been doing anything obvious so I chatted on with my seat mate. The mystery cleared itself when I got off. "Do you have a sister that works at the 24th St. Garage office?" he asked. "Why, no," I said, relieved,

"Why?" "Well, I lost my bet," he said, "You are certainly twins." This is the second time I've been asked whether I was a sister to a Betty, the other occurring when I took Connie down to Columbus. I should certainly meet that girl! Love, Margean

———

January 7, 1947
From YWCA, Flint, Michigan

Dear Ones: Well, Flint here I am—a pseudo-schoolgirl with books, headscarf, slacks and stadium boots. Nine men tomorrow: 7:24 to 5:06, reports, and then plan the next day's work. I really have eighteen rides tomorrow for one has to deadhead [*not inspect, just ride*] to the end of the line and then wait for the man to show up—if one could work both ways it would be so much easier.

Mr. Geise is nice but not what I expected. He reminds me of Bruce Cabot of the movies. Chatting about an hour, I gathered that he wasn't too satisfied with Allen's work, too brief and stripped to the bone. Because he wants a report that might have been written by a customer—explanation, comments and superlatives, the typical customer—he won't be dissatisfied with mine.

If I only knew this city better! I asked for and got a map of the lines, the street run times (a technical planning tool, like a schedule on interurbans), a book of the street stops, and other things necessary to my way of planning runs. Work is limited to daylight hours because of the need to catch badge numbers. Can tell more about this Communist-infested nest of men after tomorrow, if I'm not stranded out on Dort Highway or Flushing Road.

I believe I told you that Greyhound has the FBI at work here, a fact garnered from the Burleigh-Prater-Worst conference. Mr. Geise asked me to keep an eye on three men. Shall oblige. Love, Margean

———

January 11, 1947
From YWCA Residence, Detroit, Michigan

Dear Ones: Well, all hell today at the office conference. In the first place, I didn't know there was one until I stopped in. I worked all morning on my itinerary and, try as I might, I couldn't keep it down to 40 hours.

JP called me in to discuss the St. Ignace driver incident. He gets mad every time he talks about it and it's just a waiting proposition while the

96

union brings up its case. JP says that if he's rehired, two inspectors will always be on his tail.

The second part of our conversation concerned the other inspectors, their training and their drawbacks. The talk ended with me being assigned full time to training. I am to write a training manual, which I think should have been done long ago.

Then the conference. Some blackguards (Frye? Docker? Hobb?) are "padding" their payroll and teaching others how. Boy, did some people squirm I bet. What a 40-hour workweek consists of—well, I don't have to worry about that. New line, North Star covering Grand Rapids, Cadillac, then north to Charlevoix, for a possible extension of our work. Sling about "favoritism" aimed at me! Ella has quit (I just knew her husband would need her as a cook). Oh yes, Mr. Prater made some crack about my "vamping" Mr. Giese at Flint. "Why, Mr. Prater," I said, "He's old enough to be my father!"

Almost everyone left mad, but definitely! Mr. Glatz and I rode down the elevator together and chatted for about a half-hour in the cold. He's mad because Allen didn't complete five investigations and he's stuck with them. I learned the reason I got FTC (Flint Trolley Coach)—Allen wasn't doing enough work up there. Glatz and Prater are like that—hiss in the same pot —and Glatz said that JP relies on me the most of any in the office. "I can't understand," he said, "how a girl your age can be so stable and work so hard." From him, that's a great complement.

I took the book Joss sent to the office and everyone from JP down went into raptures over it! I have to go to bed: I have an awful headache from all the excitement today. Wonder why I have to be bonded? Love, Margean

---

January 15, 1947
From YWCA Residence, Detroit, Michigan

Dear Ones: A very full day at the office garnered much information. One, the St. Ignace driver has been rehired! He has produced a waitress in the bar who has "volunteered" my description: needless to say, there's been another scene here. JP thinks it's a "deal" with the union, since the driver no longer denies the report, he just "doesn't remember." JP is going to find out for sure if it is a union "deal" or an out-and-out repudiation of my report. If the former, nothing will be done except "open season" on the driver: if the latter, there'll be a "fight to the finish."

JP brought the driver's personnel dossier to the office. He is 34, separated, two children, and a union member in excellent standing. Employed since 1944, he has had eight accidents, five of them "at fault." He has had fifteen inspection reports, twelve of them with serious cash fare and ticket shortages, besides numerous instances where the company found he hadn't turned tickets in and billed him for them. In the words of his regional supervisor "he's not a good risk." I forgot to say that the "barmaid" who "volunteers" to identify me is the assistant dispatcher's wife. JP thinks it's a put-up job! I know it is!

Second, all hell is breaking loose on the Detroit-Kalamazoo division. At the Battle Creek terminal, there was $150 stolen from the safe, missing tickets, a little deal the ticket agents fixed up for supplying Fort Custer soldiers with girls, illegal sale of liquor, pocketing of freight money, etc. Employment applications investigated by our office were disregarded, porters and ticket agents being hired with these results! Allen says it looks like there'll be a lot of new applicant investigations, as about everyone in Battle Creek is being fired! Mr. Glatz tells me that there'll be a housecleaning in Kazoo just as soon as Battle Creek is cleaned up.

I nearly fell over with surprise. Do you know that my record is missing only four out of thirty scheduled men in a month? It's on the office bulletin board with "Can you top this?" This does not lead to love from the others. Love, Margean

———

January 16, 1947
From YWCA, Flint, Michigan

Dear Ones: According to the paper, the labor situation here is by no means settled. You remember that the Union head and two others were fired: the Union refuses to sign a contract until they are reinstated. Tomorrow more trouble as an "all day meeting" of drivers has been called, another name for strike.

Had dinner today with Mr. Giese's secretary. I expected a pretty young thing: she's pretty (very), but not young, having a daughter my age and a boy fifteen. From her appearance she could be anywhere from 28 to 40, a lovely woman!

Starting Monday, I shall stay in the city learning Detroit suburbans better so I will be capable of teaching them. I have the days all planned out. There's a note on the board that 4 to 6 suburbans will be considered a day's work, so I shall catch eight men the first day, nine the second, and eight the third. Then I shall take a day off to recuperate! Love, Margean•

January 17, 1947
From YWCA. Flint, Michigan

Dear Ones: It's 8:00 and day is regretfully breaking. It's cold, about 24, with a chill wind blowing. People look, and probably are, frozen, including yours truly, Inspector 767. I'm at a truck stop at the end of the line: my cup of coffee could float an egg and they're playing that "Nicaragua" song over and over. By 8:20, when I'm due out, there'll be enough light to see a badge number and get to work on the nine men I have scheduled. Let me see: at 8:00 brother is at work; Dad is sleeping; Mother is doing milk dishes.

Late last night the contract was signed—I don't know what concessions were made beyond a cent an hour raise: instead of $1.20, they now make $1.21. Out of this a special union assessment will probably take all joy.

Yesterday for an adventure, I explored the Civic Park line discovering a place where they serve the best hot chocolate. What makes it nice is that I step right from my "cup" onto the coach with no wait on cold corners. This makes seven lines that I know. I find I can get everyone on those lines except drivers on a small cross-town shuttle through a northern residential section.

The more I think about the intriguing situation at Kalamazoo and Battle Creek, the more I wish—I'm just afraid that JP won't ever let me go, even if an opportunity arises! Must quit daydreaming and get to work. Love, Margean

---

January 19, 1947
From YWCA Residence, Detroit, Michigan

Dear Ones: Arrived back in Detroit amid mild weather, spring breeze, and January thaw! Even an old sweater would suffice on a day like this.

What a piece of work I came back to—clothes and hair washing, ironing, mending, etc. I am still in the midst of mending, buttons and snaps having mysteriously loosened or detached. My roommate is out, giving me space to spread dresses and thread about while listening to wonderful music.

Flint has settled back to normal now that the Worst influence has left: the 73 men are reduced to 32, a nice workable margin when I add February's due men.

I really must begin another letter to Joss: it's a painful process with parts jotted in this city, stuff added in that city, and the whole polished and put together here.

More people think I'm French! One of the girls, who's getting married, asked me up to see her things, when she suddenly burst out with, "Are you French?" "Why, no," I said, "why?" "Well, the way you dress," she described, "the dark hose and colored shoes, the conservative dresses." And she came out with Dad's favorite word—"chic". Just call me "Frenchie". Love, Margean

———————

January 20, 1947
From YWCA Residence, Detroit, Michigan

Dear Ones: Well, the St. Ignace incident is settled, a union deal. He is back to work under the following conditions: he will not ask for or receive any pay for the time he was fired, November 26 to January 10; he will try to improve his accident record; he will not converse with passengers; he will not discuss company business; he will not drink while in uniform. In return he is rehired and holds a regular run leaving Bay City at 6:45 p.m. and Detroit at 11:45 p.m., hours during which I shall be careful to stay out of the terminal.

I said I never wanted to see him again, but JP said I ought to practice my right hook, and Mr. Glatz says I ought to make a point of dressing up, walking up to him and saying "Do you remember me?" and using that right hook. At least, there's no longer the repudiation of my report—and no longer any necessity to worry about him.

I got ten days' overnight pay from January 1-15. $70, making my two week salary $195. Those 75 cent YWCA rooms certainly pay off. Love, Margean

———————

January 21, 1947
From YWCA Residence, Detroit, Michigan

Dear Ones: It's 7:15 a.m. and the wind has blown me all the way up Washington Boulevard to the bus station and will probably blow me from

7-Mile to Utica Road half a dozen times today. I look like a bobby soxer in slacks, stadium boots, and fur-lined coat—let's hope the truant officer stays home today!

9:20 a.m. Roads are terrible, our rain of yesterday having turned to ice. All runs are behind schedule and I'm cooling my heels in Mt. Clemens.

I did a mean trick. I paid my fare to Utica Rd. but overrode my destination 25 cents worth into Mt. Clemens. It's the driver's fault though: I didn't know what Utica Road looked like and he didn't announce it. He'll be given hell for not checking his receipts and catching me when I got off. I feel sorry for him, he was so good natured and jolly! I'm afraid, though, that he's getting away with money by not issuing receipts for school-kids riding half fare.

By the way, Mother, when you and I went to Jackson, I sent in the report about the matron taking my nickel, unlocking the pay toilet, and not putting the nickel in but pocketing it instead. Yesterday I got a note from Mr. Radcliff saying that the woman I described supposedly didn't come on duty until 3:00, and this incident occurred at 1:06. Now he wants me to try again to see if they're working the hours they're supposed to. Lucky me! Remember her, Mother, she was the one sleeping in there when we went to Jackson.

12:10 p.m. So cold—about 14 with a 20-mph gale blowing! People are scurrying about with skirts flying, collars turned up, noses running, fingers cold, feet cold, cheeks red—everyone good natured because all are in the same boat.

I'm running into more shady deals today. My last driver just wasn't issuing any receipts or tickets: on top of that, he overcharged me a nickel. Ella rarely turned up stuff like this.

Stopped into the office today and learned that Mrs. Farr and Mrs. Thomas, our other women inspectors, had been asked to quit and have: they weren't doing enough work. This leaves seven of us—me the only woman. Love, Margean

———

January 22, 1947
From YWCA Residence, Detroit, Michigan

Dear Ones: I'm down in my periodic "dumps". There's no earthly reason why I should be, everybody is nice, I'm getting enough sleep, and I'm well. Still, I'm tired and blue: this morning I took two calcium tablets, a vitamin pill, an iron capsule, and some iodine. A regular hypochondriac!

I know what the matter is. I need to get out on the road: these suburbans bore me and I always get blue when I'm bored!

So: I shall not be home next week, I'm going to fix a nice, long trip, preferably up North where I can go now that my St. Ignace drinking man is working regular hours. I shall go up where the snow is five feet deep, where men are men, and men need inspection. Or: I shall go South, where C&LE calls.

Miss Santini tells me that my suburban reports are much better than Ella's ever were—moreover, and it surprises even me, I'm getting my men! I can't get too good at it or they'll keep me here to clean up the backlog.

Well, I've fixed my blues fine and dandy—my roommates and I walked 27 blocks downtown and rode back on the bus. What a workout! Love, Margean

———

January 24, 1947
From Argonne Hotel, Lima, Ohio

Dear Ones: At last back on the road and what a relief after a week cooped up in Detroit. The inactivity bores me—suburbans bore me. In Lima last night I went to a show, the first in ages, "A Scandal in Paris" with George Sanders, enjoying it immensely.

Guess who I met today, and me in slacks and boots looking like a school kid? It happened like this: I was wondering whether or not I had gotten my scheduled man so, to set my mind at ease, I called Mr. Polk, personnel head of C&LE, who we are to contact for such things.

"It's about time an inspector called me," he said. "I've got some special work and a run bid for you. Where can I see you?" Well, that nearly knocked me over, there being no instructions about such a situation. I kinda laughed for I was in the library across the street, and said, "You can practically see me right now: I'm in the library." "Swell," he said, "I'll be over inside of ten minutes." And he was.

The more I come in contact with officials of these companies, the more I like them and want to join the "select" company. They're my sort of people, just common everyday folks—that's the way I found Mr. Giese in Flint and now Mr. Polk in Dayton. Before we parted I learned he was born and raised on a farm and was a driver for twelve years before getting into the administrative end. He's just the sort of man men like to work for if my snap judgement holds true.

After going through my special assignment, we gabbed about drivers, buses, companies, his work, my work, for a fascinating two hours of "shoptalk". I learned one startling fact: these men actually like to be inspected and drop into Mr. Polk's office to see "if I had a checker report recently!" I nearly fell over with astonishment, for our men regard us as "rats" and "professional snoopers" according to a conversation overheard by Frye. Well, anyway, I promised to see what I could do about that list of extra men he gave me.

My special was a check on two drivers, one for driving and another for cash fares, bringing me to Columbus tonight. My day was to have ended at 3:40 this afternoon; instead it ends at 1:55 in the morning.

Oh, that reminds me. "What's your number?' he asked. "767," I said. "Then you're the one who sent in a report that won a lot of respect." "What was in it?" I asked, for I'd written only good of these perfect angels. "Why," he said, "You put in a report that a driver wore brown-green-white striped non-regulation sox, and it's gone all over the line that those inspectors sure look you over." I repeat, an inspector's paradise down here! And to think I might have been a teacher doomed to the boring, stifling, and mind-destroying regimentation of culture.

Next time I come down here I shall wear my fur coat and make a better impression, but until then I remain, Your daughter, Margean

———

January 28, 1947
From YWCA Residence, Detroit, Michigan

Dear Ones: Because I was due to leave Dayton at 7:20, I was up, dressed and hurrying along the street at wondering where to grab a bite to eat. Just a block from the station, I came across a cafeteria where I shall always eat when in Dayton. The prices were staggering—grapefruit, 10 cents instead of 15 cents; fried mush, 5 cents; French toast, 5 cents instead of two pieces for 35 cents; hot cakes, 15 cents for three instead of 25 cents; cereal, 10 cents instead of 15 cents. I broke my fast on the first two items.

Our 52-degree spring weather of yesterday is over: it's only 40 this morning and, because I'm going North, the prospects are for colder weather.

Had an interesting ride yesterday seated next to a deaf old man. He was a carpenter, 70 years old: his wife died back in 1916 and he raised his family of four boys and two girls alone. Now the boys are all carpenters and he takes turns living with them. What pleased me was the fact I didn't have to keep up my end of the conversation—he couldn't hear me.

When I hit Toledo last night I found that my room hadn't been reserved—full up. So I trotted to the Y—these hotels don't know what a good customer they're losing.

One part of the Battle Creek scandal broke today when they grilled one of the men. He has a prison record for kidnapping, armed robbery, breaking parole, and a long list of other offenses.

Into the office today, but I've promised myself that I won't work tomorrow. Just one month from today and I'll be 19. I feel ancient already. What will I feel like when 20 and 21 roll around! Love, Margean

---

January 29, 1947
From YWCA Residence, Detroit, Michigan

Dear Ones: It pays to be nice, but in this instance I didn't know it was going to pay off. About two weeks ago at Sunday tea, Mrs. Anderson and Mrs. Tolsin had guests so I offered to do their dishes (at tea, everyone is supposed to wash their own). Anyway, I washed and cleaned up the tables putting things away. Maybe that had no bearing on the following, but I think it did.

When I got back in town, I was hurrying to my room to read your letters when Mrs. Tolsin stopped me. "How'd you like Charles (our janitor) to clean out that junk closet next to your room and you could put a lock on the door?" Well, I nearly fell over: I'd been hinting around for ages that I'd like some place to lock up my papers and wondering if I'd dare put a lock on one of my drawers.

So, early this morning, Charles put a bar in the closet, we waged war against the spiders, and I "papered" with brown wrapping paper and thumbtacks. Then this afternoon I "moved:" I never realized I had so many clothes. Now I have a locked place for my clothes, coat, suitcases, and business papers! Anyway, my day off has been singularly full when I meant it to be empty and restful.

I think I told you that two reports of mine are posted in the office to be read by the other inspectors. If JP keeps doing that, they'll love me— love to cut my throat, that is! The most important report is on how to plan suburbans that I wrote after working them for three days. Others work them much more than I, but never get their men, while I who seldom work them get every man I've planned for. JP has penciled across the top: "Inspectors: read and digest." Cut my throat? They could probably cheerfully murder me.

104

You know, it's a funny setup in the office right now. Glatz, Worst, Allen, Frye, Hobb, Docker, and Lawson ranked in the order of importance, according to Miss Santini. Not quite in that order, for she ranks me as equal with Glatz in my field—me as inspector, he as investigator.

I'm the only woman now and think I shall be for some time, as JP is fed up with catering to whims, and "illnesses" and "can't work" that he got from the other women. Thank the Good Lord, he can ask me to work any day, any time, anywhere, and I can go whether or not I feel well, whether or not I want to go, or whether or not I'd planned to do something else. In consequence, I stand on exactly the same footing as the men in personal contact, special assignments and pay. In addition, I can pry—that isn't the word—am told about investigations with full details, of which other inspectors have only an inkling. Work is SO fascinating!

For logical reasons, there has been only one special assignment that I have refused. Just after the St. Ignace driver was rehired, and before I knew definitely what hours he was working, JP asked me to take a special in Flint where drivers were going by people flagging them on Flint's street corners. To do that, one whole day I would have had to stand in Flint and flag them down, see if they'd stop, ask some silly question like, "When does the next bus come?" and send them on angry. My objection was this: what would happen if the St. Ignace driver happened to be driving one of the buses? He could probably run faster than I. Anyway, JP said he should have thought of that and assigned it to Lawson who hasn't done it yet. Love, Margean

January 30, 1947
From Courtlandt Hotel, Louisville, Kentucky

Dear Ones: What a day to start out! The biggest ice storm since last month, when, if you remember, I was also out. At 7:15 this morning, traffic was in an awful snarl. I thought the ice was bad, but when we reached Toledo, it was terrible. Coming so soon after the last storm, trees had no opportunity to mend their stress and strains. With a coating of one to two inches of ice, there was wholesale destruction of trees as large as the walnut in our front yard. In town, limbs had fallen across parked autos and branches scraped along the top of the coach as we passed. Poles, put in to replace those downed by the last storm, were broken and leaned at drunken angles along the road and in the fields: at one place we counted

36 consecutive poles down. Wires that hadn't been pulled taut after the last storm now looped in low arches or were broken.

And what did it do all this time? Well, from 1:15 yesterday afternoon when I got back from my shopping, until 4:30 this afternoon when I reached Cincinnati, it rained! During the night it was that half-frozen pebbly-rain that raps on the window and coats everything, but today it was honest rain —the kind that always keeps me company in the South.

I was the only one on out of Detroit on a run that usually has two or three sections! "Hey, don't sit back there," says the driver, so I parked myself up front. When we picked up nine people in Monroe I started my report and felt more at ease. The driver, a fellow about 30, married and with a four-year-old daughter, talked mostly at first about the ice and damage. Naturally I led him on about his work, his reactions, etc.

"I never kick," he said, "Why should I ? I start to work at 7:30 and drive until 4:30 with 34 minutes off for lunch and rest. I get my meals and hotel room free. And do you know how much this pays, driving one way from Cincinnati to Detroit?" he asked. I knew but thought it best not to say. "$17." He works three round-trips to Cincinnati a week, with two days off, making six one ways, or $102 a week: $408 a month, $5300 a year —besides, his safety bonus of about $20 a month, a two weeks' vacation with pay, and thirty days' sick leave with pay. He leaves Detroit at 7:50 a.m., reaches Cincinnati at 4:30 p.m.: leaves Cincinnati at 3:40 a.m. and arrives in Detroit at 12:30 p.m. If that isn't a swell job, I'd like to know what is! It puts you in the "upper medium middle class," pensions you off like the railroad, and is a job that most of the men are crazy about.

The further South we got, the greener the fields became and the more water from last night's storm stood in them. Along the Dixie Highway, U.S. 47 between Cincinnati and Louisville, one sees hills, hills, hills, and beautiful old homes. And, what I just love, almost every farm is fenced with a white board fence, and instead of being white and red, the buildings are white and green. Beautiful.

Crossed the Ohio River and paralleled it for about fifteen miles, during which I saw a rear-paddle steamboat pushing a raft—shades of Tom Sawyer.

After thirteen hours of riding and two of writing, I'm tired. Love, Margean

January 31, 1947
From YWCA, Dayton, Ohio

Dear Ones: Had two close shaves today. Between Louisville and Cincinnati while stopped for a flagee, a lumber truck without brakes almost ran into us turning off the road just in time and flying into the field. The second occurred between Cincinnati and Middletown when some dumb woman left her car parked right in the traffic lane while she went calling —bet you 2-to-1 she didn't have a whole car when she got back!

My faith in humanity had another shot in the arm today. I am so lucky. Sitting in my room in this Y without anything to do, I decided to see if there was a radio in one of the downstairs parlors. There wasn't and I downheartedly stepped into the elevator and started to push the button for the third floor when someone beat me and I went clear to the fifth floor permanent resident hall. A girl with a suitcase was there, and as she got in I asked her if there were a radio in any parlor. She said no and asked me how long I was going to be here. Telling her for the weekend, she said that she would be gone for that time, and that I could take her radio and leave it at the desk when I left. So I have been listening to music all evening and thanking my lucky stars that there are such nice people in this world! Love, Margean

———

February 2, 1947
From Southern Hotel, Columbus, Ohio

Dear Ones: Had a full day yesterday: four inspections, a terminal, a special, and lots of report writing. Two were re-inspections requiring very close attention to cash fares; the Middletown terminal was filthy; and the matron at Dayton was stealing money. I ran into bad driving, abuse of equipment, and loitering.

After finishing the reports, I telephoned Mr. Polk and relayed my information. My special cash fare re-inspection had his peroxide blond along, and his cash fare transactions were mighty peculiar: in fact, Mr. Polk tells me that the next time I hit Dayton, both of my drivers will probably be looking for new jobs! In the Middletown terminal inspection I found a fire hazard and a filthy mess, which Mr. Polk is going to tend to. There will probably be a new matron next time I hit Dayton. This is what our office likes—action on our reports!

We then chatted about the blond (whom Mr. Polk has warned the driver about several times), and the "sweet nothings" she had whispered into the driver's ear while I listened. Mr. Polk got a good laugh when I mimicked her, "O darling, you're so cute." The driver is about 40, has a moustache and is anything but cute.

After this long talk, I went to the Virginia Cafeteria for dinner—meatloaf, bean salad, corn bread, and peach cobbler for 49 cents.

Tomorrow my applicant investigation comes up—a woman ticket agent in Flint—which will carry me to Delaware, Leonardsburg, Marion, and Findlay, Ohio. I'm slightly apprehensive about plunging into it just from the reading and without any training or anything beyond Mr. Glatz's "See what you can do with this." About a week or so ago, Frye came into the office full of talk about inspectors that he'd overheard between a driver and a woman who was going to be a ticket agent at Flint. During this conversation, we were called several uncomplimentary terms, which made JP boil, or at least simmer hard, with rage. This is the same woman. So with Glatz's preliminaries, Frye's report and whatever I pick up, I'm afraid her chances dwindle. Love, Margean

------

February 5, 1947
From YWCA Residence, Detroit, Michigan

Dear Ones: What do you think of the paycheck, $204.52. The man at the bank who always cashes my check asked me, "Which boss's knee do you sit on!"

Mr. Glatz took me out to lunch today and I learned a lot. Kalamazoo has problems. And, there is talk of Mr. Burleigh, our President, leaving for a bus company in Chicago. JP may not be here long: (where does that leave me)? JP calls Miss Santini, Mr. Glatz and myself his "crutches" —hard telling what he calls the rest. Radcliffe is on his war-horse. Glatz says this would be an opportune time to put in my two cents worth with Radcliff. He wants me to go over JP's head and see Radcliff on my own, telling me that Radcliffe "would jump at the chance to get you." (But that would mean going over JP's head and I have the loyalty to stick with him when the going's rough, like now.) I have no doubt that if Mr. Burleigh and JP go, Glatz will get JP's job! What else is going on??

This payday everyone but Glatz and I had worked only 40 hours. By the way, he and I are getting per diems we aren't entitled to as compensation for hours. More news when I hit home. Love, Margean

------

February 14, 1947
From YWCA Residence, Detroit, Michigan

Dear Ones: Wonderful run back and into the office today. What do I find but two people to train—a woman next week and a man the week after, so, I planned out our activities for a week.

Then there was a nice note asking me to "dash" off a section for a training manual. That took three hours, but I did just what was wanted at the first try. Good if I say so myself! I have another section to write on the lines that I will do Sunday.

JP called me in to congratulate me on getting the driver at C&LE fired (Mr. Polk said it was a job well done); to ask me to write the section of the manual on planning and runs; to train two people, making close notes; then, to gab about the extension of our office.

Relative to the last, we are in for increased territory: one of these fine days we add Central Greyhound—Chicago, Grand Rapids, Muskegon, plus lots of Indiana and Illinois points; King Brothers in Ohio between Dayton and Cincinnati; and North Star. I garnered a lot of information of interest. What a department this will be a year from now!

One funny thing: JP asked me if I could picture clearly in my mind the Grand Rapids terminal. I said, "Yes." "Do they have any ash receivers?" he asked. I thought, conjuring up a mental image of the terminal: "No," I said. "Swell," he said, "Hobb's got me into a nasty mess by saying they were dirty." Lord, I hope I never do anything like that. On a terminal inspection if I can't remember an item, I just leave it blank and never guess.

Mr. Glatz came in then with his Kalamazoo report: Thank God, the terminal manager hasn't been doing anything! The restaurant and its employees have been guilty of contributing to juvenile delinquency. Glatz dug up a case of statutory rape on the property involving a porter who was fired. He has to go back because of a porter who is on more than good terms with the girls. It is hell when we're held partially responsible for the moral activities of our employees, but I guess it's justified because of our close contact with the public.

Believe the 37-year-old woman I'm to train will be good. When I get that training done, I am to make a survey of our drivers, making a "composite" slip for each man. Will take at least a week, so I'm stuck in the damn city for about a month. Love, Margean

---

February 17, 1947
From YWCA Residence, Detroit, Michigan

Dear Ones: I'm exhausted! The teaching of children was nothing compared to the demands of teaching in this field. Until yesterday I had little appreciation for the amount and mass of detail which one must be able to call upon in this work. Because it was so long ago that I went through that nerve-wracking period of initial adjustment, I had forgotten what a strain it can be for a new person. I explain, explain, reiterate and reiterate.

But Mrs. Zauer is a very good pupil, slow but sure. She remembers, she can apply her information to a new situation. It will take the full training period. We get along well. I work with her from 8:30 to 5:30, and then go home, write reports, make an outline of what we did, make an outline of tomorrow's work and make a list of questions to ask. This takes at least four hours and I am dead when 10:30 rolls around.

Met Mrs. JP yesterday. Not pretty, but very, very nice. Love, Margean

—

February 20, 1947
From YWCA Residence, Detroit, Michigan

Dear Ones: Today is the first time I've been able to relax: my student is coming along grand. When I think back to the sloppy training I had, I can really appreciate that I am doing a good job. When I get through with Edith Zauer, she will have been told and hence, should be able to cope with every possible circumstance I could foresee. I have only to teach her suburbans and then take her out to practice and critique.

A little about my student: She's a tall blond, 37-year-old. She is a widow: her husband was a race car driver who died of occupational disease —crack-up. She has a boy of 15: when he was five, he had a brain tumor removed. For two years he lingered on the brink of death and was never left for a moment. The operation removed part of the skull and he wears a special helmet: you can imagine the extreme care that lad must live under. The really tragic part is that the operation left him a spastic. Edith is reconciled to the inevitable—just trying to stave it off as long as possible.

As of today, Hobb is fired. Why was Hobb fired? Well, reasons are numerous, but the most important is this: He was buying tickets on the bus, say from Detroit to St. Ignace, by way of Lansing; he would inspect on the part of the ticket from Detroit to Lansing, then sell or turn in the portion

110

between Lansing and St. Ignace, meanwhile billing the company for the entire Detroit-St. Ignace ticket! Did he make money! What a thing to have on one's conscience! Love, Margean

---

February 22, 1947
From YWCA Residence, Detroit, Michigan

Dear Ones: Made a trip to Fostoria with Edith, having a heck of a lot of fun and learning something—here is one person who definitely has been infected with my "fun" bug. No news. Yes, I have. I am getting over a terrible cold. Can you imagine the strain of talking all day with a "gravel" throat and running nose. That's why at night I have no voice and die when I hit bed. Love, Margean

---

February 24, 1947
From YWCA Residence, Detroit, Michigan

Dear Ones: JP and I had a long talk today: every time we have a long talk, it ends up in pats on the back and more work. Of course, our first talk concerned Edith, who I have sent up to Flint alone. So far, so good, is the verdict—slow but sure.

Next, we jumped into the case of a driver whose report has been grating on my nerves since January. On December 19 I rode with him, got 7 cash fares, and he reported none—a perfect discharge case, as this was the fourth time this had happened. I had beefed and beefed because no action had been taken, but I didn't get any place until I took it up with JP. He hit the ceiling as to why this hadn't been brought to his attention —a perfect example of work our department digs up. He telephoned here —telephoned there—raised <u>hell</u> with a couple of department heads and came up with the information that the reports had been delayed past the 14-day action deadline. JP <u>hit</u> the ceiling, "What the hell do they keep an inspection department for?" I sit scared at the flurry made in this huge corporation—I certainly caused a big splash by the little pebble I threw in! I can't explain the "freeze forms" which will now have to be used by other departments, but it's more work for them.

How does more work for me come in? Well, once a week I have to check the returned audited forms for cash fare discrepancies and substitutions—making a record of every suspicious transaction. "The only one with brains to read between the lines," was the nice way he put it. He sure gives me a workout in the ins and outs of this business at our level. But, when will I get out of town?

Maybe next week after finishing with Edith, I can hit Flint for some much wanted overnight pay. If she doesn't make the grade, it won't be because I didn't pour out my heart. Town bores me! But I'll probably have a man to train!

I'm planning on getting some red shoes for my birthday! Love, Margean

---

February 27, 1947
From YWCA Residence, Detroit, Michigan

Dear Ones: You know the kimono housecoat you made me? Well, I got so many compliments on it that today I bought a gold kid belt to set it off. It's my birthday present to myself. Glamour is my motto!

Tomorrow Edith and I leave for a special on equipment abuse.

Allen is stuck up in North Bay territory in a terrible snowstorm on a special I would have gotten if I hadn't been training. My luck!

Next week Mr. LaVroe and I have several dates: he's more on the ball in this business than Edith. Which isn't saying a word against her, she knows why we do things the way we do, he will just do them. But it's the why that makes it interesting.

I took out the company insurance today. For $32.50 a year I get $2100 worth of life insurance, $15 weekly sickness and accident benefits, $5 daily hospital expense benefits, and $10-$150 for surgical operations. $2.70 will be deducted each month from my paycheck.

It's nerve-wracking in town. My feet itch. Must go to bed and wake up age NINETEEN! Love, Margean

---

March 3, 1947
From YWCA Residence, Detroit, Michigan

Dear Ones: I'm sitting on top of the world! Imagine old, humdrum, practical me getting roses, red ones at that, from friend Joss across the sea! Isn't that the true Continental touch? Can you imagine anything more exciting, more glamorous, more wonderful than receiving such a beautiful gift? A card, yes: flowers, unthought of!

"Who is he?" "How did you meet him?" I'm quite the belle of the Y this evening: everyone knowing before I stepped in the door and they —and I—nearly fell over when I opened the box. Eight long-stemmed red roses. Mrs. Tolsin gave me a beautiful vase to use and they are "enshrined" on my table. "They look out of place in this room," said dour Nancy—but they're beautiful. Don't the darnest things happen to me?

I think you would enjoy the little adventure that Edith and I had on Friday. We were scheduled to leave Springfield at 11:52 a.m.: the first section came in at 12:20 p.m. "The second section is an hour behind me: I'm full." We waited an hour-and-a-half, 2½ hours in all. When the double came in there were two seats on it: one, a plump woman, who I couldn't displace with my elbows, grabbed; one, Edith got. Me? On the big "Silversides" the seats are about a foot above the aisle, making a small ledge near the back seat. Me? I got the ledge. Two <u>kind</u> men, who were more interested in our looks than our plight, gave me pillows to sit on. I made myself comfortable. The load was mostly truck drivers, near-drunk ones at that. Edith, with her blond hair, and I, with my most sophisticated dress, attracted much attention. In fact, we were the center of so much attention, we could hardly get our work done. More fun!

Mr. LaVroe is 26 years old—an Army investigator—lives with his Mother and is strictly on the ball! In fact, he's too sure of himself, and I'm doing my best to dampen this. When you're too sure of yourself—when you relax your caution—you make mistakes! Love, Margean

———

March 5, 1947
From YWCA Residence, Detroit, Michigan

Dear Ones: The main purpose of the office conference today was to tell us that henceforth we would be paid once a month, on the first. JP said it would be difficult for some inspectors to stretch their pay over a month, whereupon Mr. Glatz said, "Well, we've always got Worst to borrow from."

Mr. LaVroe and I get along just fine. What a brain: JP with less education! He, too, is in for terminal work: he tells me that he and I are liable to be transferred together—so we had better get along. We had a three-hour layover in Port Huron yesterday and he took me to a show— strictly business, 20 cents each—the only one open.

Today I told him I didn't know anything more to tell him and kicked him out on his own with orders to ask me if anything or any questions came up. His brain and mine work in the same way: hence our, shall I call it business-admiration, for each other. By the way, I believe I failed to mention the salient facts garnered from his application and our talks: 26, Catholic, career Army officer, personnel and administrative training, with a typical officer personality. If he and I were transferred together, we could make a terminal hum: the way we work clicks. I jumped about "fifteen stories" in his estimation when Mr. Glatz told him one day how old I was: he was dumbfounded. Incidentally he didn't resent being trained or told things by a woman which has made it immeasurably easier for me! I'm a good teacher and I can't stump him

He and I were called into JP's office this morning for a "gab-fest". Mr. Thomas DeVroe and I were in a deep discussion about how bus companies make money and where we were liable to expand. JP heard us talking and yelled for us to come in and let him join the conversation. So, for about an hour, Tom and I discussed, learned, absorbed, and advanced our opinions on Greyhound corporate structure, policies, acquisitions, and future developments. It was immensely interesting—and I appreciate JP's efforts to make us more versed.

Allen got back today from Sault Ste Marie and the Canadian Nickel Belt Special. I believe I mentioned that the superintendent had requested someone to come up to check into some mighty peculiar cash fare deals and details. Two men were fired immediately. The superintendent wants a follow-up in four weeks and Allen gave him my Inspector 767 number. JP heartily endorsed his suggestion. So about the first week in April, yours truly turns northward for the first time in four months, for a very important special on which, I'm forewarned, it is almost certain that I'll be turned up.

All next week I shall be in Flint. The week of the 16th, I have another trainee: the next week I'll spend on C&LE; and then the first week in April —North. I got praised to the skies for my training so far—made excellent use of my time and planning. Love, Margean

———

March 9, 1947
From YWCA, Flint, Michigan

Dear Ones: Sunday morning, a nice time to write because both roommates are sleeping or, at least, trying to as my assorted drops of keys, books, and shoes will permit. I have little to write about—just a mass of trivia.

One: To start: my down-in-the-dumps trivia. I pour out my soul trying to train two people and as long as they've got Mama to look after them, things run smoothly. One day, just one day, I leave to get some work done on my own, and they make a mess of their work! Am I to blame?

Two: Friday I had an interesting special. Because several complaints had come to C. Keith, Superintendent of southern Michigan men, that a Clare-Detroit driver was driving in an apparently intoxicated condition, Allen was sent up on Thursday and I on Friday to look into the situation. Although I had most of the Clare bars under surveillance that afternoon, I saw nothing (Allen and I are the only ones who know what he looks like): but his 5½ hours of driving were atrocious and could easily make any nervous person think he was drunk. We had three near accidents: his judgement of speed and distance was poor but his quick reactions made me think him sober.

Three: I did a foolish thing yesterday: I bought myself a white carnation for no reason at all. Pinning it on my coat I felt like a million dollars—was it so foolish?

Four: Yesterday afternoon, Beverly and I were shopping for soap when we saw gallon jugs of apple juice—not cider—at 29 cents. We bought a jug!

Five: Spring is here! Except in Clare where snow was two to four feet deep.

Six: It's a month since I've been home and the way things are shaping up, it'll be another month before I see the green grass of home again. Love, Margean

———

March 10, 1947
From YWCA, Flint, Michigan

Dear Ones: Flint is a welcome sight, but the most welcome sight will be the $42 attached to my paycheck! I have $12 in my piggy bank which holds $20. When it's full, about in time for Easter sales, it's going to buy two dresses and a pair of shoes.

Another of those crystal-bright days with a brisk March wind blowing. Makes one glad to be alive. Took my sheet music along this trip and played to my heart's content last night. Sunday evening went to "Cloak and Dagger" starring Gary Cooper: thought it asinine. If I finish early today I'm going to "Till the Clouds Roll By"—but only if in time for afternoon prices. Love, Margean

March 12, 1947
From YWCA, Flint, Michigan

Dear Ones: I did see "Till the Clouds Roll By" with lots of Jerome Kern's music—at matinee prices—enjoying it immensely. Then at night I sat in a tub and soaked for about an hour: comfort, but yes!

Spring continues: drifts are dwindling and children have spring fever. Me, too! Today it's going to rain much later today, I hope. I'm also hoping that the North country in April will be decently mild.

Today I dug up the most underhanded, totalitarian, dictatorial thing I've ever heard of! This evening—on one day's notice—the Flint Trolley Coach union is holding a meeting and is going to charge every absent driver $5. Why? The company fired a man. It went through grievance and mediation and he still stayed fired, so now the union wants to take it to arbitration, which costs $100, and hasn't the money. I heard this real early this morning and telephoned Mr. Giese who hadn't heard it yet and could hardly believe his ears: I just got through calling in again, and it's true. Love, Margean

———

March 15, 1947
From YWCA Residence, Detroit, Michigan

Dear Ones: I arrived back to all the usual tasks: hair washing, clothes washing, ironing, mending, and a jug of apple juice which showed suspicious signs of no longer being apple juice. My hair is washed, ironing and mending wait, and the apple juice which is no longer apple juice, is filling a glass beside me as I write. My roommates were glad to see me and I know I'm home.

Did I tell you employment is tightening up in Flint and Detroit? In a city of 125,000 only one column of "help wanted" for both sexes! Several people I talked to said that the only place where work could be found was Pontiac. The tones and comments of "the man on the street" in Flint were nasty.

I shall be very happy when my little radio comes: Flint would have been more pleasant with music, however, I did see three movies. I also read three books: *The Last Time I Saw Paris*, *Short Stories* by Erskine Caldwell, and the *Delicate Ape,* the latter a political book regardless of the title.

Tomorrow the girls and I are going for a walk: we don't know where we're going, but blisters will develop. The last time we went for a walk it was in a blizzard and Nancy got a cold that sent her to bed. Spring fever is in the air: I have found a place at Clark Park where bicycles are rented—we shall take advantage of this later. Three days of beautiful spring weather were too good to last, for today saw a snow cover here and a sleet storm in Flint. Love, Margean

---

March 16, 1947
From YWCA Residence, Detroit, Michigan

Dear Ones: Oh, do I feel awful: the top of my head is splitting—each noise is magnified a thousand-fold. Bed would feel good, but I've a million things to do—which is why I'm sitting on the bed. If I'd lie down, I wouldn't get up. I've started to lose weight again—a springtime occurrence I guess —anyway, my hearty winter appetite is gone.

Speaking of spring, morning brought back winter, and I was awakened by Beverly's alarm clock and kept awake by ambitious early Sunday risers shoveling and scraping snow. So, I got up: no, I sat up and fell flat back again. I'm cautiously crawling around today hoping to go to Windsor tonight. But I don't think so, I still feel awful. Love, Margean

---

March 24, 1947
From Hotel Ojibway, Sault Ste. Marie, Michigan

Dear Ones: I had millions of things to do before leaving Detroit yesterday at 10:20 a.m. I had to order my glasses, get a check cashed, get traveler checks, get a ticket, and get on the bus. I accomplished all except the third with a margin of five minutes. My hair and clothes were flying as I steamed into the terminal with a bag under my arm and two in my hands, bumping into everyone. No t-formation, but an unplanned attack is often just as effective!

I'm real pleased with my glasses: only $20.61 for the two pair. And you'll like my new frames.

From Detroit to Gaylord it rained, getting colder by the minute. Everything was bleak and dreary with snowdrifts getting bigger and deeper as we headed north. We heard tales of how hard the winter had been on deer and that the only remedy would be a couple of open seasons on does. After Gaylord, it snowed harder and harder, and the drifts got higher and higher, and the wind blew with more and more vigor until we could hardly hold the road.

In Mackinaw City we had starter trouble and almost missed the ferry. In St. Ignace we had motor trouble and almost missed the Soo bus. My worst adventure happened in Sault Ste. Marie. Just before leaving Detroit, I received a collect telegram that the hotel had no rooms. With the weather getting worse by the minute, this loomed larger and larger in my mind, but when I walked in and said that I'd telegraphed, they let me have one. Love, Margean

---

March 25, 1947
From St. Charles Hotel, Sault Ste Marie, Ontario

Dear Ones: I'm snowbound! I called Mr. Schlafman at Sudbury and was supposed to start there at 10:45 a.m. So gathering my things, I hurried and made the first, last, and only ferry to Canada today with the wind whistling in my ears, my fingers frozen around the suitcase handle, and the cold reaching all of my anatomy!

With only ten minutes to go, I rush into the station and am calmly told that there will be no bus today! I frantically find a telephone booth and call Sudbury again. "I've cancelled everything," Mr. Schlafman said, "we've had about ten inches since you last called, on top of the five to six feet now. And I'm still trying to find two buses on the road." So, with luck, I start tomorrow.

As you can see, I found a room and am resigned to my fate and $7 a day for doing nothing! Worse things could happen: for instance, I could be working and have the bus stopped in the middle of nowhere!

Tonight I'm going to a movie, "A Song to Remember". And if I get lost in a snowdrift up here, you can dedicate my memorial to "A Margean to Remember". Love, Margean

---

March 25, 1947
From St. Charles Hotel, Sault Ste. Marie, Ontario

Dear Ones: You've never lived until you've spent a day in a small town hotel—preferably in Canada. The owners and their children live in back, and the kids and a bulldog keep scampering and pattering up and down the hall. The wonderful smell of their family dinner and supper fill the air while I must plunge out into the cold for mine. In the room directly over me a harmonica and a guitar give out with the latest from the Deep South. If you wander into the parlor, you find assorted plants and rockers and bulldog's tail.

Out the parlor window pass the town's activities: everyone jaywalks. Bored with watching this, you don your heaviest and brave your way to the post office for stamps and the library for books. The library is closed, so you bend your sail and are blown back to your hotel. Out comes the embroidery until bedtime. I'll die if I have to spend tomorrow here. Love, Margean

---

March 26, 1947
From St. Charles Hotel, Sault Ste Marie, Ontario

Dear Ones: If you've never spent an afternoon in one, you should by all means wake up in one. What a conglomeration of sounds! The gurgle of the flushed toilet, the crying of a child down the hall, the guy practicing his harmonica, the squeaky boards punctuated with footsteps—it's a good thing I went to bed early.

I'm sitting right beside the only telephone in anticipation of the call from Sudbury. You have no idea how slowly time passes, especially when the call will be anytime between 8:00 and 10:00 a.m. Well, the call came: I am to meet Mr. Schlafman during my thirty-minute layover when I get to Sudbury. Just like in spy stories, I am to get off and walk slowly to the back of the coach—could anything be more exciting, especially when you don't know what he looks like?

Six to seven feet of snow in Sudbury! A huge storm in Toronto! What luck! I do have to spend another day here. I hope the movies change. I keep dodging the driver around town, reminding me of the time in Port Austin when I had to write standing up in the post office.

I can't even get back into Michigan—no ferry—so I sit and made $7 overnight pay. Because the mail isn't going through, I must telegraph

Detroit and let them know where their infant is. And I can remember saying I'd like to get stuck here! Love, Margean

---

March 27, 1947
From King Edward Hotel, North Bay, Ontario, Canada

Dear Ones: At long last I start moving north. The temperature is 20. Because it's a <u>warm</u>, sunny day, I'm taking it for granted that you have the same with maybe a 45 reading instead. Still, because there's no telling whether I'll spend the night in a bed or a snowdrift, I had a lunch packed—enough for three people—for 35 cents. What did I get? Two lumberjack-sandwiches, cheese and egg salad, pineapple pie, two cookies, and an orange. Snowdrifts—here I come!

I am sorry to bid good-by to my nice little room here at the St. Charles. I shall miss the noises and the activity. Oh, yes, I almost forgot: yesterday was the little boy's birthday and I got invited to the party. Beer, coke, pretzels, cake and a card game of Pedro—was I plied with questions! Where in England did I come from? Where was I going? What did I think of it here? It is so easy to fall into Canadian speech patterns: I love to listen to them talk.

Just a half-hour. I hope the bus is warm. I hope Mr. Schlafman isn't too difficult to pick out and up. More tonight. Love, Margean

---

March 28, 1948
From King Edward Hotel, North ay, Ontario, Canada

Dear Ones: I should have said tomorrow morning for it took me three hours to write my reports yesterday. What a ride—not that the driver did so much wrong, but that he had so long to do it in. Like all my Canadian men, he was swell in his handling of passengers, but the roadwork!

Luckily the snowplows had been through and fifteen-foot drifts and banks lined our path. Can you imagine our gravel road at its worst complicated by frost heaves every fifty feet? Anyway, he took them at almost 45 mph, while I hit the ceiling figuratively if not literally. We broke the air brake hose going into Espanola and had to rely on the handbrake thereafter. If it was cash fares they want, they got them—18 out of a 62 audit, or one quarter of my load—only four looked suspicious.

120

I picked the six-foot Mr. Schlafman out of the crowd at once. I slowly walked to the rear of the coach and around the corner—fifty seconds later we were shaking hands and saying, "It's about time." He had a nice itinerary made out with tonight finding me in Little Current, Saturday in Sudbury, Sunday in Blind River, Monday at the Soo, and Tuesday at 8:00 p.m. in Detroit. Another $49 overnight pay. A room has been reserved for me in Sudbury so I'm all set.

The day is beautiful—sun shining brightly—cold, about 20 and I leave at 1:30 p.m. Love, Margean

---

March 28, 1947
From Hotel Coulson, Sudbury, Ontario, Canada

Dear Ones: The end of a very exciting day—the end of the first month after my 19th birthday! What an adventure today—listen!

We left North Bay at 1:30 p.m. bound for Sudbury. About 20 minutes out, our motor blew a gasket. Anyway, it stopped and wouldn't start, only rumble like forty-eleven parts had broken, and this the first run for our reconditioned motor!

Three men—an Indian, a banana inspector and a machinery salesman—and myself were on. "Does anyone want to ride or walk back to North Bay?" We all elected to stay. The driver left: little did I realize it would be three long hours before I saw his charming face again.

I got out my embroidery. The men got out a bottle. The coach got colder: the men got mellower. As the conversation became friendly, I put on my "British freeze" and the atmosphere chilled. Besides my embroidery, only twelve cars and three trains broke the monotony.

Having little else to do but think and let my imagination run riot, I remembered all the sudden that I was loaded with money—$35 in Canadian currency, $65 in U.S., $10 in my bra, and $70 in traveler checks! What to do: my body might not be found for weeks: in fact, it might not be found at all! So, opening my little brown cosmetic box, I stuck in my two pocketbooks and locked it. After all this stewing and preparation for the END, our driver came back.

Having called Mr. Schlafman from North Bay I knew there was a room waiting for me, so I checked into the Coulson. Fifteen minutes later he raps on my door and we go over the reports to date, which proved satisfactory and complete. After gabbing "shop," he leaves for Greyhound

League bowling. I make out my current report, and after his bowling was over we go out to dinner.

At a little dump on a back road—all roads in north Ontario are back roads—we have spaghetti and chicken, different and delicious, and more shoptalk.

Then he has to show me the office here and the garage—me apprehensive every minute that a driver would show up! He has a nice setup and is putting on a 300-mile service North in May.

Then back to my Canadian home at the Coulson where I am writing this. Did I say an adventurous day? I had a wonderful time. Love, Margean

---

March 30, 1947
From Hotel Coulson, Sudbury, Ontario, Canada

Dear Ones: I hope you have a map and can see where I'm at—Little Current on Manitoulin Island in Georgian Bay on the north side of Lake Huron. The late President Roosevelt had, and Mr. Burleigh has, a camp up here: in fact, lots of millionaires who want to get away from civilization come here. I didn't want to get away from civilization—the do's and don'ts of people providing my livelihood.

Came in last night on the crookedest, narrowest, driftedest washboard of a dirt trail. It was drifting badly and I was apprehensive lest I be snowed in again. But morning broke bright and dazzling with no wind so my worries were for naught.

I stayed at an out-post of civilization called the Manitoulin House and nearly became a "post" myself. The radiator was pounding out heat at a terrific rate if you got within two feet of it you cooked. To counteract that, the curtains stood out ten inches from the window flapping in the gale coming through the cracks in spite of a storm window's dubious protection. Under the door came a stiff breeze from the hall. This would have been bearable if the washbowl had been near the radiator. As it was, I received blasts from the door and window, and none of the benefits of the pounding and gurgling of the radiator. Putting a spare blanket around my shoulders, I sat on the side of the bed near the radiator roasting my feet into blissful comfort while I wrote reports.

That essential job done, it was time to turn in: that is, after I'd washed. At the washbasin, I finally coaxed out lukewarm water that in the Arctic chill of my room felt like boiling. I took off only my dress and hose and popped into bed—on the side by the radiator—and with the aid of three extra blankets, was soon drifting off.

I would have drifted off much sooner, but! Let me digress a little. Only registered hotels in Canada are permitted to sell liquor, and the Manitoulin House isn't registered. However, this doesn't prevent guests from buying liquor by the bottle and having it in their rooms.

This was what was taking place in the room next to mine. From the noise, there must have been several men in there! Someone was telling "Herb" why he didn't like him and "Herb's" ancestors were described in detail! The conversation was not cosmopolitan! I drifted off lullabied by the bumps of "Herb" as he was evicted and roughly assisted in his descent of the stairs. I excused this unseemly conduct: this was Saturday night in a lumber and trapping community and, obviously, they couldn't know a lady was in the next room!

Morning broke with the thunder of fists on my door and a cheery "It's 7:30 and you wanted to be called." My eyes were greeted by a dazzle of sunshine. I took the wind direction and was surprised to find it abated. Loath to leave this comfort all at once, I advanced a foot. Deciding that this pussyfooting wasn't becoming to a farm-raised girl who was once a steady visitor to an outhouse, I threw all caution—and blankets—to the wind, greeted the day, and dressed in nothing flat!

Calm was spread over the hotel. I descended to the lobby where a wrinkled old man took my $1.50 for the pleasure of staying there. Then to the dining room where, instead of a menu, I was brought a glass of grapefruit juice and a bowl of cereal and was asked how I wanted my eggs. Such service! I wasn't even certain I had wanted eggs, but if it had to be eggs, it had to be eggs! Two beautiful fried eggs, toast, bacon and coffee were next placed before me. I had qualms—but that's why they always give you the check at the end of the meal! Calmly resisting the voice of financial panic I ate, nearly falling over when I got the bill—50 cents!

By then, it was bus time and out into the dazzle I marched, down a crooked block and into the station where the owner was breakfasting on grapefruit and toast. I bought my ticket and the bus arrived. The driver entered and said he had to have his morning "bracer". "What's this?" thinks I. He walks over to the jukebox, drops in a nickel and the horrible strains of "Open the Door, Richard" prove a most effective "bracer".

We started back over a road now complicated by fresh drifts: through country where you shoot wolves from a wind-blown snow-sled over the frozen waters through a land where wilderness is wilderness, and men supposedly are men through a land of logging operations with the logs neatly piled by creeks waiting for the thaw and the yearly boom down to the KVP at Espanola.

My driver related the news, gossip and local color during the entire trip. Your traveling companions? My first was the son of the woman who owns most of Manitoulin Island. He is a famous hunter, friend of the Indians, and the biggest bootlegger in Canada. About four years ago he was bringing in liquor when the officials caught up with him: jumping the train while it was crossing a bridge, he escaped and made his way to Detroit where he stayed until the heat was off. Because of this and his hunting prowess, he frequently makes the headlines and pictorial pages of the Toronto Star, while his yearly visit to California provides copy the rest of the year. And what did I see? Not a hard gangster, not the smelly hunter that this would lead one to expect—instead, a rather nice looking, unprepossessing chap in heavy clothes with a friendly voice.

Next came an Indian. He looked like an ordinary Indian and he works for the Canadian Pacific Railway on night shift at an out-of-the-way curve. One day last week he came home early and found a visitor with his wife. She is recovering, and it is definitely certain that she'll live!

Next we passed the log house where three Indians <u>had</u> lived. Last week, a husband, his wife and the wife's sister lived there: this week only husband and sister are left. Last week they had a party with a jug of liquor for refreshment: wife accused sister of taking away husband and knives flew. Husband staggered out to be found sleeping it off in a drift; sister was found sleeping it off; and wife was found sleeping permanently – her throat slit! People are looking forward to the trial. Love, Margean

April 2, 1947
From YWCA Residence, Detroit, Michigan

Dear Ones: I was greeted like a long lost friend who'd hibernated in a snowbank all winter, and nothing would do but I had to sit down while they plied me with questions! Everybody dropped into the office today and registered degrees of surprise at seeing me un-thawed and with only a runny nose. The most persistent raze was astonishment that I'd not picked up a good, unused lumberjack after staying away so long! The cards and letters with my adventures were tacked on the board with "appropriate" comments added by thoughtful members of the office! We had quite a celebration!

As always, there had been changes—Pat has quit under Doctor's orders for migraine. Mr. Polk has asked that I be sent down for a special in Dayton next week that should keep me there quite a while. This week I'm doing that survey at the office, which means a lot of typing and poring over audited forms.

Look how much they took out of my check. $35.50 income tax! $40.70 deducted! Only a measly $209 take-home pay! How do they expect a working girl to live? What's my bank balance now?

I got my glasses. Very chic. My sunglasses are very dark and distinctive, as you rarely see rimless sun-lens. You should see the red shoes I got! Love, Margean

---

April 4, 1947
From YWCA Residence, Detroit, Michigan

Dear Ones: Well, hell broke loose today as rumors of company change have surfaced and Mr. Burleigh has left! What with one thing and another, my day proved very informative. What amazes and pleases me is that I'm a confidant of all sides.

My survey is progressing nicely and appears to be just what JP wants. Edith came in and we went out to dinner. She's just about ready to quit. Miss Santini is riding her over things she knows nothing about. I stick up for Edith and try to keep off some of the fire, as does Allen. Allen, too, is just about fed up with the whole outfit. And, I might as well say that I'm ready for a change. I feel stifled, have little initiative, stagnating, intellectually starved. By that, I mean the work no longer holds the unexpected.

All this is leading up, so be patient. You know North Star Lines inquired about and asked for our services on the basis of two runs I took with them. A letter was sent, but the contract for our service must have been pretty steep for the small company and they are still undecided. The same thing happened with Short Way Lines. Allen has applied for a license to open an inspection operation and it should come through in about a month. He would have a small set-up operating on an equal basis: he wants two people beside himself and wants to know if I'll make the second. It's something to think about on a purely business angle and makes me proud that he'd ask me. He can do it, too: until Glatz came along, Allen was sure of a promotion within Great Lakes Greyhound.

How the currents and crosscurrents are flying with the factions trying to get me on their side! The only thing now is for my "luncheon" to take place! Then all the cards, so far as I'm concerned, will be on the table.

1. Allen's offer: salary $350 a month and my own boss.

2. Glatz's offer: salary a probable $300 a month.

3. Schlafman's offer: salary a probable $250 a month with advancement if I change my citizenship.

4. Mr. Radcliff's offer: terminal? traffic? traveling agent?

5. JP's offer: stay with him?

How my brain is whirling? What should I do? The first offers independence, wider experience in the field and could take me back under Mr. Burleigh into the American system out of Chicago covering all the U.S. The second offers a continuation of the present, only I don't think I'd like to work for him. The third offers what I want to do with the disadvantage of citizenship and distance, but a swell superior—and Allen thinks this has great advantages if I'd rather stay with the company instead of going into a "working partnership" with him. As yet, four is vague, but I would guess with the advantage of a permanent location with a settled life and the disadvantages of a probable cut in pay, prejudice against women and my age. The fifth is just a possibility. In connection with the last two comes the question: have I worked my head off for nine months for nothing?

For the last few days I've been batting these around and am going nuts trying to weigh the scales! I wish both of you would write. What are your opinions? I must be good. So far, three people have come with out-and-out offers for my services, and the value they put on these services leads me to only one conclusion—I must have something to offer that makes each overlook the fact that I'm a 19-year-old woman.

I can't come home to talk, I'm loaded with a survey and a special South that'll consume this week. Dad, write and send it special delivery so I'll get it on the double—by Saturday night, because I don't know when I'll leave. What is the best for my career—for it's fast developing into that. You know my mental and physical capacity better than I do. How would I turn out? Love, Margean

———

April 8, 1947
From YWCA Residence, Detroit, Michigan

Dear Ones: Had a talk with Miss Santini and the outcome of the examinations is up in the air—Great Lakes putting in a new bid for JP's

126

services. Another result of this talk was an interesting piece of news—which I had already surmised—that she and Mr. Glatz are getting married! Our office has been a hotbed of romance, three marriages and one in the future.

This noon we went shopping at a sample shoe store where you get broken lots and cancellations at much lower prices. She has real tiny feet and got two pair that cost $30. I got some everyday ones with a 1½-inch heel for $6.50.

JP dropped in before leaving for Ann Arbor and told me to go to his Personnel Office at the 24th Street Garage to finish my survey. Miss Santini calls there and says she's sending over a "clerk" to look into some records. So I work this week at the 24th Street Garage—next to my little boys! Love, Margean

---

April 10, 1947
From YWCA Residence, Detroit, Michigan

Dear Ones: Finished my survey today—quite an enlightening process as I had the run of all the personnel files and was able to "snoop" to my heart's content. Out of curiosity, I looked up the terminal manager at Kalamazoo. What a background! Six years of college and university to learn the transportation business and then he started at the bottom: one year as starter at the Detroit terminal; three years as ticket agent and auditor; and two years as traveling passenger agent; and finally Kalamazoo where he's been for about five years. If I could only follow in his footsteps! Who knows where I'll be at 37, as he is!

If I do say so, the survey is very complete and most informative. I wish JP would take me to the meeting where he's going to spout at length about the "we told you sos" and "how comes" I dug up! This will be the first big meeting since the change in top men from Burleigh and Morrow, and the new ones probably won't be so sympathetic. Maybe some action will result. I hope so.

Got a call from Miss Santini asking me to head down to Valley Greyhound because we're resuming inspection on that line again, and she seems to think I ought to start it off. Boy! What a check I'm going to get! Love, Margean

---

April 14, 1947
From Gibson Hotel, Jackson, Ohio

Dear Ones: A lovely ride down: spring is about three weeks advanced here with trees budding, baby pigs running, and lambs steady on their feet. The beef cattle in the pastures still carry their shaggy, rough winter coats. The sheep look naked! Everyone is plowing and, inside of a week, oats will be in.

Interesting people filled my day. Just south of Marion, a woman got on carrying a long flower box. Her son had dug up an Indian skeleton—so she thought—and she was taking it to the museum at Columbus. One woman I sat with was a nurse who takes "out" cases and she told me all about herself, her sister who's going to have a baby (although she's got a lung collapsed from TB), her brother who's studying medicine at "State" and some patients.

But the man I sat with from Columbus to Logan took the cake. He was such a nice ordinary fellow! His wife had just had a serious operation and he'd been off work this week, but his sister came up today so that he could go home. He worked in a trouser factory in McArther and had eight acres a "five minute drive from town." He had one cow that just had a calf, two pigs, three hundred chickens (ten died), fifty peach and apple trees, a large garden, 3½ acres of pasture, a seven-room house, a small barn and a medium-sized chicken-coop. He has one dog (part hound and collie), rats (who ate his cat) and termites: the first he feeds scraps, the second, arsenic. He likes egg and onion sandwiches. During the war he was an MP at the "concentration" camps for both Japs and Germans in Montana and California: in the latter place he got his dog.

Before the war he laid and tested pipes for the natural gas "stepping-up" station at Sugar Grove. To find where the leaks are, you walk over the line until you come to a place where absolutely no vegetation grows—that's the leak: you dig down to the pipe and find the hole (oh, I forgot: you smell the dirt to find out for sure before you dig). Then you wrap a band of rubber around it and clamp it on: you can't weld or solder it because the pressure would blow it off. Back in the deep woods, they'd find places where a ¾-inch hole had been bored and capped where bootleggers had tapped the line for power for their stills. His wife is coming home next Sunday. Don't I meet the most interesting people!

Oh, I forgot about something that happened in the Columbus terminal. I walked in very business-like about a half-hour before bus time, sat down and started watching people One old woman, all painted up to look 40, came tripping in on three-inch heels. By the way she walked, I knew her

128

feet were killing her. What did she do but put her hand on the seat in front of me, pull off both shoes and barefoot up to the ticket window. I guess my face must have been a picture of suppressed laughter and surprise: I held it as long as I could and let out a loud chuckle. <u>Everyone</u> looked at me and then looked at her—the entire terminal burst out laughing: but she calmly replaced the shoes and strolled out with a haughty air instead of throwing them at me as I deserved. I was thoroughly ashamed of myself, but it was just like a movie happening in front of me.

I looked up across the aisle and this <u>handsome</u> Romeo was laughing at me. He came across, sat down and said, "Someone ought to have had a camera to record the expression on your face." Before we could delve deeper into this, my bus came and I had to run. Another bit of unfinished business.

Back to my talkative man: he was telling me all about the inspectors that they have on Greyhound. Now I didn't know anything about them: did I? I was thinking on the way down that there couldn't be many more than 100 in the U.S. With just eight people, we cover most of the mid-west and lots of Canada: so multiply eight by about ten big divisions and you get 80. And I'm one of them

I'm writing this in Logan where I'm stuck until 10:20 p.m. It's black out, no stars, no moon with dark clouds scurrying along. The town is brilliant—red, green, blue and white lights up and down Main Street. Every one jaywalks, traffic is slow and people are friendly. Logan is just two hours away from Jackson where a bed awaits. It's a very crooked road. Love, Margean

---

April 18, 1947
From Southern Hotel, Columbus, Ohio

Dear Ones: It's time I break my silence and report on my few activities. My last ride on Monday resulted in the firing of a man: he charged me 30 cents for a $1.38 ride for some unknown reason, and the company didn't like it. My ride on Tuesday turned up some mighty peculiar money deals that have to be returned from audit before I can translate them. The other runs were dull.

My reaction to the country between Athens and Pomeroy on the Ohio River, which I saw for the first time yesterday, was one of speechlessness. Not since I went to Washington have I seen such pressed-together hills. Pomeroy is a river town—one street along the river and the rest piled up under over-hanging rock-cliffs—a town that Mark Twain could have written about. A quaint little rear-paddle boat was pushing two coal barges —and the day was so lovely—and the hills were so green—and there was a shower on the way back—and there was a beautiful rainbow—and the sun came out and set fiery red with rain-rays all around!

I got a spring coat today: black gabardine, very plain, very good, 100% wool and very much on sale. I have always wanted a gabardine coat because they look so neat. I am thinking of buying three fur-skins to dress it up.

I have been trying to write a descriptive essay about the night bus from Louisville: so far it should be torn up, scattered to the winds and forgotten. But it's got a good foundation and everything in it is true so I shall stick with it.

At this moment I'm trying to decide if I want to walk four blocks down to a pet store and look at the puppies in the window. I think I shall. Off to the puppy windows. Love, Margean

---

April 20, 1947
From YWCA Residence, Detroit, Michigan

Dear Ones: Back in town, a wet, drizzly town, but still it's home. I once thought it was awfully big, but it really isn't. Of course, I have to walk only three or four blocks and I'm lost but it isn't as frighteningly large as once it was.

Today I had planned to do many things, the most important a walk to Clark Park and a bicycle ride if the rental shop was open, but this steady downpour has spoiled my whole day.

I feel very lonesome: here I have a new coat and a beautiful up-do (which I'm praying will last for the office tomorrow), and nothing to do. I even put some perfume behind my ears and it smells tantalizing. Nancy went to her sister's wedding last night and hasn't come home; Beverly is sleeping; and I want to go to the Oriental Gardens and have fried shrimp! My lament—all dressed up and no place to go.

My brain, typewriter, and I worked on that essay today and whipped it into something presentable but still amateurish. I really ought to do something about the woman who took off her shoes, or about the character who talked to me from Columbus to Logan, or about the woman with the skeleton. I am including the essay with this letter so that you can see what I see. Love, Margean

130

NIGHT BUS FROM LOUISVILLE

It's famous among transportation circles, this night bus from Louisville. Leaving Louisville at 8:00 p.m. bound for Detroit, it stops in Cincinnati at midnight for a half-hour, in Dayton for ten minutes, and in Bowling Green at 6:20 a.m. for breakfast. You might call it an express, it makes the best time; you might call it the truckers' bus, they compose most of the load; but you'll probably end by calling it "night bus from Louisville" like everyone else.

It's famous for its passengers. Night after night it's loaded with "haul-away" drivers and their girl friends. Naturally there are others—the commuters in Kentucky, the businessmen, the distance travelers—but ask any bus driver and he'll say, "Night bus from Louisville? Hell, we run it to get the haul-aways back to work the next day!"

What intrigues the occasional traveler is the ritual used in loading, a ritual unique to this run. The haul-aways step up, hand over their tickets, unbutton their coats, and circle around—the driver being free to take into custody any bottle he can see. To make the driver feel that he's done his duty, they let him confiscate three or four bottles, but there's method to their madness. At Cincinnati the drivers change and the confiscated bottles are returned. When the ticket and open coat routine are enacted the second time, few bottles are seen and the party takes its second wind.

But this is getting ahead of the story. At Louisville, the haul-aways and their girlfriends make for the "bleacher" or rear seat and the last three doubles. The girls all look alike—a bleached beef-trust that wears slacks —and are usually headed for jobs slinging hash in Detroit. The fellows are the muscle-bound type wearing flashy belts and jackets. Alone, just a bunch of lonesome individuals: together, men, women, and bottles, they set the character of the night bus from Louisville.

Assorted giggles, dirty stories, and sounds of kisses float up to the front, while the driver flips on the lights occasionally to keep the situation under control. Sometimes one of them will have a guitar, a harmonica, or an accordion; after proper liquid stimulation, songs—all sorts of songs— drift up. Usually starting with cowboy and close harmony, they move into "The Man Who Comes Around" and "A Huggin' and A Chalkin'" with bigger and better verses. Of course, sometimes the gang goes maudlin and sings hymns.

Reactions of the other passengers to this startling assortment are varied. Strait-laced old women turn up their noses and murmur "vulgar". Businessmen get out their private bottles and attempt to persuade their seat companions to become sociable. Gradually the whole load takes on the friendly air of one big happy family getting happier by the minute as the miles click off.

If the driver happens to snap on the light about an hour out of Dayton, he'll find almost everyone asleep with heads cuddled on shoulders, arms wrapped around each other. The bleacher and rear seats breathe in unison. Little happens the rest of the trip, and the sweepers measure the success of the night bus from Louisville by the number of bottles that roll out. Love, Margean

———

April 22, 1947
From YWCA, Dayton, Ohio

Dear Ones: Into the office, no notes in my folder; gave Edith an oral quiz; worked out a week's work. No sign of JP.

Yesterday I had to take a final ride with Edith: she had it all figured out to Talbotville, Ontario, a place where I've never been. On the spur of the moment, she looked up the population and it was 17,000—large enough to window shop. Talbotville turned out to be a crossroad with twelve houses, a gas station, and a Greyhound Post House. Where were the 17,000?

We scooted into an antique house until the driver left, and then came out to look over the situation and lay down our strategy. It was plain we couldn't stay here for three hours. We had to go to the john and went over to the gas station but the door was locked. Edith went to get the key and came back with the information that it was out of order but we could use the men's: we did.

Our strategy consisted of walking three miles to St. Thomas, which I knew was large. We had walked down the highway about a block when a big Packard pulled up, and a fellow asked if we'd like a lift and what were we doing at this God-forsaken crossroad. Well, we were antique buyers and had come up to look at some pieces in this shop here, but they weren't authentic—so naturally, our store couldn't buy them. We had a good time yesterday. Love, Margean

———

April 24, 1947
From Hotel Henry Watterson, Louisville, Kentucky

Dear Ones: From my talk with JP it's quite certain that he's not leaving, which means I stay.

132

He delegated to me (besides Flint Trolley Coach, C&LE, and extra men) the responsibility of doing all inspections for this special survey of his. This means setting it up, choosing who I want to double with me, checking the reports when they return from audit, and sending my copy of the man's record, plus the new reports, plus my and JP's comments to Mr. Budd, the new president. And it all has to be done in sixty days or less if I can. My shoulders are broad.

Had a lovely trip down yesterday. Lettuce, onions, and tomatoes are up, and tobacco seed is planted. Love, Margean

---

April 26, 1947
From Hotel Henry Watterson, Louisville, Kentucky

Dear Ones: Well, I got turned up today, became known. I had purchased a ticket from Louisville to Hamilton Boulevard that meant I should have continued out of Cincinnati north with a new driver. When we arrived, I bought my return to Louisville, south, and scooted out of sight till an hour later when I was scheduled out. At 1:00 p.m., I breezed in, out to the loading platform and practically into the arms of my previous driver. With a "you're a checker and you can't fool me" look in his eyes, he said, "Kinda late ain't you? You know, lady, the last time I had a ticket to Hamilton Boulevard, it turned out to be a checker!" With an innocent, surprised "what's that" look in my eyes, I said that the announcement wasn't clear in the restroom, when was the next bus due out, and what was I to do? He didn't believe me, I just know.

Just then in pulls my southbound bus and I left in a hurry, ostensibly to have a "stop-over" made out but really so he couldn't point me out. I took the trolley across the river to Covington, Kentucky, took my hair down, changed glasses, bought a box for my coat, and caught the 3:00, hoping by so doing to remove any identifying marks like an upsweep, dark glasses, and black coat. No one looked suspicious on the 3:00. Love, Margean

---

May 5, 1947
From YWCA Residence, Detroit, Michigan

Dear Ones: Hurray! I get the first room that opens when a girl moves out at the downtown YWCA. So sometime in the near future I move!

Contrary to my expectations, the office conference didn't produce a blow-up, chiefly because JP didn't allow any opportunity. He hit some hot and heavy, but none affected me. One thing he said was very interesting: "I'm really ashamed that I haven't advanced some people to the point they deserve." I hope he gets some ideas! Love, Margean

---

May 7, 1947
From YWCA Residence, Detroit, Michigan

Dear Ones: Who would ever think it would snow today? While I was in Bay City, I heard that they had seven inches in Cadillac. What a nasty, cold day!

I had a pleasant surprise, the driver gave me a nice ride considering his bad record. With the fellow coming back though, you nearly had your $12,000 insurance!

I'm all enthused about moving but can't do anything but wait. They're notoriously slow about moving out of the Main Y. Everything is ready to move and I could go on an hour's notice—but it'd take all day to trot across town with loaded suitcases. I don't know how far ahead to pay my rent here. I have some dresses that need cleaning, but I don't want to clean them until after the wrinkling mess of packing is over. No news. Love, Margean

---

May 12, 1947
To parents from YWCA Residence, Detroit, Michigan

Dear Ones: To the office yesterday, my survey finished and good if I say so myself. I hope I get a pat on the back but shall have to wait a week to find out. My lovely schedule down to Louisville went to naught when Miss Santini asked me to go on a special to Valley where we have resumed inspection. Are the others going to love me—first chance at the field, and I grab off 17 for re-inspections (they've only got about 50 men)!

This afternoon I'm going to work some suburbans out to Pontiac and make a terminal inspection. It has a very bad reputation and Saturday will be a good time to check on it. This morning I spent pressing, playing the piano and writing letters. Love, Margean

May 13, 1947
From YWCA Residence, Detroit, Michigan

Dear Ones: You should have been here this morning! First, I drag myself from my warm bed at 4:00 a.m. and dress without waking my roommates. At 4:25 I was out on the Boulevard when I decided there would be time for coffee at Sam's as there would surely be two trolleys, one at 4:30 and one at 4:45, and I could catch the latter.

Accordingly, I had a cup of coffee and at 4:35 was standing on the Boulevard again. No trolley: my bus was due to leave at 5:10. Still standing there at 5:02, I decided that desperate measures were necessary! Lifting an inexperienced thumb, the first car stopped. He turned out to be a traveler from Toledo who was memorizing the Mason ritual. So, while he was whisking me downtown, I held the book while he recited what he'd learned. He deposited me in front of the station as my bus pulled out and I got it. Love, Margean

---

May 16, 1947
From YWCA Residence, Detroit, Michigan

Dear Ones: Was showing Miss Santini my embroidered peacock today, finished at last, and JP wanted to know what I'd take for it.

Mr. Budd is holding up our North Star inspections—sulking because JP didn't consult him? JP's mad!

Mr. Adamson and I went to Clare and back yesterday. Today we worked suburbans. The other day four of us got on one man—Curtz, Allen, Edith, and I—a survey with three cash fares paid by inspectors! The driver better be right.

Tomorrow I'm going down to the Main Y to hep up Miss Maloney about my transfer. Can hardly wait to move—I want to so badly! Love, Margean

---

May 17, 1947
From YWCA Residence, Detroit, Michigan

Dear Ones: Congratulate me! I shall be moving the first week in June or before. Hurray, hurray! This means I'll have to spend money on an iron and a radio. Who cares! After almost a year, I'm where I want to be.

Have decided not to tell anyone here that I'm moving. Shall start a new life completely—no close friends—no roommates. Love, Margean

---

May 18, 1947
From YWCA Residence, Detroit, Michigan

Dear Ones: Everyone's at church, leaving me and a radio with good programs. Dreamed some more about the joys of living at the Main Y —swimming and a nice, cool building! It poured last evening with both roommates caught out and coming in dripping, then we bored each other the rest of the evening. As usual I'm bored stiff sticking in town. Love, Margean

---

May 20, 1947
From YWCA Residence, Detroit, Michigan

Dear Ones: You should have seen me this morning. Up at 5:00 to catch a 6:25, out of the house still groggy, and out on Grand River to the first railroad crossing there to await my driver.

My driver had plenty to upset him: coach #1 had a leaking airline; coach #2 had faulty brakes; and coach #3 had faulty steering rods and gears that refused to mesh properly. Coach #1 got down to 38 lbs. of pressure before he sent an SOS; coach #2 got two blocks out of Lansing terminal when he put on the brakes and I hit the baggage rack; coach #3, despite its gearing faults, got us to Mt. Pleasant.

I had quite a diversion on the way up. The fellow behind me had a pet groundhog. Coming from South Carolina to his Mt. Pleasant home, he had started three days ago. Thirteen days ago they had gone hunting, and their dogs cornered and killed the mother groundhog. They found her three babies, and this passenger kept one.

He was just like a fat rabbit with the face and teeth of a squirrel and a little flattened tail. His paws could grab a-hold of your finger. Including his tail, he was about ten inches long; his coat was a pretty silvered brown and gray. They make awfully nice pets if you get them young.

I held this little baby from Lansing to Mt. Pleasant and fed him. By himself, he held a small size baby bottle with a nipple. He drank and drank, and got rounder and rounder, his stomach sticking out so far he could hardly grip his bottle. They aren't called hogs for nothing. Then he curled up in the corner of my elbow and slept. Love, Margean

136

May 22, 1947
From YWCA Residence, Detroit, Michigan

Dear Ones: I move Monday and I dread the thought of toting my things across town! I still don't know about my room, what it looks like or how much. Tuesday I'll buy an iron and a radio.

I have put in 39 hours in three days this week! Next week, Frye and I are going to Indianapolis on a special, my first time in that territory. Don't know when I'll get home. Would certainly like to see the garden. Love, Margean

May 23, 1947
From YWCA Residence, Detroit, Michigan

Dear Ones: I think I told you when I called, that if Mr. Glatz is in town, he'll help me move, which is wonderful. Monday, moving day, Frye and I leave at 7:45 a.m. for Bowling Green, arriving back at 2:07 p.m.—so that fits in fine.

Today Frye and I went to Mt. Clemens and got our survey man. It's the first time he'd ever been there, and he nearly fell over from the mineral bath sulfur odor that fills the air.

I've had a lot of fun doing these doubles with various inspectors and learning how they conduct themselves on the road. Frye, being one of the old ones, is very good. Yesterday we were nearly being killed by one of my bad boys, when I felt a tap on my shoulder. Looking around, I see it's Frye's hand with a note in it. Hardly daring to take my eyes off the road, I opened it: what had he written but "Prepare to Die, You Greyhound Rat!" I nearly split, and the woman sitting with me asked "if she'd missed anything!" Love, Margean

May 25, 1947
From YWCA Residence, Detroit, Michigan

Dear Ones: A wasted day: Mr. Hoppe crossed me up by asking that I get to Bowling Green to catch a double, and then there wasn't one! And I gave up a planned day's work for this!

Packing tomorrow and what a job! Nancy has lent me two suitcases which will give me four. Then I have six pairs of shoes, books, and knickknacks that have to be toted somehow. If Mr. Glatz doesn't help,

I'll be at my wit's end. Evidently Mrs. Anderson has told several that I'm moving and, much to my surprise, I find that I'll be missed—everybody bemoaning the fact—which makes me feel good.

Played piano this morning before work and enjoyed myself immensely —shall greatly enjoy a grand piano to practice and thump on without disturbing anyone. Have found my playing has improved—to my ears, anyway.

I've decided to buy a cactus and, maybe, frame my peacock to decorate the room. I have a single for $6 a week. Do you realize that's $312 a year, instead of the $468 with all the meals I miss, that I have been paying. The savings will be substantial. Speaking of meals, JP told me how to make Johnny cake—make it only half-inch thick. Makes it good and crisp. Sounds good. Love, Margean

---

May 26, 1946
From Main YWCA, Detroit, Michigan

Dear Ones: It's a beautiful, beautiful, room—a single with a view over all downtown Detroit, including the river with its boats, and across to Windsor. Miss Santini saw it and fell in love with it; Beverly saw it and fell in love with it. The maple furniture looks new. The floor has green-leafed carpeting. There are new drapes of red, blue and yellow flowers with green leaves on cream background. There is a lavatory, a large closet, a chest, bookshelves, a four poster bed with a dusty rose bedspread, a desk and a chair, and an easy chair upholstered in green plush. Room 933 at 2230 Witherell, Detroit—my home!

Mr. Glatz, bless his soul, helped me move, and I got everything in one trip saving wear on mind, body and feet! Miss Santini helped me tote things up. It's now 10:30 a.m. and I have everything packed away with plenty of space for all my junk.

Tomorrow I settle down: hunt for an iron and radio for D.C. current; buy a cactus, which I'm determined to raise; buy a picture frame for my peacock; find the piano—and, at 5:10 p.m. go on a short trip to Lansing.

To the office today planning and got JP mad at a superintendent, not me—when I showed him a beautiful case of driver stealing which Joe Lane had requested where nothing had been done. There's something rotten in Battle Creek again! Don't know all the particulars yet! Really stinks! Worse than the previous odors! Love, Margean

June 3, 1947
From Main YWCA, Detroit, Michigan

Dear Ones: Last night I saw one of the best movies ever! It was "Fantasia". I have never seen anything like it! Oh, the music!

Went to Bowling Green with Frye today. We were standing in the station waiting for our bus when a man comes up, gives Frye a card and tells us that for $16—including bus fare to Detroit, blood test, license and taxis to the station—we can get married. JP roared when we told him!

Am anxious to go South because of the new region. Allen got turned up there last week. He took a ride through Bedford in the morning and noticed a driver was standing near the station. When he came back four hours later, the driver was still there: he pointed a dramatic finger at Allen and said, "There's your inspector." I wonder what's the rest of the story?
Love, Margean

———————

June 6, 1947
From Main YWCA, Detroit, Michigan

Dear Ones: The day before a big trip is always filled with excitement —packing, getting sufficient forms, getting the room cleaned up. This day is extra full though because I have five men to catch.

Read an exciting book this week: "Storm" by George Stewart. It's the story of the birth, maturity and death of a storm, and it's effect upon companies—telephone, water supplies, airlines, road maintenance, etc. —and about a dozen people. Thought-provoking as I'm out in so many storms of all kinds!

I'm just breaking even this month—$1.10 left and 75 cents will go for tickets. What made it tight was paying for my room a month ahead before getting paid. Of course, I haven't robbed my bra but still I came close.

Later: Got paid today. Because of my long trip, I'm not sending $150. Notice how my sticking in town has hurt the amount. Love, Margean

———————

June 11, 1947
From Hotel Severin, Indianapolis, Indiana

Dear Ones: This will be sort of a diary letter that I will add to:

June 7: Made a long trip today—almost ten hours, mostly through low, dark, good farm country rolling in parts and sweltering in a 93 temperature. Still, I had lots of time to look around. The country is soaked: all drainage ditches have been opened and are starting to overflow. The river at Bedford, through which I pass tomorrow, is rising two inches an hour today! And it's poured all day! No roads in danger so far, they say.

Thirty minutes after getting off, I was sitting on the Bloomington-bound coach, numb in the rear despite the protection of a 15 cent pillow. Our first man was alright—Fred did him; the second man was terrible—I did him! He swore a blue streak.

June 8: Bloomington to Evansville is through gently rolling, good farm land. Honeysuckle and roses grow wild along the roadbanks and perfume the air, especially at night! First cutting of hay progresses—lots of chopping—but corn is only an inch high, mostly not planted.

Evansville is an old city, like Grand Rapids but on level ground. It hugs the Ohio River. Fred and I had a four-hour layover so we "covered the water front." It's a narrow park: a pontoon airplane gives rides; red wagons sell popcorn, candy and hot dogs; people sweat. We sat on a hotel veranda overlooking the park, wrote our reports and listened to boastful talk while babies played in back of our swing. Later we had dinner in a cool restaurant where for $1 we had spaghetti, yams, corn, jello salad, apple cobbler, rolls and iced tea.

June 9: We made a trip to Paoli, saw a show and returned, having gotten our two survey men. Got back in at 12:45 a.m. again. Tired!

June 10: I made another trip to Evansville with a 45-minute turnaround.

June 11: Several things amaze me about Indiana: low restaurant prices, no sales tax and the ill dressed people—including me. It's entirely too hot to care—85-95 degrees. Have been working like mad 18 hour, 17 hour, 12 hour, 15 hour days. Am at last up-to-date and shall mail this today. Love, Margean

———

June 12, 1947
From Main YWCA, Detroit, Michigan

Dear Ones: Had an interesting ride from Indianapolis to Dayton. A drunk woman was on—a bottle rolled up and down the aisle: another drunk woman swore at the driver and was put in her place!

140

Shall be back in town Saturday, and a good thing because my clothes and I look grimy! Had a pleasant surprise when several of the clerks knew me when registering last night. This Southern Hotel in Columbus is on my regular beat.

Had my hair cut this afternoon, and saw "Duel in the Sun": wonderful, both. Love, Margean

———•———

June 15, 1947
From Main YWCA, Detroit, Michigan

Dear Ones: The end of a very, very long day, but then I suppose I <u>did</u> rest, not doing much besides ironing and piano playing. Office will be a welcome sight tomorrow—there's always the wonder of "Where will I go next?"

It's pitch black out and the bright red "Crowley Miller" and "Hudson" signs seem suspended in a bottomless pit. The park paths are lined with lights, and lights in some office buildings make me suspect that someone is either cleaning or getting a jump on tomorrow. My clock is ticking away, and the alarm's set for 7:15. So—goodnight! Love, Margean

———•———

June 20, 1947
From YWCA, Flint, Michigan

Dear Ones: June 18: This will be another diary letter. As usual, nothing has happened: Flint is <u>always</u> dull! Though, we almost ran over a little boy who fell with his bike right in front of our trolley. A woman jaywalked in front of us, and two people in the trolley fell when the driver braked to avoid hitting her. Good reaction times from the drivers!

June 19: Another "as usual, nothing happened day" with me getting bored at and with Flint. Not even one bright or funny spot to brighten my day. I imagine people probably think I'm nuts coming into their stores to sit and then popping out at such odd times as 1:23, 10:47 and 11:36.

June 20: I got 29 men in 3½ days. Love, Margean

———•———

June 21, 1947
From YWCA, Flint, Michigan

Dear Ones: Today I had to get up to Saginaw to meet Adamson for a survey. There was only one hitch for both of us—there were no regular men to go up on and we had to rely on second sections. So, at 9:30 a.m., I took my battle position, namely the Durant Hotel's window in the ladies lounge that looks down South Saginaw Street up which my bus had to come. The first bus was due at 9:41, and promptly at that time one of those big, beautiful monsters rolled into view bearing a most welcome sign, "Bus Follows".

So I scooted downstairs and took up my advanced battle station in the doorway of a loan company, where I could venture out to observe whether the enemies' advance scout had moved and whether my second section had come into view. The scout pulled out, and the objective pulled into view. So I rolled up my sleeves and firmly grasped my weapon—suitcase—and prepared to do battle with the people between the door and me. The only casualties suffered were dirty looks as I clambered on, the third when I should have been the fortieth: we had a standing load: I had a beautiful seat. Love, Margean

---

June 22, 1947
From Main YWCA, Detroit, Michigan

Dear Ones: To resume my story. I got to Saginaw at 11:15 a.m. and sat myself waiting for Adamson who would arrive between 11:15 and 5:56 depending on the chances for doubles. He pulled in on the 1:15 double and we compare luck: I had a "never-inspected" and he had a re-inspection.

We had a layover until 5:58 so we went to see "High Barbaree" with Van Johnson. We then pushed and shoved to get with our survey man back into Detroit—made it!

I learned one startling piece of news: a conference is scheduled for Thursday. Santini gripes? News of Central? Will someone be fired? Will JP resign? Will our department be dissolved? There are so many possibilities. Love, Margean

---

June 25, 1947
From Main YWCA, Detroit, Michigan

Dear Ones: As you know from my call, the department is being dissolved. JP called me into the office and said he'd found another opportunity for me. We've done a lot of investigation out at Willow Run Airport where Siprionni Limousine Service is muscling in on our franchise. Greyhound has already fired two dispatchers for accepting bribes. Siprionni boys aren't nice, and they aren't particular how they get their trade.

So Mr. Keith called up JP and said that we've decided to fight fire with fire, and did he have three good men who could take care of themselves. JP said yes, but that he had something better—a good, aggressive young woman who wanted to learn dispatching and who would look good in a uniform—and wouldn't this look better than a "gang war." Well, they contacted Mr. Powell, Vice President, and he laughed at the idea, but the whole prospect hinged on seeing and talking to me.

Because of the radio connections between the buses and the airport, I would have to get a radio operator's license. Hours are 8 to 4. As yet the pay is unknown. Love, Margean

---

June 26, 1947
From Main YWCA, Detroit, Michigan

Dear Ones: Mr. Glatz says, "Hold tight, get some security." He also said that American Buslines—Mr. Burleigh's—was a good one.

I just saw Mr. Keith. He offered me $200 a month as radio dispatcher: $250 if I'd "hustle" trade away from Ciprionni; $280 if I were successful. Future—radio dispatcher for the new 17th Street combined operations garage when it's completed in 2-3 years. Pay then about $300.

HOWEVER, he said that if he were in MY shoes he'd take Burleigh's offer, regardless. Love, Margean

---

June 27, 1947
From Main YWCA, Detroit, Michigan

Dear Ones: Well, I saw Mr. Radcliffe and Mr. Lyons this morning. He had nothing to offer me but ticket agent work that starts at $140 a month for a 48-hour week. There is a $10 raise every six months until the ceiling of $205 per month is reached. I could have my choice of Flint or Battle Creek stations. Naturally, I said I'd let him know next week.

I'm enclosing a map of the American Busline territory. It is connected with the National Trailways Bus system, Greyhound's biggest and most serious rival. I have just finished writing to all the YWCAs in Chicago to see what a change of room would involve.

It's 12:30 and hotter than Hell! I'm going on the roof to think and burn. Love, Margean

———

June 28, 1947
From Main YWCA, Detroit, Michigan

Dear Ones: This _is_ the fateful morning. I am partially dressed—hat and stockings—and have a few minutes to kill before putting on the rest in this heat.

Yesterday afternoon, Allen, Edith and I went out for dinner. You'd think we were employed. Well, I've got news. Allen and Edith are going to be married! Isn't that wonderful! Two people that I've always liked very, very much. She's seven years older than he is but I guess that doesn't make much difference nowadays. Anyway, I'm very, very happy for them.

This is an awful feeling—no job with the department dissolved—and I don't know what to do with myself. I can't eat because it's too hot. I have taken one bath and two showers every day—then I lie on the roof and fry in oil. I play the piano. It's too hot to go uptown. Men lie on the grass in the park. Birds take sand baths. It should rain. Radio says 89 today, which probably means 95.

Later: Mr. Burleigh had to put off my appointment until 1:45 this afternoon when I am to meet him at his suite in the Book-Cadillac. It's almost that now.

Evening: Well, you know what happened! It was a beautiful suite: the card on the door said $14 a day. We discussed details over a "Tom Collins." I hadn't spent my days entirely in idleness: I had spent my time digesting his territory.

It boils down to this: I work directly for _him_—not his company, but _him_!

My first job will be to check Flint public opinion on the extension of the Flint Trolley Coach franchise that he owns. My reports go directly to his Detroit office here, marked "personal." No one is to know what I'm doing. No one on Flint Trolley Coach is to know I'm there. Reports are to be made in duplicate. I'm to keep one copy. I'm to sign myself, "Mr. M." Salary is to be $250 a month with a bonus at the end of the job in Flint (about September 9 when they vote). Then I can go to either San Francisco or Chicago where I either set up an investigative service for the company, or continue working for him.

Flint will be easy: I know the city: I know where to contact the different classes of people that need contacting. I have made up my mind the kind of "form" I shall use in reporting.

Incidentally, I'm to call Chicago if I "need or want anything!" Love, Margean

----

June 30, 1947
From YWCA, Flint, Michigan

Dear Ones: Wasn't I lucky getting a room right off the bat? I just walked in and asked, and they had half of a double. And guess how much a week: $3.45! Will I save money! I paid for a month, $13.80.

So I got to work. Bought a box of typing paper, carbon and a bunch of long envelopes. I made six contacts that resulted in five reports. I hope they are what he wants. My typing—will I have to practice!

I have to return to Detroit the 3rd to get and cash my paycheck. When I get back to Flint I'll establish a bank account so that I'll be able to cash my future checks: they never want to believe me. I should get between $450 and $500 in that paycheck. Out of that I want to pay another year on my insurance and bank most of the remainder. I probably won't receive a check on this job until the end of July or first of August, so shall retain some.

It's melting here: I could positively drop into a grease spot. Everyone is going around in cute midriff suits. But me: I'll have to be careful in my wardrobe now that I'm hobnobbing with society. I shall stick to black and gray and strive to achieve a little glamooooor, and keep my mouth shut so people can't tell how dumb I really am.

Yesterday in Detroit we had a beautiful cloudburst. It poured and poured and got blacker and blacker. Sometimes it was so dark I couldn't see beyond the Wolverine Hotel, a block away. The rain blew in gusts along the street. Trolleys were stalled. I saw the Crowley-Miller building struck by lightening. Because the wind was coming from a different direction, I could sit by my open window and watch and feel it grow cooler. It was marvelous. An hour later the sun was out.

I'd give anything to see what three years will bring. Big Business is so exciting, especially when you can see it happen. I may have to practice scrawling my signature. Love, Margean

———

July 2, 1947
From YWCA, Flint, Michigan

Dear Ones: Work here is interesting but tedious: the public can be <u>so</u> dumb! I canvass from house to house, and for every answer I get, I have asked two others who don't know or don't care.

I am to insert a germ against city ownership in everybody's ear to whom I talk. Best germs are the cost of taking over the lines and the probable raising of fares to 10 cents, this when Flint can't even provide good schools. This insidious propaganda could be problematic. The biggest problem, that I would hate to stir up, is race prejudice. A driver said that if the city got the lines, they'd have to hire Negroes, and they would with Negroes forming probably a fourth of the population. The driver said that women don't want to ride home late at night with Negroes—especially in Flint.

Of those people who do have opinions though, three-quarters favor continuation of present service. It is my opinion, even at this early date, that Mr. Burleigh's franchise will be extended by a wide margin. Strangely, the union sits on the fence, leaning a little towards city ownership if anything, while the drivers favor company ownership. Figure that out!

My first contact is usually made at breakfast, my next from a passenger, my next from a driver and so on. The old drivers are better to talk to, having individual opinions; the young ones just repeat union dogma. The old ones have been through several union changes and aren't afraid of it.

I have a nice roommate my age from a farm. The girls here are very friendly, and I know half-a-dozen already. But then, I've been here lots before.

You asked whether I was supposed to take time off in the middle of the week. I don't know. He didn't say how I was to work: how much work I was supposed to send in: or anything! And I don't know how I'm being paid. Love, Margean

146

July 4, 1947
From YWCA, Flint, Michigan

Dear Ones: Am enclosing $330: please pay a year on my life insurance and bank the rest.

Naturally while in Detroit yesterday, I learned all about the poor, inefficient, haphazard, no-good outfit hired to take our place. Wages range from 75 to 85 cents an hour with time-and-a-half for over forty hours. Only an audit and a short story of the ride are given—no specific violations! They use part-time workers in the summer. Their workers aren't trained. Glatz said the headman didn't look too bright or too prosperous. (Incidentally, I was the only one this guy was thinking of hiring). And you have to type your own reports! Our poor divisional superintendents are going to be awfully disappointed with this new setup! Greyhound has become too economical!

While I've been gone from the Detroit Y, I have received two telephone calls from someone named "Wally:" I don't know anyone with that name! I've been raking my brains trying to think who it could be. [*And I never did find out*]!

If I'm sent to Chicago in September, I will have a private room in either the West Side Residence or the McGill Residence of the Y. Both include meals. The first is $10.80 a week, the second $7.50. So I'm all set —if I'm sent to Chicago. Love, Margean

———

July 8, 1947
From YWCA, Flint, Michigan

Dear Ones: Naturally I forgot some things I wanted—my AAA hotel book, my green purse, my black shoes, and my embroidery floss.

My feet are sore! I walked blocks out Civic Park way where a Flint Trolley Company fight is raging, to see how the wind blew. Favorable. While out there, I stopped at a house where a man was fixing a tire and asked my question about the FTC franchise. He turned out to be a driver! I hurriedly said that I was from the Flint Journal and scrammed. I hope he forgets about it.

I had a delicious dinner, cottage cheese stuffed tomato and a pineapple salad. I got to thinking about the cookies I used to make, my carrot and peanut ones, the peanut butter ones, the brownies and the cakes. Those days are gone forever, I guess.

Went to see "California" and "Stairway to Heaven:" both good, the last great. I'll be glad when my roommate gets back—she's really a live wire.

Mother, remember you can come up here and stay with me anytime you feel like it. All you have to do is get on the Indian Trails at Galesburg and come. Love, Margean

---

July 10, 1947
From YWCA, Flint, Michigan

Dear Ones: I've got a mystery on my hands, an unsolvable mystery that's driving me simply crazy! When I went to Detroit last week, I told you I'd had two telephone calls from someone named "Wally." I have never known anyone named Wally. Then today I find a picture postcard in my box that had been forwarded from Detroit. It said: "Dear Marg: Tried to get a-hold of you a few times last week, but had no luck. I'll drop you more cards as I go on. Wally"

What really puzzles me is that it had my Detroit room number on it. Who in the world do I know, or have met, that knows me, knows my room number, and can't remember all my first name? It has to be someone I've met in the last month since I'd moved to the downtown Y; it has to be someone who's traveling; and it has to be someone who is interested enough to "drop more cards as I go on." I have lived like a hermit for so long I just don't know who it could be!

Got that wonderful book "Inside U.S.A." by John Gunther. It's one of the most talked about, exciting, wonderful books to come out this spring. I've been waiting for it ever since I knew he was writing it a year ago. I'll send it home when I've finished—only a thousand pages to go—and you must read it.

It's almost noon. I got a call from Chicago—Mr. Burleigh—but I wasn't here to receive it: damn! I wish I knew what he wanted. Love, Margean

July 10, 1947
To me from J.B. Hooper, Southwest Michigan Properties

Dear Miss Worst: Enclosed is an employment card commencing you with the Flint Trolley Coach, Inc. on July 1, 1947. The information shown thereon was obtained from the one you had completed for Great Lakes.

Will you please sign this and the exemption certificate also enclosed, and promptly return both in the envelope herewith.

I presume you understand that your connection with FTC should be treated as confidential, being known by Mr. Burleigh, yourself, myself, and no other persons.

Yours very truly, J. B. Hooper

—■—

July 12, 1947
From YWCA, Flint, Michigan

Dear Ones: I'm agog with enthusiasm and everything else. It seems my life is composed of secret after secret. I have to keep all the enthusiasm bottled up in me. You are the only ones with whom I can share my life.

Got some real valuable "information" today from one of the FTC union men, one I recognized from the strike. Tomorrow I intend to write a summary of the "status quo" to date. I can't see why they don't start propagandizing now.

We dedicated our new kitchen here at the Y last night—cookies and coffee. We have a Frigidaire, gas stove and a very modern gleaming kitchen. So any canned goods you don't need could find a home!

Am going to the Presbyterian Church tomorrow with a bunch from here. Will wear my blue dress with red cape; however, anything I wear is too dressy for Flint! You should see the hordes downtown today.

Wrote a long summary report of the situation to date. Love, Margean

—■—

July 14, 1947
From YWCA, Flint, Michigan

Dear Ones: What did I do today? Nothing but ride buses and ask people "Do you think they'll get their franchise?" I'm really proud of the summary report I wrote. I wish I'd hear some word on the acceptability of my work. This throwing bricks at a wall is monotonous! Love, Margean

———

July 18, 1947
From YWCA, Flint, Michigan

Dear Ones: Had a note in my box this afternoon telling me to call Detroit and reverse charges. So I did. It was Mr. Hooper who wanted to tell me how fine I was doing and to give me two questions to get information on. He also said Mr. Burleigh was very pleased. After going through his and Mr. Burleigh's hands, my reports are sent back here to Mr. Lucas. I bet he wonders who "Mr. M" is!

Mr. Hooper is Mr. Burleigh's man, taking care of Mr. B's private interests—namely, FTC and Southwest Michigan Properties, that means Burleigh and Co.!

Had good meals this week—me cooking! I love cooking again.

Got a letter from Kalamazoo schoolmate Beverly. She's going to summer school and planning to marry this fall. She says that I should do graduate work, there are three eligible PhD's on campus—young and handsome. Makes me homesick. Love, Margean

———

July 19, 1947
From YWCA, Flint, Michigan

Dear Ones: I was absolutely stunned by the news that Uncle Lyle is dead. I'm so very glad that I got to see him the last time I was home.

I don't like the questions I'm asking now. They don't lend themselves to statistical analysis the way my own did.

It happened today. I've been wondering how soon it'd be before I asked a driver twice, "Do you think they'll get their franchise?" And it was today. He said, "I thought we decided that the other night?" And I said,

150

"Well, it makes a good topic of conversation." I just know he thought I was trying to pick him up!

What a day here! It rained cloudburst—hard three times, and I was out every time and was very wet by the end of the day! Love, Margean

---

July 19, 1947
From YWCA, Flint, Michigan

Dear Ones: Received another mysterious postcard from the mysterious "Wally." I quote: "Dear Marg: I'm sorry for not writing more. But as I travel I hardly take time off to eat. I'll tell you all about my exciting trip when I return. It is wonderful out here, but certainly hot. Really doesn't seem hot to some, but it's got me drinking water hour after hour. It's not bad in the evening, really the only time to enjoy this place. Wally." It was mailed from Phoenix, Arizona! Who do I know that was going to take a trip west?

Overcoat weather today. The reason for this unseasonable cold escapes me. Thursday a Greyhound bus burnt up between Pontiac and here. I know the driver, rode with him while he was in training and again a week before our department was dissolved.

Got some nose-plugs and went swimming last night, the plugs really making a difference in my enjoyment. I am surprised that I still remember how to swim, not doing any last year and not being in the water since college classes.

How did you like plowing through those boxes I sent home? Any surprises? One of these days I must go shopping for a trunk, maybe at Penny's where I saw one for $10.

You have never seen car jams until you've been in Flint on Saturday. And the crowds reminded me of the streets in some Southern towns. Love, Margean

---

July 20, 1947
From YWCA, Flint, Michigan

Dear Ones: Went on a blind date last night. Did I look snazzy! Dancing, late dinner and home. I am positively ashamed of myself that I cannot dance better! Ironed two hours this morning—five dresses, my good coat, two slips. And our room looks fairly presentable again. After dinner am going to see "The Hucksters". Love, Margean

———

July 22, 1947
From YWCA, Flint, Michigan

Dear Ones: Approximately fifty more days to spend in this God forsaken town. Then what? Scares me to even think about it. I <u>hate</u> moving!

Yesterday I got on a bus at the end of the South Saginaw Street line, and the driver said to me, "You sure get over Flint, don't you?" It doesn't take drivers long to catch on when you're seen in the same area going different directions all the time. Didn't go near a bus today, went house to house getting comments instead. A Citizens Investigation Board to study the situation has been set up and I say I'm representing that. Boring work. Gee, people are dumb—drivers and unions aren't.

We're having broiled liver and onions for dinner tonight plus vegetable salad and peaches. Last night we had broiled hamburgers, stuffed tomato and melon. I <u>so</u> enjoy cooking again. Love, Margean

———

July 27, 1947
From YWCA, Flint, Michigan

Dear Ones: A lovely day yesterday. Marilyn stayed in bed until 12:30 giving me a chance to get my work done. At 4:00 we rented bicycles and rode four miles out to her aunt's place. I thought I would absolutely die before getting there because we went so fast. Anyway, we arrived and I was revived with two Band-Aids for my blisters and a glass of ginger ale. For about an hour we gabbed—real home folks. Her uncle is a mail carrier. Then her aunt fixed coffee and cinnamon rolls and we wolfed them down. The way back didn't seem so hard and long for some reason and we soon steamed into port. I can't understand why it was so hard to walk when I got off. We both staggered! We went home to spend an exhausted evening reading and sewing.

Yesterday received another postcard from the mysterious Wally, postmarked El Paso, Texas. "Dear Marg: I didn't forget you. I've been very busy and couldn't get even two winks of sleep. I'm resting—and very

152

comfortably—at the air-conditioned Cortex Hotel. It's sort of lonesome but I'll be back Monday for work—see you. Wally." I sure wish I knew who he is. [*Still do*].

We're going out to chop suey dinner and then to "The Perils of Pauline" this afternoon. Love, Margean

---

July 29, 1947
From YWCA, Flint, Michigan

Dear Ones: Fixed a cheese omelet tonight. I'll make one when I get home.

Got my ticket today. I asked the girl if I could look at Russell's Guide [*the bus bible of schedules*] and she nearly fell over. I guess no "civilian" has ever asked to look at one. So I plotted my course, got my ticket and shall leave at 6:05 p.m. Have sent a note to Detroit that I shall not be here this weekend. No objections. Am reading "Inside U.S.A." like mad so that I can bring it home. 200 pages to go: fear I shall not make it! Love, Margean

---

August 7, 1947
From YWCA, Flint, Michigan

Dear Ones: All packed! I have one trunk, two suitcases, a cosmetic box, a typewriter case and a radio. I can't decide just what to take to Chicago first. I would like to take everything but the trunk. It took me about two hours to pack. The last time it took me at least six hours, but with clothing to an irreducible minimum it was a shorter process.

Answered Edith and Allen's letters. As yet they're not married, and both are anxious to get back on the road. Maybe I can do something for them in Chicago. I wouldn't mind working with them. See you soon. Love, Margean

August 9, 1947
From YWCA, Flint, Michigan

Dear Ones: Mr. Hooper called this morning for me to hang on for another week because Mr. Burleigh will not be in Chicago on the 10th, instead he will be in Oklahoma! This weekend, however, he will be in Detroit, and Mr. Hooper will call me Monday and tell me of the plans.

This procrastinating and uncertainty almost makes me wish I had taken Mr. Keith's offer at Willow Run. So I have another week here. At least, I'm packed! Love, Margean

---

August 11, 1947
From YWCA, Flint, Michigan

Dear Ones: Naturally I'm very excited again. Who wouldn't be with the definite assurance that one is going to travel "coast to coast?" Let me list the cities again: New York, Washington, Cleveland, Columbus, Pittsburgh, Louisville, Toledo, Indianapolis, Memphis, St. Louis, Des Moines, Kansas City, Topeka, Tulsa, San Antonio, Austin, El Paso, Albuquerque, Santa Fe, Phoenix, Las Vegas, Salt Lake City, Cheyenne, San Diego, Los Angeles, San Francisco! And of course Chicago! Coast to coast!

Mr. Hooper said that Mr. Burleigh wanted to see me before I started in. Naturally I wasn't bright enough to ask "started in what?" And he came through with the vital information that I would be based in Chicago. What will I be doing? That is what preys on my mind. The suspense is killing me.

Somehow we got to talking about Mr. Burleigh's summer camp near Little Current, Ontario. I told him about being up there this spring, and he was properly impressed. Mr. B. has asked him to go up there with him sometime this or next month. What an experience for anyone who has never seen that country. So we chatted: me growing more excited by the minute thinking about the possibilities—the things I would see— the country I would travel—the people I would meet. I hope I do all my traveling by bus. After all, it is the only way to travel and see the country. Anyway, we finally finished.

A week to go: I'm still packed, living in three cotton dresses. And not living very high either. It will seem nice to dress up every day—wear hose all the time—have my hair up—be the career girl.

Down to earth! The girls got home last night properly enthused about their times at home, their boy friends and what they were going to do next weekend. I didn't get to sleep until about 11:30 when they finally quit jabbering and, consequently, I didn't feel any too chipper when I got up at 6:30.

Riding buses has been dull today. I did discover a driver's girlfriend though, but because I'm not here for that sort of thing, I could be justly amused instead of justly critical. She was too young for him.

I always ride on three lines—Detroit Street, South Saginaw, and Corunna Road. These give me the upper crust, the Negroes, and the laborers. Anyway, the drivers are coming to think me a native: they always say "good morning" to me like every regular rider. I haven't made the mistake of repeating my questions to any of them since that one time.

Tomorrow night, I'm going to a meeting for "Bus Improvement" that's being held across the street at the Flint Journal. More fun. Love, Margean

---

August 13, 1947
From YWCA, Flint, Michigan

Dear Ones: Received a call from Mr. Hooper this morning and I'm to meet Mr. Burleigh in Detroit about 9:00 Saturday morning.

I'm going to be mad if he keeps me here any longer. I've twice told the McGill Residence in Chicago that I was coming. I'll be out on my ear both here and in Chicago if somebody doesn't make up his mind. I don't care if he is a millionaire. I'm going nuts trying to keep organized!

I'm going to have to take a 6:15 a.m. bus to get down there to see him. I'll have my hair done Friday afternoon. I'll make an impression.

I'll telephone as soon as I know anything. Let's hope you can come either Saturday afternoon or Sunday: Sunday would be nice and perhaps you could bring either Aunt Christie or Grandma along for the ride. Love, Margean

---

August 18, 1947
From Chicago, Illinois

Dear Ones: Well, it is American Buslines/Burlington Trailways now —my company! My head is swimming with all the activity of today. In the first place, make up your minds not to see very much of me. At present, I won't be seeing the farm until around September 15th.

So far, my schedule is solid until August 30, and by solid, I mean ten-plus hours on the road each day! Next time I'll plan my own trip and it will certainly be in easier stages! Mr. Johnson was overly anxious for me to cover the road when he made out that itinerary! But from August 30 on, when I'm in Dallas, Texas, I'm on my own and shall not work so hard.

As you know, I have the same conditions Greyhound offered me, but I think the future will be brighter. Talk was in the wind about setting up a special department. I think they had little idea what inconvenience my coming would be—a special person, special accounts, and multitudes of reports. The reports are to go to Mr. Burleigh and the three of them will look them over and, probably, criticize.

I met John Tigrett, Vice President, a youngish man, about 34. My contacts with him and Pete Johnson will be very close, especially with Mr. Johnson who was Greyhound manager at Grand Rapids for twenty years and knows a lot of the people in Kalamazoo that I do.

At Dallas, I revolve a whole week getting all the dope possible on Dixie Sunshine Lines and Continental Trailways. This is my real assignment! They want something on the order of the Greyhound divisional reports I wrote that Mr. Burleigh had seen. Whether they are going to break franchises or buy them or just snoop, I don't know. Only all three of them stressed absolute secrecy, discretion, and carefulness.

My room here at the YWCA would have been nice, fully as nice as in Detroit. But henceforth when I'm in Chicago, I'm to stay at the Congress Hotel, one block from work, where good old American Buslines has some of its personnel living: Miss Wilson, Mr. Johnson, and now me! So, darlings, let's hope I make the grade! This is SO exciting!

I'm to give the lines the works! Drivers, ticket agents, rest stops, lunch stops, terminals, equipment—and other companies—just as I'd done before. I have a feeling that they haven't been satisfied with what has gone before (if anything) so I hope I give them what they want.

The train ride to Chicago was hellish! My first train ride and I was never so disappointed in my whole life! It was just like riding three or four hours on a Detroit trolley car, only rougher if anything. Me for buses.

Must do my homework—two new rulebooks to memorize. Incidentally, Mr. Burleigh says to buy Greyhound stock! Love, Margean

August 20, 1947
From Castle Hotel, Omaha, Nebraska

Dear Ones: The end of a long, long, long day with eighteen hours of work. Reports are finished and sent so I can at last relax.

The speed with which all vehicles travel in Chicago impressed me. We were out in half the time it would have taken in Detroit, then onto the road and a battle against sleep. Starting at night, I didn't have much opportunity to observe Illinois. At Rock Island where one crosses the Mississippi, I was fortunate that the bridge was barred while an oil barge went through. This offered an opportunity for everyone to get out and look and for me to recheck my load.

I was disappointed in Iowa—where was all the level, black land I had expected to see? Instead, long ridge after long ridge undulated out as far as the eye could see. After getting to the top of a ridge—as high as Schram's Hill, but not as steep—you'd see a broad valley with other ridges running into it and, up the road a mile, the next ridge. In short, the land's much more rolling than I had expected, but nowhere is the slope so steep that the land can't be cultivated and all forms of power machinery used.

Views were more clear and distant than in Michigan, the air more clear and it's hotter—102 today!

Crops? Corn, corn, corn, corn, soybeans, wheat, alfalfa. Pigs, pigs, pigs, cows, sheep and a surprising number of horses. As a rule, the land doesn't begin to compare to ours—barns are unpainted, houses look in the dumps—and this the second richest agricultural state in the U.S.!

Near Council Bluffs a new feature comes into view—the bluffs. And guess what they're made of—loess, or wind-deposited soil, feet deep. Down 20, 30, 40 feet will be the original soil, which, if the loess is removed, produces as if it had lain on top for years. The remarkable feature about this loess (which is, by the way, fertile and productive) is that when cut vertically it doesn't crumble. Hence you have road scenery of 20-foot walls of dirt, with the road running through, with never a break or a slide. Even rock won't do that.

Towns are few and far between, forty-five minutes apart, and traffic is surprisingly light except for huge semis. Railroads are already becoming more important in the life of a town.

From Des Moines to Omaha, an American-Burlington Safety Engineer sat with me—why do company people always sit with me? I gleaned interesting facts from him: all drivers are high school grads or above; all drivers take psyco-physical tests (all the latest gadgets); their union is the Railroad Brotherhood. More progressive than Greyhound?

Omaha is a dirty, hilly, and all around unlovely twin to Grand Rapids. Population 228,000. Cheyenne tomorrow. Love, Margean

——

August 22, 1947
From Plains Hotel, Cheyenne, Wyoming

Dear Ones: Don't ever move out to that God-awful Nebraska country: that is, don't unless you can pay $225 an acre for irrigated Platte Valley land. Eastern Nebraska was a continuation of Iowa—corn, mostly irrigated. West of North Platte, the real West begins—no trees.

At Cozad I passed through the alfalfa center of the world, miles and miles of it, all irrigated by large pumps. It is cut and chopped while very green and wet, and then hauled to mills where it is dehydrated in what looks like huge revolving boilers. The process gives off a heavenly aroma like our barn loft when we have put up hay. After dehydration, it is compressed into bales and shipped to areas unable to grow good grass—like Arizona —for the farmer that keeps only one dairy cow. Incidentally, Nebraska is the state where one county has eleven millionaires—airplane ranchers!

Cheyenne is lovely. Twenty miles before you get here, the night air is so clear one can see the street pattern! I never saw a main street with such a multitude of different colored lights—a regular jewel box.

It's cold this morning—60 degrees—a welcome change from the Plains' heat. As our altitude increases it grows progressively colder, and I'm thankful that I have a coat along. Incidentally, I passed the center of the world—the hundredth meridian—yesterday. Love, Margean

——

August 23, 1947
From Salt Lake City, Utah

Dear Ones: I've lost track of the days. Yesterday was monotonous: Wyoming is monotonous: time is monotonous. I got so sick of sagebrush and the eternal whitened-green of the landscape. Towns are 80 to 100 miles apart and there's nothing but a railroad track to relieve the view. The landscape and towns look exactly like my Sudbury country, except there's more rain in Canada.

Highway 30 isn't even paved! It's an oiled, dirt road! And it's all under repairs, so we were on detours two-thirds of the time. Rough!

All yesterday it rained at different places in our view and we ran into showers twice. It's so queer when one can see showers fringing down at different parts of the horizon, and then watch oneself run into one.

Cold, about 55 or 60 all day and I nearly froze! Elevation ranged from 6,500 to 6,700 feet. We went forty-five miles up-hill from Cheyenne, then five miles almost straight down into Laramie. How the bus labored! Laramie is a pretty town of brick and stucco houses and contains Wyoming's university.

Salt Lake City is beautiful. The last four hours last night were through awesome, rugged terrain, and then this valley, all ringed with mountains, opened. Right now I'm looking at them from my hotel window. Love, Margean

---

August 24, 1947
From Hotel Golden, Reno, Nevada

Dear Ones: Another day through God-forsaken terrain is finished, and today I expect to see good country. I saw a few mountains yesterday: the highest elevation at 6,970 feet was nothing to get excited about. So far, I much prefer the rough and colorful trip East.

The only thing pretty about Nevada is its towns. Such color and activity! They do wear cowboy boots and hats, but I haven't seen a gun yet. A slot machine for every man, woman, and child—a bar for every four people. Spike Jones is playing at Elko this week, a town possessing all of 3,000 people and 3,000 tourists. My room here directly overlooks a gambling establishment that has been in full swing ever since I arrived. Right now I can hear them calling out numbers this Sunday morning.

Yesterday we saw a roundup—about a thousand head and five cowboys. Six miles out of Lovelock, we had a flat tire. Because it was an inside tire he drove on it into Lovelock, where we waited forty minutes. But everyone had a hilarious time. A man and his wife, about 70, were on, and he was the most henpecked husband anyone had seen. Her nagging kept everyone in tears. When one driver left, he asked how long they'd been married: "Seven years to the wrong woman," was the old man's reply. Love, Margean

---

August 25, 1947
From San Francisco, California

Dear Ones: God's country? Eskimo country if you ask me. Fur coats, fur scarves and wool coats are the order of the day. A nasty, wintry blast blows one up the hills and whips skirts about. Where, oh, where, is warm California?

Yesterday's run was worth all the discomforts of the trip. Crossing Donner Pass at 7,230 feet, we were in the heart of mountain country and winding roads. At the summit one looks down at a beautiful lake in a cup fringed with pines about a thousand feet below. The road over the pass was a feat of engineering skill—especially the bridge.

California is beautiful so far. The Golden Gate Bridge was ten miles of twinkling fog lights, two levels of them. The lights and searchlight on Alcatraz Prison island shown brightly. Midnight-blue is the only color to describe the bay. And then hilly San Francisco!

This morning I had to rush around in search of an American Express Office to send stuff to Chicago and to observe the scenery. Dresses are definitely long here, and everyone dresses to the hilt. Me, I'm in a sloppy raincoat.

In Reno, I had wired for a $2.00 room, but all they had to give me was a gorgeous $5 suite. It was the first chance I had had to take a bath. So soak I did and washed my hair.

My driver yesterday cussed a few passengers out: I was so surprised and it made my report interesting. Love, Margean

---

August 26, 1947
From Hotel Hayward, Los Angeles, California

Dear Ones: Yesterday's trip was wonderful. Now that I've seen it, I wouldn't mind living here—and neither would you, because along the roadside I saw several herds of cattle, good ones. Then mile after mile after mile of vineyards, then orange groves looking like a Sunkist ad, and then palm trees! Beautiful small homes, all modern architecture. And beautiful little towns. No wonder people love California. It has only one serious drawback: it's as cold as a chilly, fall day. One needs all the blankets possible and a coat at 5:30.

The first thing I need to do when I get time is buy a slack suit and some sandals. The next time I carry so much in my suitcase, I'll have my head examined! However, it's the big supply of forms that makes it real heavy.

I hope I have enough money. I have $158.41 left, and it goes approximately $15 a day for tickets and everything. Send $100 to Dallas. Love, Margean

———

August 23, 1947
Air Mail, Special Delivery from Mr. Tigrett, Vice President
Miss Margean Worst, Hotel Hayward, Los Angeles, California

Dear Miss Worst: I have just read one of your interesting inspection reports.

I have forgotten whether I told you before you left, but we would like very much to have a detailed report on all rest stops, both as to size, cleanliness, lighting, odors, etc.

We would also like to have your observations as to whether certain of these rest stops could be eliminated without inconveniencing the passengers.

Very truly yours,
John Burton Tigrett, Vice President

———

August 27, 1947
From U. S. Grant Hotel, San Diego, California

Dear Ones: You will be receiving a package from me soon, but don't go into raptures! It contains a very dirty dress that badly needs tossing into a washtub after six days of constant wearing.

The nice thing about this job is the bargains one finds. In Los Angeles yesterday, I found precisely the slack suit I wanted, $8.95, marked down from $17.95. It's black serge and will wear like iron—all it needs are permanent creases sewn in. By the time I get home, it will be ready for the cleaners!

There were beautiful stores there. I wandered around until my feet hurt and then went to eat. I looked up a cafeteria mentioned in the AAA book, it had many levels, lots of greenery, and a baby grand piano player: the food was even better than Greenfields!

About seventy miles today were along road fronting the Pacific where long rollers dashed in, cresting and breaking on the beach below. Although there were no birds like our barn swallows visible at Capistrano, there were thousands of blue-white birds similar to parakeets: maybe, those are their swallows.

San Diego is stunning! It's the combination of white, low buildings —rarely above four stories—and bright light that makes them so attractive. For instance, my hotel is all white and fronts on a palm park. I would not object to being sent here! Love, Margean

---

August 30, 1947
From Jefferson Hotel, Dallas, Texas

Dear Ones: Received and cashed the money order without any trouble, but would probably have had difficulty if you had asked a hard identification question. I am so dead tired! I am through with a twenty hour—not including report writing—day.

Presently after three hours sleep, my head still swims, but it is too hot —104—to sleep. Although I have a fan, I'm skeptical about sleeping with it on, having heard that that's a good way to catch cold. Sweat is running down my back and perspiration drips from my brow. As it's only 3:00, there're four more hours of sun before cooling off. And you'd be surprised how quickly it cools.

Yesterday's run was just mile after mile of ranch country, until Odessa and Midland when I was in the heart of a Texas oil field. I forgot to mention the irrigated country I saw in Arizona, New Mexico and Texas where I saw miles of a certain plant before I realized it was cotton.

In order to forestall suspicion, I have developed a beautiful Texan brand of speech. Never can it be said that I don't talk like a native— usually one of the original settlers—witness my success in Canada.

I simply can't stay awake any longer. Love, Margean

September 2, 1947
From White Plaza Hotel, Corpus Christi, Texas

Dear Ones: Another Labor Day has passed—with me laboring! After four days in Texas, I'm beginning to wonder why people live here. I

162

melt into a grease-spot each day. Towns, except for Austin, San Antonio, Corpus Christi, and Houston, are Podunks of the worse order—worse than Dighton, worse than any Michigan crossroad I've ever seen. Dirty, one-story, tumbled-down buildings; boxcar-built houses on posts, with one missing; wardrobes hanging on the front porch. All sorts of people. Heat. I wouldn't live here!

Everyone has been saying that the weather is right for a hurricane, and when a few clouds gathered and lightening began to web the sky and thunder to roll, I thought I was in for an adventure. It was just north of Houston in the midst of lumber camps, that it began in earnest with a regular cloudburst, hail and wind, but nothing of true hurricane proportions. We were driving into it at about 30 mph (couldn't see to go faster), and it lasted one and a half hours at the same furious rate. The driver was magnificent in his handling of the coach!

The triangle of Dallas, San Antonio, Corpus Christi, and back to Houston and Dallas, encloses much farmland—most in cotton or just waste land. I could recognize no other crops. Apparently the cotton was ripe for long rows of Negroes were bent over picking it. Growing only twenty inches from the ground, it was backbreaking work!

At Corpus Christi I stayed in this White Plaza Hotel. Right next door, high, imposing and trying to overshadow the White Plaza, is the Driscoll Hotel. Years ago, so the true story goes, this "Mrs." Driscoll was a permanent resident at the White Plaza, a convenient location for her amours. However, because of her activities, the White Plaza was beginning to get a bad reputation and asked her to leave. It must have been a stormy scene, for it ended with some famous words on her part, "I'll go: but I'll never rest until I build a hotel right next door that will be so much bigger and so much higher, that any of my men can pee on your roof!" And she did! Love, Margean

---

September 6, 1947
From San Antonio, Texas

Dear Ones: It's been ages since you've heard from me I know, but I've been through one time-consuming, worrisome adventure after another.

It all started in Amarillo where my room wasn't waiting, and I wound up in a small boarding hotel located for me by the Y. The second adventure —which isn't through yet—was forgetting my suitcase keys in Paris, not finding it out until Shreveport, and having to have my suitcase "jimmied" (as yet I haven't a key and am having to carry it tied with twine because it won't latch). Today, I hope to have some keys made. This will never happen to me again!

The third adventure occurred in Tyler where I was on a "Man-on-the-Street" program. It was fun and they got a kick out of my earrings and "Kalamazoo"—down here they don't think there's such a place. It was also profitable: I got a $5 compact and a $1 jar of cream perfume! Maybe the fourth adventure would be the horribly hot weather: 114 in Childress when passing through and 110 most of the rest of the time. I'm dying by degrees!

I like the people down here. Every male from three up calls you "Ma-am" and you're treated like a lady. The drivers are wonderful—my old Great Lakes Greyhound bunch could take lessons from them! Where else is each passenger thanked for riding and told to "be sure and ride again with us soon?"

I think I've seen more of Texas in a shorter time than any other person ever has—West, East, North, and South! I'd love to set up the inspection service for the combined operations of Continental and Dixie Sunshine. Four people and I could do wonders. In layout and type of business, they resemble the C&LE (Cincinnati and Lake Erie) layout that, if you remember, was my baby!

As I'm not on the road today—just report writing—I sent my clothes to the cleaners and had my hair washed. This is the first time in three weeks that I've had time to relax and it's too hot. With my clothes at the cleaners, I'm running around in slip and bra, plus my raincoat. Needless to say, I'm uncomfortable.

For once I'm getting my full of shrimp—a shrimp dinner is 50 cents.

Counting per diem, I'm making $460 plus a month. They even cover my time in Chicago. Love, Margean

———

September 7, 1947
From Jefferson Hotel, Dallas, Texas

Dear Ones: The end of a long and arduous trip is at last in sight and the interesting portion of it begins in Chicago. As always, the getting-back-to-the-office portion of a trip is the most interesting, and I hope, in this instance, that everything has proceeded to their satisfaction, information and hopes. In other words, I hope I have delivered the goods.

My luggage is on a jaunt of it's own, the porter having neglected to remove it in Palestine and it continued on. Did I squawk! It should be here tonight or by 10:00 in the morning—if not, I'll just have to wait for it. My luggage will never be the same. I must get a utilitarian piece, something with a compartment to fold clothes: this mess of everything together is not to my liking on long trips.

I hope I'm met by cooler weather. If everything goes well, I shall see you the end of this week or the first of next. Love, Margean

---

September 16, 1947
From Congress Hotel, Chicago, Illinois

Dear Ones: Into the office with everyone so busy that they could pay little attention to me beyond saying that I was doing a good job, be more descriptive on my terminals and take a trip East. They want me to get a good feel for the lines. So, it's Toledo, Pittsburgh, Harrisburg, New York City, down to Washington D.C., then to Columbus, St. Louis, and back into Chicago. Unfortunately, the nicest part of the trip, through the mountains from Washington D.C. to Columbus, will be at night.

We won our franchise election in Flint 3-1: my percentage wasn't high enough. However, this was more than a franchise vote; it was a very effective protest against the way that the CIO has always tried to run the town. I feel elated to have had a part in it!

My cold is miserable, but tonight Hulda Wilson (Mr. Burleigh's secretary), Ilo, (Mr. Tigretts' secretary), and I are going to the House of Eng for dinner. It's a Chinese place, the best in the world they say, where each party is in a draped-off room by itself—and the drapes work by electric eye and whoosh, there's a waiter! So that's where I'm going instead of getting twelve hours' sleep! Such are the demands of society! Love, Margean

---

September 19, 1947
From King Edward Hotel, New York City

Dear Ones: This will be a diary letter that I will finish in New York. I did a beautiful piece of work yesterday—tore rest stops apart—then went to bed at six in the evening.

Right now I'm in Toledo at the ungodly hour of 2:30 a.m. I'm sitting in a hamburger joint waiting for the station to open so I can leave at 3:00.

You should see the conglomeration of people roaming the street—cops, taxi drivers, September-May romances or, more likely, illicit trade. This is the end of the line for lots of Great Lakes freighters and their whistles and horns were my lullaby.

Saw some real good farmland between South Bend and Toledo: Indiana and Ohio farm landscape is always pretty and prosperous looking. It was boring, though: no conversation; no unusual events; no nothing!

New York: dare I say it's really not so large after all, just a bigger Chicago with a little faster traffic. Ten miles away and you're still in woods —then over miles of huge bridges and under the Lincoln Tunnel and here I am.

Pennsylvania was lovely—all hills and prosperous looking dairy farms with hex signs on the barns. The Pennsylvania turnpike wound though all those hills! Hours of toll road with six tunnels that take minutes to get through even at 50 mph. Allentown was a quaint place with flowerpots, vines and blooms on the lampposts.

As I told you, Hulda, Ilo, and I went to the House of Eng, a wonderful place: soft lights; intricate Chinese architecture; black-bloused Chinese waiters! Mr. Eng himself saw to our comfort and hovered over us (he knew Hulda and Ilo), and we had a scrumptious repast. Conversation was interesting to say the least—all the idiosyncrasies of our bosses and all the gossip that makes big business seem awful common and little. Love, Margean

—•—

September 20, 1947
From Emmitsburg, Maryland

Dear Ones: I didn't make it to Washington D.C. after all, and it adds up to another of my adventures. I passed through much of historic America yesterday—Philadelphia, York, Gettysburg and right through the Peach Orchard Battlefield. Until you've seen the East, you can never appreciate the town layouts.

Finally I got to Emmitsburg, Maryland, (smaller than Galesburg), where I was to transfer in twenty minutes for Washington. All day it had rained and misted. For one and a half-hours I stood on the corner of the square to flag the bus down, getting wetter, and madder, and hungrier as each second passed. So I said, "to hell with the bus. I've got a bad cold now!" I found a tourist home and holed up. I leave at 5:42 for Columbus. On the radio downstairs, they've got a hell-fire preacher—but still it rains!

166

While sitting in bed this morning, I drew up a form for rest and lunch stop inspections. We didn't have one before, and I'm proud of it. I'm staying in bed as long as possible because I have to stay awake all night.

I have been in twenty states in thirty days! That should be a record of some kind. Love, Margean

---

September 22, 1947
From Southern Hotel, Columbus, Ohio

Dear Ones: In Columbus trying to stay away from my driver who also stays at this hotel. I've been trying to figure when he's due out and can't. I'm dead tired but my room won't be ready until 7:30 a.m., and by that time I'll have my second wind and will be ready to have my hair done. In other words, I'll go to bed about 5:00 this afternoon

I forgot to tell you some things about New York: you see nine men for every woman on the streets; dime stores stay open until 10:00 at night; women wear the longest skirts, only about ten inches from the ground.

Standing in the rain must have helped my cold—it's practically gone. Love, Margean

---

September 29, 1947
From Congress Hotel, Chicago, Illinois

Dear Ones: A lovely ride back on the train. Met Ilo last night and accompanied her to supper, but only as a conversationalist.

They now want one of my in-depth reports on Mo-Ark so I leave tonight for Omaha, then to Springfield, to Jefferson City, Missouri, to Willow Springs, Memphis, Florence, Alabama, Chattanooga, back to Springfield, St. Louis, and Chicago. All reports seem to be satisfactory, so all is going well. Love, Margean

---

October 1, 1947
From Pickwick Hotel, Kansas City, Missouri

Dear Ones: It wasn't a blinding snowstorm that met me when I was up at 1:00 a.m., instead a torrential downpour accompanied by multi-colored lightning and assorted degrees of thunder. Orange and red lightning thrill me!

When I come home for brother's wedding, it would be a good idea to have my teeth looked at. Please make an appointment. Love, Margean

———

October 2, 1947
From Jefferson City, Missouri

Dear Ones: A glass of Pepsi-Cola, a sleepy Southern town, a temperature of 85, and a long layover—who could ask more. I sauntered around Salem here, and got the natives to gaping and buzzing "Who is she?" Everyone is so nice and hickeyfied. A stranger always creates a sensation here, in Galesburg one wouldn't be noticed.

A long layover, this one from 1:00 p.m. to 6:45, can be mighty boring and time can drag. But seated in this hotel and listening to the homey conversation is anything but boring for scandals and gossip unfold before my ears! Prices in this little burg amaze me—meals, 40 to 65 cents, sandwiches, 10 to 30 cents—but, then, people don't have the money to spend.

Missouri is pretty, especially the wooded, rolling part I saw today. The ever-present sawmills and sawdust hills give one clue to their livelihood. Haven't seen much cultivated land: most farming is dairy, and that not very good. Buildings aren't as bad as those I saw in Texas. The road was fair, but in a couple of days I get onto unpaved ones.

You should hear the comments about my Halliburton luggage. Everyone from drivers to passengers comment on it and all want to know how much it was. "It's awfully expensive, isn't it?"

It's going to be so strange to come home to just the two of you. Home's not like it used to be, is it? And, Lord only knows where I shall eventually settle. Love, Margean

———

October 5, 1947
From Hotel Reeder, Florence, Alabama

Dear Ones: 165 miles of red <u>dirt</u> road masquerading under a U.S. highway number! I was bruised and shaken when I arrived, but at least I got a good look at the "Deep South." I am thankful I was not born a horse here. The poor specimens I saw had all their ribs showing and were munching the poorest excuse for hay—on the other hand, the mules were beautiful and I didn't see a skinny one.

Although I expected it, the amount and rate of erosion stunned me. Bringing it vividly to mind and very thought-provoking was the sight of fencing and fence posts dangling in the air over a 20-30 foot gully! Cut just this summer, our dirt road was washed and gullied and, during yesterday's cloudburst would have been impassable. Everywhere that one looked, the South's boasted red soil was showing its leached sides. On a hillside slice, there would be 4 to 8 inches of topsoil and grassroots, and then the color would range from brick red down the color scale to a pasty gray. So sad.

165 miles of board, log, and tarpaper shacks inhabited by poor people, white and Negro. It's so different to ride the buses down here. All the family, from the latest to the oldest, ride. When mealtime comes, the babies just reach in and grab and nobody pays any attention. By the way, if you were selling bras down here, you'd go broke!

Practically everyone pays cash fare, and I get a memory workout keeping track of where each gets on and then gets off. They come running out of their shacks furiously waving and we miss at least half-a-dozen every trip. When you're running late and come to a station, one is sure to bound out at the last minute and, when the driver asks for their ticket, innocently say, "Do you have to have a ticket?" The drivers are saints!

True to my unlucky star, it always rains when I head South. I've been in two God-awful cloudbursts, plus it rained one night when I wasn't on the road. Last night, Saturday, was one of the cloudburst nights, but everyone was in town. Little Podunks, smaller than Galesburg, would have one to two thousand (well, I do exaggerate a little) standing around. And, as God-is-my-witness, it took us fifteen minutes to get through Marked Tree, a town the size of Augusta.

What with the rain, the road, the crowds and a broken air pressure indicator, we were over an hour late into Memphis. That air pressure indicator had me really worried. At one time, the pressure went down to seven pounds, and we could hear it hissing out. The driver tinkered around, pumped the accelerator, and hit the dial—any one of which, or combination of all three, put the pressure up to 55 pounds. Every time the driver sounded the air horns and/or slammed on the brakes, the dial innocently continued to show 55 pounds.

When I hit Florence this afternoon, I wrote up a flock of reports and decided to see a show. And, always when I decide thus and so, something happens to defeat my plans. In this case, it was the Methodist Church —no movies are allowed on Sunday. So everyone, except myself, sinfully transported themselves to the other side of the river to revel in the sinful temptations of the soul found in a box of popcorn and a silver screen.

Another thing irks me: I dragged my winter coat along, and the thermometer playfully cavorts in the 80s! I look asinine, but I did need it for the 30 degrees between Chicago and Omaha when a flat tire held us up for an hour-and-a-half in the middle of nowhere.

Another "everything happens to me." Last night when the sky announced that the cloudburst was through, I slouched out in search of dinner. I relaxed for a good meal and then was greeted by a blanket renewal of the storm, fireworks and all. After twenty minutes of waiting with no let-up, I dashed, coatless, the three blocks to my hotel with the fireballs rolling down the street (well, maybe I exaggerate), and then it stopped.

Enough. As you can see, this letter was written from sheer boredom and a lack of popcorn in town. Love, Margean

---

October 7, 1947
From Hotel Reeder, Florence, Alabama

Dear Ones: Having pored over several schedules and finding a 2:00 a.m. bus out of St. Louis, I beg leave to inform you that I shall arrive in Kalamazoo about 7:30 Friday night. Notice that this entails the most disagreeable task of rising at 1:00 a.m.—with such fervor do I love my home!

Noticing as I have, the extraordinary shooting frays and state-patrol escorted buses mentioned in the papers, I now know why I was pulled off the Southern Trailway assignment.

Chattanooga was magnificent. In fact, this entire TVA area (I'm in the Muscle Shoals district and saw Wilson Dam) is rich in scenery. Love, Margean

---

October 18, 1947
From YWCA, Flint, Michigan

Dear Ones: Well, back in Flint to check on Mr. B's personal business —Flint Trolley Coach—and to offer observations and suggestions. How I hate Flint!

To be perfectly fair, however, I did find some enjoyment. The weather has been glorious, and every night has found me at a movie making up for lost time during my coast to coast and Southern trips. But today! I had to

170

work in a leaden rain that soaked everything—raining when I got up and, tonight at 9:30, still pouring. Well, another nice thing, everyone here at the Y was glad to see me—where have you been, and all that sort of thing.

For two days, I have been working on a FTC summary report. I have found a half dozen things that cause accidents, found five ways to get on without paying a fare and/or paying a dishonest fare, and have three solutions to offer plus many more things for him to chew on as he polishes up his baby. What more can he want? Of course, the only sensible thing is to give the town back to the Indians—a suggestion probably original with me. Love, Margean

---

October 21, 1947
From YWCA, Flint, Michigan

Dear Ones: Today I did what I've been meaning to do for months —bought one of those portable Silvertone radios. It works like a charm. I've had it playing over my shoulder all day, and now it is plugged in. How heavenly to have music wherever I go! No more lonesome hotel rooms. Love, Margean

---

October 30, 1947
From YWCA, Flint, Michigan

Dear Ones: Where, O where, had my Manferd gone. Here it is, way past the middle of the week, and still no Burleigh. So I continue to rest my bones and to ride buses. Today I turned in Report No. 141, and am finding difficulty in seeking out unchecked drivers. The next time I come to Flint, I'll probably be made an honorary driver! Everyone will know my face.

Which reminds me to tell you that coming through a territory too often is a real invitation to being known or turned up. I don't think Chicago is aware of that. Without the run-bid sheets and other things that we had at Great Lakes Greyhound, it is more risky planning a trip. Of course, on the lines we don't own that they have been having me report on, it isn't a factor: but I like to stay below the sight and "a-ha" line no matter where I'm at.

So my Flint days are running like this—up at 7:45 a.m., on a bus at 8:05, off at 10:30 when the rush hour is over, back out at 1:10 and in at 5:00. Then its report writing, embroidery, and to bed at 11:30. Such a boring routine! Of course, it's not the twenty-hour endless days, either! Love, Margean

---

November 10, 1947
From Congress Hotel, Chicago, Illinois

Dear Ones: Great to have been home and, just as sure as I zipped in the fur lining, I'm sent South! It's California, Texas, Missouri and "call me collect" from there for the rest. I will not be home for Thanksgiving—the way things look now I'll be eating turkey in the South somewhere.

Hulda Wilson, Mr. B's secretary, has secured an apartment, tired of living free at the Congress. Mr. Johnson's secretary is taking a job in New York, and he is running around in circles. Because of this, no one has been available to make out my expense account checks, and they're four weeks behind!

I am trying to fight off a cold.   Love, Margean

November 12, 1947
From Hotel Keystone, McCook, Nebraska

Dear Ones: After a series of maddening mishaps, I am here. My first night out gave me two bad drivers who kept me scribbling in my little notebooks—especially when we ran into a snow and sleet storm.

Yesterday coming into Omaha, I played rummy with the fellow across the aisle with everybody kibitzing. He was no dumb player, but I beat him nearly every time. Good training at home!

Then, yesterday when stepping off the elevator of the Castle Hotel in Omaha, I slipped and nearly broke my neck! My knees and one elbow have beautiful bumps streaked with blue and lavender. My radio-case will never be the same—two corners are off, and it is splintered in two other places. I can hardly walk! Doctor said, "No bones broken."

The country is pretty dried up—lots of pigs and feeder cattle around, and corn pickers look like medieval dragons out in the fields. Love, Margean

---

November 13, 1947
From Plains Hotel, Cheyenne, Wyoming

Dear Ones: A monotonous ride yesterday, no fault of the two excellent drivers who got deserved pats on the back. The sky and later the stars were beautiful. Denver was so-so, but then I didn't have an opportunity to explore. It seemed to consist of railroad tracks!

Today I have a 14½-hour ride into Salt Lake City. The best part of the ride, the approach, will be at night, worse luck. According to my radio, the temperature here last night in Cheyenne was 20 and the forecast is for snow on my entire run. It might get real bad going into Salt Lake City, what with the mountains, curves and passes—they'll have all day to fill up and drift. This is all, probably, idle fear; before, when I didn't have a radio, I would never have given it a thought! Love, Margean

---

November 18, 1947
From Hotel Hidalgo, Lordsburg, New Mexico

Dear Ones: I'm having a deuce of a time with one driver. I had him last August, rode with him on the 17th and then ran into him as a relief driver yesterday. He is now ahead of me in El Paso, and I'm afraid he'll be in that station when I arrive. Remember what I said about being sent into an area too soon! Anyway, how I dread 10:00! Love, Margean

---

November 19, 1947
From Crawford Hotel, Big Springs, Texas

Dear Ones: My dread was for naught! Finally arrived here where your letter was waiting.

My seat companion was a slightly deaf, well preserved woman of 38 who told me her life history. This was her second marriage and all her trials and tribulations were pathetic. People sure do live in private hells, don't they. All the troubles of others make me appreciate the fact that I have none. Here I am, having a three-week or more "vacation" in the South for free, receiving an unbelievable living allowance, a great salary and an expense account besides!

What wonderful weather I had in California and Arizona. I sweated out my cold before it had a chance to fully develop. It started due to lack of sleep, because after I had had two good sleeps, it left me. Here in Texas I ran into a lot of unexpected rain and a coat feels good at night.

I'm running low on money. They are five and a half weeks behind on my expense checks and one paycheck. I could sure use some of it. In all probability I shall have to telegraph for money—so be prepared. Love, Margean

---

November 21, 1947
From Kingkade Hotel, Oklahoma City, Oklahoma

Dear Ones: Called Chicago today. Mr. Burleigh wasn't in (in Washington D.C., to be exact), but I talked to Mr. Tigrett and I'm to call him Sunday to find out my setup. From what he said, I believe it will be the strike-bound Southern Trailways: you know, rifle shots, police escort, bombed terminals and all. Aren't you glad my insurance is paid! But then, nothing has happened there for a month, so don't worry!

Today gave me my first smoking driver on this trip. I found out why that one driver I saw so many times just chews gum now: he was fined $42 for smoking. I'm glad I was able to give him an A-1 report this time. Twice I heard the story of what happened to him. Incidentally, he is one of these excellent Texan drivers and, now that he doesn't smoke, one of the most perfect.

This is the third straight day of rain that means that you may be knee-deep in snow. Five inches were reported in the Oklahoma Panhandle, and I'll probably run into it tomorrow on my way into Missouri. I'm hopeful that I can continue in this relatively warm tier of states while you stumble in snowdrifts.

Went to a hilarious show tonight, "Where There's Life" starring Bob Hope. Am back in my room with the radio working full blast—which reminds me, I worked a couple of wires, pushed on a couple of tubes, and it works on current again. I'm still carrying around the bruises of that fall, though.

Saw a gory, horrible, nightmarish accident today! Just a few miles north of Paul's Valley, a small pickup had collided on the slippery pavement with a gas truck so we were rerouted. Terrible dirt roads here in Oklahoma —twin red-mud ruts that lead nowhere. Love, Margean

November 23, 1947
From Hotel Seville, Springfield, Missouri

Dear Ones: Got your lovely, long letter today. Evidently there are still no checks from the office. The last time I figured, they were approximately $550 behind, not including my salary.

Called Mr. Tigrett today, (who, incidentally has the thickest Southern accent) and I am to head down to the strike-bound Southern Trailways to check on the total number of runs they're sending out. Southern has put out a statement that 80% of their runs are going through, and I'm to find out if this is so. This means Jackson, Mississippi, for three or four days and then to New Orleans. This also means standing on a street corner, or in hotel rooms if I can find ones overlooking the stations, for 24 hours and seeing how many runs go out and come in. It will then be easy to compute the percentage.

Friday I'm to report back for further instructions, which will probably mean going on the Missouri Pacific line. I am agog with curiosity over these assignments—do they use the information to break a franchise, are they in a buying mood—why are my bosses so nosy that they're spending all this money?

Have a great Thanksgiving, I shall be working. Love, Margean

November 24, 1947
From Wm. Len Hotel, Memphis, Tennessee

Dear Ones: Leaving Springfield with a chilly wind and predictions of snow, I headed South and will be in Jackson, Mississippi, tomorrow. It was very chilly riding and, due to a faulty transmission, there were comments raised on the possibility of sitting in a cold bus if it broke down. Luckily, we made it with both overdrive and third and fourth gears gone—late, to say the least!

Bought my ticket for Jackson. Since there's been no violence for about four weeks, there's no reason to feel apprehensive—especially since we have a police guard.

The more I think about it, the madder I get over all the money they owe me. The figures I quoted in my last letter refer only to overnight pay, and not to tickets which will run near $200! Love, Margean

---

November 26, 1947
From Hotel Heidelberg, Jackson, Mississippi

Dear Ones: I'm feeling blue—a combination of not being home for Thanksgiving, and a miserable cold, stuffy nose and sore throat. Mostly the latter! Almost December 1st and no coats are needed—well, in the evening, it does get a little chilly but, all in all, it's quite pleasant.

What a day I put in! Over to the terminal at 5:30 a.m. counting runs and the number of people on them until 12:30. Off until 4:00 then back until 6:30, leaving 12:30 to 4:00 and 6:30 to 9:30 to cover tomorrow. Nothing happened: The two pickets paced back and forth, the two cops paced back and forth, buses came and went.

Everyone's tired of the strike. Most of the strikers have found other jobs: they're washed up as far as driving for other companies is concerned, and everyone has conceded that the company broke the strike. Just estimating, I'd say that service is 85-90% of normal, and will be normal as soon as drivers are available and trained.

I maintain that you can spot a Southerner in any crowd. But today with them all around, the main characteristics were more evident: rope-tied luggage, no tie, silk dresses and half-sox. Love, Margean

---

November 28, 1947
From Hotel Heidelberg, Jackson, Mississippi

Dear Ones: Called Chicago and made my report about Southern Trailways. Was told to take a few rides around and then come North. This will take me to New Orleans and Shreveport, then up to Memphis, St. Louis and Chicago. So just a few days more where coats are unnecessary and it's balmy spring with just a little chill in the air.

My cold is a jim-dandy despite spending as much time in bed as possible. Each night I take a scalding bath and pop into bed, hoping that it will be gone in the morning—but the inevitable has stayed. Love, Margean

---

November 30, 1947
From Hotel Heidelberg, Jackson, Mississippi

Dear Ones: Have covered a lot of territory—making a regular three-sided triangle out of Louisiana—in a very short time since I last wrote. 90% of that journey was either swampland or second growth forest.

Nothing could be blacker or more eerie at night! Cows, horses, mules and pigs wander over the highway causing frequent application of brakes. One driver jokingly said that the company was going to let them paint little signs on the buses (like they did on planes during the war) to tell the public how many animals a particular coach had killed! It would be just like riding down U.S. 12 with signs "Cattle at Large" posted all over. And the roads – dirt and ruts!

Had an adventure yesterday. At Alexandria, a man told me to move over, he wanted to sit down. I did, for the bus was going to have standees and I would have had to anyway. Shortly after starting, he passed out and I didn't know whether he was drunk or sick. As he went under, he kept sliding down and over, until he had his seat, half of mine and my shoulder. Enough was enough! I made frantic motions for someone to tell the driver, and a standing man finally tumbled and stopped the driver.

Back they came and pinched, poked and slapped this disgusting drunk awake, made him get in his own seat (instead of kicking him off), and we started again. Five to seven minutes later we stopped for some cash fares, and my drunk heaved: not on me, thank God, but on the woman across the aisle, the man in the aisle, and the aisle! Now, enough was enough! The driver got him by the nape of his neck, another man got him by his belt and with a heave-ho, he landed in the ditch. The driver Okayed his ticket stub, stuck it in the man's hatband, and we left. Love, Margean

———

December 1, 1947
From Wm. Len Hotel, Memphis, Tennessee

Dear Ones: How would you like to see your darling daughter? Well, if you stay home Friday night, she intends to come home. At present, she gets into Chicago at 5:30 p.m. and will take the first train on which she can make connections, probably getting her into Kalamazoo near 10:30.

I forgot to mention that they were cutting sugarcane in Louisiana. It's the most gosh-awful-looking contraption, cutting a six-foot swath head on, and looks something like a beetle's head with nippers. You can smell the sugar refineries for miles. Also, I forgot to mention the long ride over Lake Pontchartrain, which was posted—"No fishing and No crabbing."

Saw "Nightmare Alley" tonight, a gruesome thing! But I'm now back in a warm hotel room with my radio on. Someone will probably pound on the wall for me to turn it down—they did in Cheyenne.

Anxious to get home and tell about the wonderful country I've seen. Also anxious to get back to the office—when I left, there was a terrible scandal that broke the day before. The Assistant Treasurer had signed Vice-President James' name to too many checks and cashed them himself! Love, Margean

———

December 8, 1947
From Congress Hotel, Chicago, Illinois

Dear Ones: I'm confident that I will be home for Christmas. Met Merle Morrow (you may remember I met him a year ago when I met Mr. Burleigh) and will be working with him in Springfield, much as I hate to hit that Mo-Ark territory so soon again.

There was a big hullabaloo over my absence—Tigrett and Burleigh sending me out for four weeks when Pete Johnson wanted me for signing affidavits and for some special inspections! They had a regular shouting match! My reports are <u>excellent!</u>

I had three-day measles this weekend! Love, Margean

———

December 11, 1947
From Congress Hotel, Chicago, Illinois

Dear Ones: Off to Denver, with a nice letter of introduction, to confer with a Mr. Hensel about inspecting his territory. If anything goes wrong starting back—such as a flat tire, or something that would make me late —don't worry. Shall be a Christmas present, one way or the other! Then it's back to Chicago on the 29th and down to see Mr. Morrow in Springfield, Missouri.

Have received all checks except a big one which must be sent from Flint Trolley Coach, and a big one for last week. Both of them will be sent home.

Am dead tired: got in this morning at 6:00 and my last sleep ended at 10:00 yesterday morning. Shall post this and get to bed. Love, Margean

December 15, 1947
From Cosmopolitan Hotel, Denver, Colorado

Dear Ones: I'm finally here, arriving 11:15 last night. It's 56 out, a beautiful day—a lovely day for travel—and I'm hitting the road to Salt Lake City at 4:30.

Went to Mr. Hensel's office this morning. He turned out to be a handsome man of about forty, a typical transportation executive with whom anyone would enjoy working. He outlined the work he wanted done, got the names and badge numbers, gave me a letter for Mr. Merrell in Reno and made hotel reservations at Salt Lake and Reno—plus gossip. I always enjoy gossip: it frequently allows me to put two and two together with what I see and hear on the road for special reports which is the sort of work that Pete Johnson likes me to do.

Mr. Merrill will be the man with whom I shall work at Reno where he is manager. I have twenty men I shall try to inspect. In March or April, Hensel wants me back to inspect the Black Hills-Billings district. Love, Margean

---

December 17, 1947
From Riverside Hotel, Reno, Nevada

Dear Ones: Hit Reno last night about 11:00 and wondered which of the lean, handsome men standing around was Mr. Merrill. So over to the hotel, checked in, and fifteen minutes later he called from downstairs. Down I went: he turned out to be lean, handsome, and 35-ish, tickled to death to have an inspector at last!

My God! What goes on out here! Drinking and gambling in uniform, driving while under the influence of liquor, kickbacks and payoffs for unofficial stops! And poor Mr. Merrill has been run ragged trying to convince Chicago that the situation really exists. (This must be why Pete Johnson was so anxious to get me out this way)!

For example, yesterday, before I knew about these problems, we made a stop at Wells, Nevada, where the station is in a combination lunchroom and bar, as are most of the stops out here. The driver sat down at the bar for a coke: I would <u>swear</u> that the bartender poured some liquor into the coke! At Battle Mountain, a driver division point, they have a perpetual card-game where I saw them playing in uniform with suspicious sized glasses on the table—they were not water glasses!

But like my St. Ignace man of last year, they get the goods on a driver, fire him and have to hire him back because of the union. I told Mr. Merrill that from my experience, my reports alone wouldn't do the job. We're going to see about one of those cigarette-package-sized cameras—that's where we'll have them dead to rights.

And steal cash fares! And open sealed company mail! And poor Mr. Merrill has the union President under him—the worst of the lot. And this is the situation I run into.

Down to Sacramento and back today: then a flag-down tomorrow into Battle Mountain where Merrill is going to drop me off at a junction for a cash fare. Love, Margean

—•—

December 19, 1947
From Riverside Hotel, Reno, Nevada

Dear Ones: I got in at 11:15 p.m. yesterday and didn't consider it necessary to get a room. So, I'm struggling to stay awake until 5:00 a.m. when I will take a cab to Sparks and flag down a driver for a cash fare. I now write this hoping it will keep me awake. I haven't had enough sleep in the last two weeks to keep a human alive, but tonight I shall get fourteen whole, delicious hours.

I'm still in a quandary as to when I'll be home but take the gifts and cards to Grandma's on Christmas Eve just in case. If I get home on Christmas Eve, it will mean days on the road with no time off thanks to my schedule here.

The other day, my trip between Denver and Salt Lake took me over a 13,000 foot pass, one of the U.S. highest, which made 7,132 foot Donner Pass, between Reno and San Francisco, look small. At night, I couldn't fully appreciate it—only the icy roads and snow. Both trips in and out of San Francisco were in pea soup fog.

To date have only a smoking violation, but this afternoon I expect to get a report on the perpetual gambling game at the Battle Mountain station. Love, Margean

—•—

December 30, 1947
From Colonial Hotel, Springfield, Missouri

Dear Ones: After swearing that I would never go out of Chicago without sleep, I did it again. But it was just so I could get a good night's sleep tonight!

Leaving St. Louis we had a people adventure. A fat, old woman, wearing scads of junk jewelry, pushed and elbowed her way to the head of the line–naturally getting my place. From her talk she seemed to have some sort of problem with her legs which were puffed, swollen and bandaged.

Although she got out twenty minutes before the bus was supposed to leave, she wanted the driver to let her on immediately. He wouldn't, so for fifteen minutes she called him everything under the sun, and mumbled and grumbled—loud enough so that he could hear.

When he did begin to load, she demanded the front seat and he wouldn't let her have it. Puffing and panting while boarding, she complained about how her legs hurt her, how she couldn't get around, what an unaccommodating man our driver was, and more of the same. Under his breath so she couldn't hear it, but loud enough so the rest of us could, he said, "Shouldn't ride buses, then."

As usual, it rained, and the highway was wet all the way. A low ceiling and muggy atmosphere will probably dampen the afternoon. Love, Margean

———

1948

I Roam the South

I am Turned Up

If We Don't Care, Why Should You

A God's Gift-to-Women Driver,

Texas Style

I Turn 20

West Frontiers

Mumps

Casanova Spots Me Again

A Spy with Binoculars

A Hearing

I Fly

January 1, 1948
From Colonial Hotel, Springfield, Missouri

Dear Ones: I saw the New Year in riding through an awful sleet and ice storm! You probably heard about it, and by the time you get this it will be past history. Ten hours in it yesterday put a few gray hairs where they shouldn't be, and made me happy that my insurance was paid.

Ice an inch thick hung on everything. Trees, poles and wires were down. Several times we hit big branches hanging down and blocking the road. We had near misses with sparking "hot" wires. Ice covered the highway from Clinton to Springfield, but from Kansas City to Clinton, sleet, three to four inches thick, covered everything. In Kansas City, where I got out, it was like walking on slippery, coarse sand that eventually melted in my heel-less shoes.

Because of the storm, New Year was quiet and we encountered no drunk drivers—in fact, no drivers at all. Only an occasional bottle rolling down the aisle indicated that the bleacher seat was celebrating. Superb driving.

It is noon here in Clinton, Missouri. I have four more hours to wait and, because of the holiday, no stores, libraries or beauty shops are open. I have absolutely nothing to do but grow sleepy. The station is in a hotel, where I don't want to go until absolutely necessary. So I'm sitting in the town restaurant where everybody is eating. Dinner $1.00 for: roast turkey, mashed potatoes, string beans, escalloped corn, apple salad, rolls, strawberry shortcake and tea.

Tuesday I had dinner with Mr. Morrow who lives alone at this hotel and spent Christmas here. I happened to remember some scandal about him this morning. Just before he and Mr. Burleigh went to American Buslines, his wife ran off (shacked up) with some bus driver. At the time Mr. Burleigh wanted JP to get some divorce evidence, but JP wouldn't, said it wasn't any of our department's business. So I don't know if he got his divorce or not. To sum him up, he's about 43, and has been with Mr. Burleigh twenty years. He hasn't the outgoing personality that most of these bus men possess, nor does he take as much personal interest in his work or men that others I know do, but then maybe this marriage thing still bothers him. He's still nice, and I learn much about the transportation business from him. Love, Margean

———

January 5, 1948
From Wm. Len Hotel, Memphis, Tennessee

Dear Ones: I can hear your laments as each day passes with no letters, only telegrams, from me. But work, that nasty word, keeps me frightfully busy: for example, today I started out at 12:30 a.m. and finished at 7:00 p.m. Then I relaxed and went to see "My Wild Irish Rose."

Today I got into Florence, Alabama, and spent time window-shopping: there, in a window, I found just the dress on a model. When the store opened, the dress was gone but I tracked it down. Naturally, it's black, long sleeved, buttons down the front, and is some sort of material that doesn't wrinkle. But, oh, what it does for me! A $17 dress reduced to $8—don't I find the nicest bargains?

By the way, having left my pen in Chicago, I had to get another: this is the $2 Ink-O-Graph pen I have been promising myself. While down here, I've had to make carbons of all my reports, and this is the only pen that will make a carbon excepting those ballpoint pens.

As usual, there are loads of cash fares down here, usually at least half of my load, so must carefully work up my audits. Love, Margean

---

January 6, 1948
From Florence, Alabama

Dear Ones: My hotel here in Florence couldn't put me up but kindly secured a room at a tourist home. This letter is on an official report form. I'm fresh out of any stationery, and there was no paper in the desk.

Had fried oysters for supper in a little cafeteria. For some strange reason have been continuing my losing streak.

These drivers are dreadful, and how they break rules: smoking, cigars, letting deadheads drive, girlfriends, etc. I'll wager that twenty days from now they'll be minding their P's and Q's.

The South is full of characters. Today we had a little ten-year-old boy traveling alone. He was chewing tobacco, spitting at an alarming rate, and even offered the driver a chew! At one stop he hopped out and returned with a big, black cigar that he puffed away on. I had my new dress on today, and looked quite too-too, if you know what I mean. The character across the aisle—fat, forty and salesmanish—kept ogling me: I didn't know I could give such cold shoulders! You will be receiving some of the books I've been reading. Love, Margean

January 7, 1948
From Wm. Len Hotel, Memphis, Tennessee

Dear Ones: Another spring-like day—early spring, but nevertheless, spring. Had a lovely trip from Florence. Tomorrow down to Corinth and back, and Saturday night up to Springfield, where they have had snow. What is that stuff?

Had supper in a cafeteria I always patronize here: two seafood patties, hot salad, two biscuits and sweet potato pie—50 cents.

My beloved radio is on the blink: it hums workably, but won't bring in a station! A little kid hit it the other day, and I could have paddled her britches! Shall see a radio doctor on the 9th.

Today's driver was the Union Agent. He kept his tickets on a ledge right by my knee and didn't take them out at rest stops: they should have been under better care. He's going to have one hell of a time explaining why he gave two men free rides. And he didn't cut a one of the fifteen cash fares or keep an "audit board:" no driver can keep that much in his head!

Did I tell you that I had a toothache? Went to Mr. Morrow's dentist and had two unknown cavities in the same tooth filled—$4.00.

Have a room overlooking Memphis' "great white way." Quite a city! Goodness, here on the twelfth floor the wind moans in a frightful manner, and I've taken to murder stories again. With no radio, I'm spending a lonesome evening looking at my reflection in the window. Right by my right ear the red Hotel Chisca sign is flashing, while on my right shoulder, the Malso theater sparkles—new jewelry style. Love, Margean

———————

January 9, 1948
From Wm. Len Hotel, Memphis, Tennessee

Dear Ones: A beautiful day with an 80 temperature: how does that compare with your blizzards and snowdrifts back home?

Have had an awful time with a stubborn cough: not content to keep me in misery during the day, it always wakes me up about 3:00 a.m. Having suffered since leaving Kalamazoo, I went to the hotel doctor today. He checked my throat, but couldn't find anything radically wrong, gave me a cold shot, and recommended an X-ray when I finally get home.

Took my radio to a shop this morning and, after a long song and dance on my part, they agreed to fix up whatever damage that kid caused by hitting it and to have it ready by 4:00. Then I wandered through the

186

stores, over to look at the Mississippi three blocks away and back to bed. I found some of my little 2"x3" notebooks which you'll be getting through the mail.

Dread the trip back tonight. Maybe he will smoke or haul a girlfriend —anything to keep me in a state of wakefulness. Love, Margean

---

January 12, 1948
From Hotel York, St. Louis, Missouri

Dear Ones: Have to cut my work short here because Pete Johnson wants me pronto!

Haven't written because I've been recuperating—from what I don't know. Part of it was the flu—mild, but flu nonetheless—and maybe part of it was the cold shot. Anyway, as I seem to get whatever it is about every two weeks, I'm tired of feeling half dead, half the time. Next time I get home, I'm going to have a complete physical. Maybe I'm "anemic," although I don't look it. Maybe I just sit next to people who have nasty germs. Maybe it's just me. Love, Margean

---

January 14, 1948
From Congress Hotel, Chicago, Illinois

Dear Ones: Into the office with everything apparently OK—no hearings, no nothing. After being told that my next trip would be over the Eastern Division with special attention to Cleveland and Toledo, I was kicked out for the day because I had been working too hard—shades of JP! Tomorrow, I am to see Mr. Tigrett and then hit the road to Pittsburgh where I am to contact Mr. Neil.

What did I do with the time off and the temperature at one below zero? I window-shopped and visited Marshall Fields. Outside of a 25 cent book, Scotch tape and a roll of film, the only other thing I got was sore feet.

Have two good books and a comfortable bed for this evening—my idea of perfect relaxation! Maybe by the time I leave tomorrow, I'll feel perfectly fit. Love, Margean

---

January 16, 1948
From Secor Hotel, Toledo, Ohio

Dear Ones: Burr. Another cold wave due tonight, down to -5. Was out for dinner about an hour and a half ago and a nasty, cold wind blows one right off the road. The weather and snow remind me of a trip last winter in Detroit. I stood out on Grand River near a railroad track waiting for a Grand Rapids-bound bus that was over an hour late. That wasn't all: we then broke down about 3:00 a.m., just north of Lake City, and walked back. I hope nothing comparable happens on this <u>cold</u> eastern trip.

I have a very interesting special assignment from Mr. Tigrett, our Vice-President. On or near April 1st, a special Express Through Service goes into effect with coaches having toilets and a "snack bar" that would eliminate all except meal stops. It's my job: one, <u>to lay out a schedule</u>, and two, <u>to select the</u> <u>meal stops,</u> "those that will give the very best impression."

By the way, our merger is going very badly due to a non-corruptible I.C.C.! Secondly, we are involved in a lawsuit in Kansas City because our low bid was accepted in the purchase of Missouri Pacific instead of the high bid of Santa Fe. If you remember, they had me go down and do a special on that line.

Shall now read my two new books. Love, Margean

——◆——

January 18, 1948
From Hotel Keystone, Pittsburgh, Pennsylvania

Dear Ones: Well, this had to come sooner or later, and, as I said in my telephone call, I don't give a <u>damn</u>. They know me, and they know my number. I knew I was being sent back too soon and without the protection I had asked for on some of the bad reports from last time! And I didn't do anything to turn myself up either. How do I know?

Well, we pulled into Pittsburgh, where there were two or three drivers to meet us and, when I got off, one driver very nicely helped me off with a firm grip on my elbow and a firmer one on my suitcase. "What have you got in here? Gold bricks?" he said. "Wish they were!" said I, and set out.

I crossed the street and went one way around a building and at its end, I caught a glimpse of one of those drivers who had gone the other way through an alley, right behind me. As luck would have it my radio strap started to slip, and I had to drop my luggage and hoist it up, thus cutting my lead.

So, just when I got to the parking lot before the hotel, came that phrase I've been dreading for two years, "Have a nice trip, No. 77?" from the man about ten feet behind me. Well, naturally, I didn't turn around, look at him and say "Yes." The only thing I could do was walk right on pretending I hadn't heard.

I walked past my hotel a block, stopped to adjust my radio strap, and, checking in a window, saw that he stood in front of the hotel. "Well, boy," said I to myself, "If you want to stand out in this -10 degrees, you go right ahead!" So I turned the corner, found a place to eat and had dinner. When I came out he had quite intelligently gone, and I registered in peace.

The only thing I dread about the whole affair is telling Pete. This trip is going to be real funny with everybody knowing I'm here, and I imagine it won't be the last time I'm asked how I liked the trip! I'll naturally tell Mr. Neil that I think I'm hot and let the responsibility of planning my trip rest on his shoulders.

What this will do at the office, I don't know. We will close our eyes to the fact, bring me out in the open, or give me a different job. What it will be, Lord knows. But the situation, from now on, will be a farce unless something is done!

This is the biggest news in a long while, isn't it? And let me reiterate I don't give a damn! Like I always told the ones I trained, it's bound to come sooner or later and one might as well have a fatalistic attitude all prepared. I'm going to a movie! Love, Margean

---

January 19, 1948
To Mr. Burleigh, 616 S. Michigan, Chicago, Illinois

Dear Mr. Burleigh: When training inspectors, I always tried to develop in them a sense of fatalism that the day was certain to arrive when drivers would put two and two together and come out with—*inspector*. And it has finally happened to me: it would make my work a farce to close my eyes to the fact that I am no longer unknown. I think I can safely state that nothing I have done, no bungling of my job, has been responsible: it's just that my face has become too familiar.

Therefore this letter will allow you time to decide my fate by the time I arrive back in Chicago. Being known on our lines does not impair my usefulness for inspection of foreign lines or inspection of rest and lunch stops, and terminals, and it is a fact, that our known inspectors on Greyhound brought in as many bad driver reports as any of the unknown ones.

If the quality and quantity of work and special assignments that I turn in justify my continuing as a known inspector, I shall be very happy. But if it does not, you, Mr. Tigrett, and Mr. Johnson have a reasonable idea of the other types of work in the company for which I would be fitted and could probably secure me something suitable. Very truly yours, Margean Worst

———

January 20, 1948
From Emmitsburg, Maryland

Dear Ones: Just a note while I'm waiting for my bus here in Emmitsburg, Maryland. I have one nice memory of this town: I got a shoe buckle fixed free—which just goes to show that a smile and a pleasant word go a long way.

By now, you have received the rough copy of the letter that will probably crystallize my "career." Whether I stay in the same capacity, shift entirely to schedules and specials, or go into a station is the big question. I hope, and believe, it will be the second. If it's the latter, I want to stay with American somewhere in the southwest.

Cold—nothing like what one expects of Maryland. Hope to be home on the 8:00 p.m. train out of Chicago on the 24th. Love, Margean

———

January 21, 1948
From Hotel Dixie, New York City, New York

Dear Ones: This thing grows funnier and funnier! Yesterday I was waiting in Emmitsburg for my New York-bound bus. Now Emmitsburg is the place where the New York-bound and Washington-bound buses branch off, and they're due at the same time. There is one street corner to wait on, no regular station.

So I am standing on this corner, freezing in the 10 degree temperature and probably starting another flu, when the Washington-bound bus whizzes through, catches sight of me and skids to a stop. Who should it be, but my friend of "Have a nice trip, No. 77?" fame! A minute later my boy comes and lets me on, after which they go into a huddle.

190

Can you imagine what that trip was like? I could hardly keep a grin off my face as I received one of the nicest runs in my life! And it'll be like that all the way back into Chicago! And I'll probably run into my "friend" again, just to make it funnier! Love, Margean

---

February 2, 1948
From Congress Hotel, Chicago, Illinois

Dear Ones: As you know per my telephone call, I'm mad! Of all the non-handling of my concern about being turned up! And after giving them two and a half weeks notice with my letter! Absolutely nothing said!

And a hip-to-ankle run appeared in the best hose I have with me. Love, Margean

---

February 4, 1948
From Brown Hotel, Des Moines, Iowa

Dear Ones: Yesterday was long and dull with no outward hint that the men knew I was on. Radio reports of road conditions leave much to be desired, with heavy packed snow and sleet reported. It started yesterday and at times made us thirty minutes behind schedule. Today it's five degrees.

How bleak it looks out in the country! Saw some herds of dairy cattle out in the snow yesterday: ice cream. We would never let our cows out in this kind of weather! Love, Margean

---

February 5, 1948
From Hotel Robidoux, St Joseph, Missouri

Dear Ones: After scaring myself over potential road conditions yesterday, I found that a semi-thaw had set in and there was nothing to worry about.

But before that, my run of bad luck with drivers set in again. I didn't get to the Des Moines station until five minutes before bus time and had to rush in after my ticket. And who would be there but my driver of day before yesterday! (I had it figured that he should have left Des Moines at 6:00 a.m.) Naturally, I didn't let on that I noticed him, but he and my driver exchanged a few words: however, I didn't get any suspicious glances, and so can't judge what was said. However, when those two get their reports, they'll know who! This sending all reports through without protection really is a jinx!

I have decided to move to Australia after reading a long article about their immigrant policy and labor needs. For example, a Sunday newspaper carried 68 columns of help-wanted. The Australian Offices here guarantee immigrants jobs, lodging, and subsidize their passage. Just think what I could do there. Meat is 20 cents a pound. Houses rent for $15 to $20 a month. I think I should get some more information.

Incidentally, I think I should get ten more shares of Greyhound stock. Love, Margean

February 8, 1948
From Hotel Roosevelt, Cedar Rapids, Iowa

Dear Ones: How many times did I walk under that ladder? Just how much bad luck can a person have? What kind of jinx is there on me, anyway? I got to Des Moines safe and sound, but who should take over there but "Junior," the one I rode with last week and who saw me the next morning. I didn't dare look at him but I bet his eyes "bugged" out plenty, and I would have given anything to hear what went on in the "conference" of drivers that followed. Love, Margean

February 10, 1948
From Hotel Iowa, Keokuk, Iowa

Dear Ones: Have had an uneventful time after the nerve-wrecking experiences with the "man from Des Moines."

In my trauma over the Des Moines affair, I quite forgot to say anything about my trip to Sioux City. As can be deduced from the name, this is Indian country and almost everyone riding is Indian. Contrary to my expectations, they do wear blankets, at least the old women drape themselves in woolens: that, sweater, dress and men's overshoes constitute the outdoor and "go-to-town" dress of most. I was absolutely appalled at the number of blind Indian women I saw. The little ones are cute and the babies are friendly.

192

How they make a living I don't know, because much of the area is reservation with all that connotes in bad land and lack of opportunity. Most of the area was too rolling and too dry for agriculture as we know it. It reminded me vividly of Indian portions of Canada.

Today, on the highway between St. Louis and Burlington I saw barnyard after barnyard of feeder Herefords. All were of marketable size, in excellent condition, and probably represented at least a $30 loss per animal due to recent market trends. In fact, that's all you hear around this section. The shoe pinches. The winter crop of piglets is starting to run about the pig lots and I saw a few premature lambs.

I hope Pete agrees to my going West next as I have a beautiful trip all worked out. That will be absolutely the last time I can hope to hit any territory unknown. Love, Margean

---

February 22, 1948
From Congress Hotel, Chicago, Illinois

Dear Ones: On my way down on Indiana Railroad, a line we purchased for part of our new Detroit routings. Will be in Indianapolis, Louisville and then home for a day about the 27th for birthday #20. Love, Margean

---

March 1, 1948
From Congress Hotel, Chicago, Illinois

Dear Ones: Headed to Los Angeles and back in ten days. Orders! Love, Margean

---

March 11, 1948
From Congress Hotel, Chicago, Illinois

Dear Ones: My, did I run up a telephone bill calling you twice. But it was so good to talk, especially after the eventful last two weeks.

Into the office this morning and had my new "assignment" explained. It entails riding buses, striking up conversations, and securing names and addresses of people willing to appear at I.C.C. hearings relative to our proposed new service between Detroit and Louisville—similar to what I did in Flint but on a larger scale. In other words, I lay the groundwork, and then a public relations man will contact these people and decide who will appear at the hearings.

Relative to the other part of my call: I was talking to Pete and reiterating the fact that my working undercover was a farce. As I told you, he said, "If we don't care, why should you?" He then went on to say that eventually my work would be exclusively riding the lines and finding fault—in other words, true efficiency work. He put it this way: if a person is told that a motorcycle cop is in a certain area, he is going to be pretty careful even though that cop may never appear. I'm going to be that "cop." This suits me 100% OK! Too, my reports have been exactly what they have wanted and never had before: so life is good!

I'll tell you more about my bus breakdown: it took place between Dallas and Big Springs about 1:00 a.m., and the principal actors were a wonderful driver, Bus 554, 26 passengers, and an unknown, but highly blessed, truck driver.

As I said, it was between Dallas and Big Springs that the bus stopped, and I maintain that when I'm on a bus that stops, it will invariably be 1:00 a.m. and thirty miles from the nearest town. The driver pulled knobs, pushed buttons, and flicked switches (while we sat in encouraging, expectant silence), but outside of a discouraging gurgle and grunt, it stayed stopped. At this point, a truck came along. The two drivers tapped mysterious places, tested fuses, crossed wires, consulted gauges, charts, and reports, and finally announced their decision—we were out of gas! Can you picture the faces and hear the groans of 26 assorted passengers—in the middle of nowhere—in the middle of one of Texas' coldest nights—when this ultimatum was delivered!

Setting out flares, the drivers left in search of relief—gas or another bus. We settled ourselves: children began to bawl, heaters breathed their last and cold, dismal thoughts occupied our minds. But we were brave and hungry—a count of available rations included candy and apples. We tried to play our radios but couldn't get any stations in the middle of Texas in the middle of the night. So, after many references to freezing to death, we shut up and tried to sleep.

Although it seemed much longer, it was only an hour later when our driver appeared with the San Diego-bound bus and the news that we were to transfer while he stayed with the bus. Through groans and hard work, we passengers got our luggage and ourselves into the other bus, only to find there weren't enough seats. Just like at sea, women with children and old women came first: this is the only time a young woman will add years to her age, but I had to stand. Big Springs was a welcome sight and we scattered in search of rest rooms and the great big pot of coffee made up for us. Fifteen minutes later none cared that we had been "bus-wrecked" for two hours.

It was here I ran into the handsome Texas driver who had turned me up and had the most enjoyable part of my trip. The minute I walked into Big Springs terminal and saw him, I knew I was recognized, and sure enough, when I transferred, my cases were in the co-pilot seats next to the driver. The driver said, "Would you mind if that other driver (my nemesis) sat with you?" And what could I say. So this ultra-handsome Casanova—this God's gift to women—who I had cost $42 for smoking—sat beside me and proceeded to tell me where and when I'd ridden with him, where I'd stopped off, and that I must work for either the Company or Markel—but he didn't connect me with the smoking report! I didn't say "Yes" and I didn't say "No:" in fact, I didn't say anything. After the initial suspicion had worn off, we just gabbed and, naturally, by devious questions and comments, I learned a lot of company affairs. I thoroughly enjoyed myself and kept a complete count and trip information right under their two noses!

After lying over in El Paso for twelve hours to sleep, I was underway again at midnight. My God, he must have camped in the station, for he was there again and I was carefully pointed out and, when it came time to board, I was again seated in the co-pilot seat and gabbed at all night. I think this driver decided I was in the clear, because I didn't hear any references after him, just gossip. The Los Angeles to Chicago portion was absolutely clear. Love, Margean

---

March 12, 1948
From Hotel Book-Cadillac, Detroit, Michigan

Dear Ones: Just a word before I start out on my night trip. Guess who's in the hotel here—and me even riding in the same elevator—Thomas Mitchell, the actor who portrayed Scarlet's father. He's here in a stage play.

Called up John Prater this morning and had a nice long conversation. He's with the American Manufacturing Corporation in Public and Labor Relations. In June he's being transferred to San Diego to take charge at that point. Had a lovely time gossiping,

Sylvia and Harry Glatz have been let out by the Hound-dog lines… ."because no action was taken on their work." Am I glad I didn't stay! Must be underway to see how many people I can pick up! Love, Margean

March 17, 1948
From Carrollton, Kentucky

Dear Ones: I guess it's apparent that I'm writing this on a bus. After changing my seat twice, once because a little girl sat by me, and once because a drunk plunked himself down, I am at last situated with an empty seat into which I hope a disgruntled hound-dog rider will flop. Until that happens, I can catch up on my correspondence.

Have been digesting the fact that I'm now 20 and in three months I will have been working two years. Neither fact seems possible! But then I get to thinking about all the changes in our family! I am going to look for wrinkles and enlarged pores tonight and perhaps invest in a jar of hormone cream, like Aunt Alice.

Spring is arriving with a bang—robins and bluebirds here; grass is greening; plowing is well underway; people are raking their lawns—all sure signs.

At Detroit yesterday, we were loaded and ready to leave when a man at one of the gates had an epileptic fit. A young fellow about 22, it took five men to hold him. He happened to be with a young girl on our bus who hopped off with tears running down her face. Hope there was a happy ending.

Our drunk is becoming sick! Love, Margean

March 22, 1948
From Congress Hotel, Chicago, Illinois

Dear Ones: As you know, tomorrow I leave for Detroit and Bay City to do the same contact work that I've done for the last two weeks. Personally, I think it's a waste of my time and their money but they do not complain.

During my absence, we filed for a Chicago, Kalamazoo, Lansing, Bay City routing so, maybe in the not too distant future, I can ride into Galesburg on one of my buses! Love, Margean

March 29, 1948
From Congress Hotel, Chicago, Illinois

Dear Ones: No one said anything about my "failure" on the Detroit-Bay City assignment, and I saw Mr. Keenan's report from the same region with the same results—no disgruntled Greyhound riders!

On my way to Denver and Montana points for at least twenty days. Please wire $100 to Denver. Being gone so long, I shall run short. Love, Margean

—•—

April 1, 1948
From Cosmopolitan Hotel, Denver, Colorado

Dear Ones: I'm here in Denver heading out to Cheyenne at 5:15 p.m. There I shall meet a Mr. Weber and receive my itinerary for the remainder of my trip. Mr. Hensel informed me that Mr. Weber would board my bus at Ft. Collins: will he be surprised when I meet him tomorrow morning!

The altitude makes my nose run, but the weather is perfect with a temperature of 75 and a wind that whips one like mad. However, I've been informed that it snows on a minute's notice and I fear for my spring coat.

Saw "I Remember Mama" last night. Don't miss it, simply wonderful.

The roads are terrible where I'm going, load limits are restricted—this means they're running "jeeps" or Kazoo clipper buses to you. Love, Margean

—•—

April 2, 1948
From New Gladstone Hotel, Casper, Wyoming

Dear Ones: Am really underway now. It was funny. At Fort Collins where Mr. Weber was to get on, the bus filled up but I kept a seat and when he got on last, there was no place for him to sit except by me. And so by me he sat. I said, "Mr. Weber?" and he jumped a mile: then I introduced myself. We conversed the remainder of our ride about company affairs.

This morning he brought over my itinerary and I am underway—Billings, Rapid City, Cheyenne, Casper, Scottsbluff and back to Denver. In Denver, Mr. Hansel has about three days work for me, and then it'll take four to five days to get back into Chicago.

Barren wasteland with lots of cattle and horses. Love, Margean
April 4, 1948
From Belknap Hotel, Billings, Montana

—•—

Dear Ones: Had a wonderful trip today, about thirty miles of it through Wind River Canyon. Before the present road was opened last fall, the road ran down the bottom of the canyon beside the river and cars could go over it only at certain times of the day—all other times, the road was under water. The road now is an improvement although so narrow I'd hate to meet a truck on it. It has three tunnels through solid rock, and that's what you see—rock ceiling, rock sides, rock roadbed. The scenery was magnificent!

Two big dams are being erected and this area is boom frontier centering on Thermopolis. I've ridden through frontier towns all day. Shacks with a Cadillac at the door. It's not just the dams but oil that has brought in the spondula!

Where the land levels out, there are farms with more shacks. To me they look far from prosperous; but from talk, I guess they too are rolling in the jack. I'm so far north, I can't decide what they raise, but whatever it is, it is irrigated.

My embroidery is proceeding beautifully and I have finished the green. It's gorgeous. Love, Margean

———

April 6, 1948
From Plains Hotel, Cheyenne, Wyoming

Dear Ones: As luck would have it, the man Mr. Weber wanted me to catch goes out today instead of tomorrow so I have to tag along, but tomorrow I'll catch up on sleep.

Yesterday I had a grand circle tour through the Black Hills. Newcastle, Lead and Deadwood are situated in mountain gulches on mean, narrow, crooked streets with bricked-up sides. At Lead, buildings of a large gold mine cover a whole hillside. Last night coming out of the Black Hills, we scared up a herd of fifteen elk feeding on a hill.

Snow was in them thar hills—feet of it, but the air was warm. The dirt road was slushy and, because of this, the motor got wet. It's miles from civilization with forty miles between towns, so we spent a disturbing fifteen minutes on the top of a windblown pass while the driver got things dry. Love, Margean

———

———

April 7, 1948
From Wheatland, Wyoming

Dear Ones: The next time I get home you will be the recipients of a used alarm clock. After fruitless searching through about twenty states and as many big cities, I finally tracked down one of those $7 Westclox travel alarms. It's a beautiful gold and ivory creation with a shutter that slides up or down to protect the glass face. In size, it resembles a large cake of oval Sweetheart soap. So you may have my old Westclox that has traveled miles, and miles and miles.

The other thing I did was get my teeth cleaned—no cavities. One nice thing about these towns, dentists are not so busy. You can just drop in and hear the gossip. The more you see of this country and its people, the better you like it: however, everybody knows everyone's business!

This town, indeed every town in Wyoming, is oil-mad. New fields, old fields and incidental drilling are going on and bring in big money. The most recent millionaire, so my dentist informed me, was a ranger who last month sold his 3,500 acres of poor grazing land to an oil company for $1,200,000. Here, also, a new pipeline is under construction and the town is filled with machinery and linemen. Although only 2,500 in population, Wheatland is booming.

Mr. Weber fouled me up on my men, and I doubled back this morning from Douglas with the guy I had going up yesterday. But I think something went wrong at the Casper end of the driver's run because they shot him back after only a seven hour layover. When he gets his bad report, he may remember me!

The roads are terrible. Restrictions, as I mentioned before, are in effect. Holes, big enough to bury someone in, invite the unwary tire. Last Saturday there was a terrible wind and sand storm hereabouts and even yesterday the dirt was blowing in long sheets along the horizon. Today the wind is blowing very hard, and I had difficulty in navigating the streets, keeping my hair on and skirt properly in place.

Have met all sorts of interesting people. The most interesting was a woman last Saturday. I thought her slightly mad until I listened in and found her to be a "Wyoming Character." She is the widow of a former Wyoming U.S. Senator, (with her land, richer than Fort Knox), and knows everybody in Wyoming. And did she look careless: her dress was black with white dots, some of which had peeled off. She wore her sox rolled above the knee and, when she leaned over to boom in the driver's ear, she didn't take the trouble to keep her rolled tops from showing. In short, she was sort of a Margery Main. She had been to a Governor's dinner in Cheyenne and was on her way home to Thermopolis—she would have looked far more appropriate on a horse!

Her latest incident was this. Wyoming car licenses have a man on a bucking bronco, a nice man with a hat in hand and a neckerchief blowing. My friend thought this too plain—so with assorted paint pots, she painted the man on all the cars at a big Thermopolis dance (everyone goes to these). Appropriately enough, they hauled her in and clamped her behind bars while they leafed through law books to find a statute against desecrating Wyoming's horse and rider. There was none. "They had me buffaloed," she said, while the whole busload listened intently. So they let her out, the whole thing having been half in fun. The driver later informed me that the incident was splashed all over Colorado, Wyoming and Montana. It was hilarious to see her sitting there, respectable hat perched on respectable white hair, leaning forward with rolled stockings showing, while she expounded just the right amount of indignation—and one could tell she had had a whale of a lot of fun out of the incident. Love, Margean

----

April 8, 1948
Postcard from Sidney, Nebraska

Awoke this morning with a mump on my right side. I hope I shall not be seriously incapacitated. Can't eat. Love, Margean

----

April 9, 1948
From Cosmopolitan Hotel, Denver, Colorado

Dear Ones: I'm writing from a bed of pain. I exaggerate; it's really not too bad. However, like the flu, it hit my lymph glands. My jaw hurts but only from the stretched skin. Until the fever broke this morning, I was miserable—now, I'm sweating and feel much better, relatively speaking. In order to venture into society, a scarf is fetchingly arranged to hide the side of my face.

You kept me too isolated on the farm! Better burn this letter. Love, Margean

----

200

April 11, 1948
From Boss Hotel, Clarinda, Iowa

Dear Ones: My God was I sick the rest of the 9th! I got your letter and my hotel reservations off, crawled into bed about 10:30 a.m. and left a call for 11:30 that night. I must have slept a couple of hours when I woke up wringing wet. I was building roads down south somewhere, and I did it until about 10:30. Then the old "got-to-work" pull helped me pick up my scattered wits.

The thought of being a sort of Typhoid Mary—or a Mump Mary— never entered my mind. With the aid of assorted chairs, I finally got my clothes on and a scarf draped around my swollen jaw. I floated down to the lobby and floated the two blocks to the Denver bus station, so lightheaded I must have staggered all over the place, partly from fever and partly from not eating.

I had an hour to wait, so invested 85 cents in an ice bag and got it filled at the coffee shop. This, with aspirin, definitely broke the fever and got my feet on solid ground again.

So I copped a whole front seat, rented a pillow, curled up, and set that ice bag on my ear. I didn't have the slightest difficulty staying awake and catching the driver smoking, not stopping at railroad crossings, and lots of other things: he will rue the day I caught the mumps!

With the aspirin taking effect, I was feeling better and beginning — typical me-fashion—to worry about my appearance. Lord knows it hurt to even open my mouth. I invested in another bag of ice, and another bag and another bag. Today, the fourth day, the swelling is almost gone so maybe there is something to that ice bag therapy! Don't let that old "dill-pickle" test fool you—you can so eat them, although they put a slight cramp in your mump! I broke my two-day fast with a hamburger and a pickle slice.

Mr. Hensel at Denver laughed fit to kill and said I'd have to pull the runs of any of his men that came down with the mumps. I feel very guilty. Love, Margean

———

April 28, 1948
From Congress Hotel, Chicago, Illinois

Dear Ones: Got my wish for a Western trip, but slightly more than I bargained for—a whole month on the road: Chicago, St. Louis, Tulsa, Dallas, El Paso, Tucson, San Diego, San Francisco, Chico; back to San

Francisco; then Reno, Salt Lake, Denver; to Trinadad and back to Denver; back to San Francisco; down to San Diego; over to Tucson, El Paso, Dallas, Tulsa, Springfield, St. Louis, Chicago. How is that for several thousand miles in 29 days! Really, near the end, I may be contacted to stay in Springfield and do some work for Mr. Morrow.

The San Francisco-Chico rides are over the new Gibson Lines we are acquiring and they want in-depth reports on the company. My Salt Lake-Denver-Trinidad runs are over the Denver-Salt Lake-Pacific Lines that I have never inspected. This latter means two rides over that 13,000 Berthoud pass.

A lovelier day to travel would be hard to find—cool, cloudy, flowers out and farming in full swing. Oats are up about four inches and corn plowing occupies most. Lots of little pigs. From Kankakee to Decatur it's flat and black with well-kept farms, richer than at home and reminds one of farms around White Pigeon.

All were solicitous of my health at the office—well, having suffered in their childhood, they laughed just like Mr. Hensel! I tell them I am the infant of the office, the infant of the company! Love, Margean

---

May 1, 1948
From Jefferson Hotel, Dallas, Texas

Dear Ones: Had a lovely trip. Turner Falls near Ardmore, Oklahoma, was at it's best. We all went "Oh" and "Ah"—it is the last real piece of scenic value until near Tucson, Arizona. Second cutting and bailing were well underway. Corn was up a foot. Cotton was showing. The temperature was 90 on this hot, muggy day. Am I glad I didn't take my other coat!

Had an interesting seat partner who had won her trip in a radio contest. Love, Margean

---

May 5, 1948
From Hotel El Tejon, Bakersfield, California

Dear Ones: I had bought a full through-fare where a stopover doesn't look so suspicious. But it happened again. Naturally I would run into the only driver—the handsome Casanova—who was capable of pointing me out. And that's precisely what he did. I can't really blame the handsome

202

boy, because I have run into him <u>every</u> time I have hit this region, but they sure move him around or he run-bids all over the place. Anyway, he enumerated the drivers with whom I last rode who received reports. He is all over the suspicious stage! I buzzed over to Trailways to get out of town and get ahead of the news.

Haven't been able to eat much due to the terrific heat which deprives me of all appetite except for coke and ice. Love, Margean

———

May 8, 1948
From Chico, California

Dear Ones: On the 6th, I made the Bakersfield-San Francisco trip, most of it in the Imperial Valley. The mountains were flower-covered. Acre-size patches of orange poppies, some yellow flower and a blue flower made one wonder how the next slope would be painted.

Such road construction—the objective to create a four-lane highway where two had existed before. With feverish activity, cats, levelers and cranes were grabbing big handfuls of mountain for fill-dirt to create new lanes to the right, or, pushing the mountain back to create new lanes to the left. All fascinating except when I could look over the road's edge without a guard-rail about a mile down to eternity and get the queerest feeling in my stomach!

The farming? In the mountains there was none. Outside of orchard groves, some hay cutting and some plowed land, there wasn't much. However, yesterday on my San Francisco-Sacramento trip, I saw lots of truck—mostly acres of cabbage.

How many times have I complained that the notion of California being warm is fallacious. Yesterday I had a coat on all day and, last night, double blankets. Love, Margean

———

May 9, 1948
From The Riverside, Reno, Nevada

Dear Ones: Had the funniest experience this evening! Got in here, wrote my reports, then decided to call Mr. Merrill to see who would be on in the morning, in case he would rather I'd lay over a run. So I called and was laughingly informed that <u>he</u> was going to drive! I joined him in the laughter! It seems that they dissolved this office the first of the month, working it from Sacramento and dispensing with his position. So we laughed some more and I told him to save me a good seat. Love, Margean

---

May 11, 1948
From Cosmopolitan Hotel, Denver, Colorado

Dear Ones: After I wrote my last letter, Mr. Hensel, who happened to be in Reno, called me. It seemed that Mr. Merrill saw him at the station and told him that I had called and the way circumstances were. Mr. Hensel said I had nothing to worry about so far as riding with him was concerned —which I already knew.

Mr. Hensel was on his way to San Francisco to inaugurate local service between San Francisco and Reno by way of our new Gibson Line and wanted my impressions of that line and our new Reno terminal.

He went on to commend me for the excellent work I did for him in the Black Hills and to ask me to come back to Denver as early in June as possible for what sounded like open, safety work. All safety-men have been done away with except me (which makes me worry about other tightening-up moves I have been hearing about). As we jabbered along, he said that he heard that I had done a good piece of work on the franchise deal—I'd like to know who's been talking about me!

So at 5:15 a.m., I was down to the station ready to go. Mr. Merrill looked very trim in his uniform and gave us a wonderful ride—he hadn't forgotten how in five years off the road. He's top man as far as seniority goes and has two good runs.

All the things we had to talk about—men, events, equipment, comparisons of Burlington Trailways and American Buslines, etc. He got a big kick out of my Texas handsome Casanova problem and told me about the run-bid roaming that a lot of drivers do. The next time I hit Reno, I'm to take a day off so he, his wife, their Pekinese dog, and I can go into the canyon country south of Reno.

When I got to the Cosmopolitan, where I've stayed time and time again, they had a gift for me—four black packs of matches with my name in gold on the cover! Love, Margean

---

204

May 13, 1948
From Columbian Hotel, Trinidad, Colorado

Dear Ones: It's 515 miles, fifteen and a half hours by bus, with three hours spent at rest and meal stops. Leaving Salt Lake, the next three hours are spent in mountains and canyons. We stopped at Soldier Springs—a pipe of water on top of a cliff—where I took some pictures and looked at three or four sheep grazing at the bottom of the canyon. A cement mine (I didn't know there were such things) and these sheep were the only signs of activity.

After leaving this rugged scenery, we emerged onto high, monotonously rolling country with occasional broken-down mountains, part of the inter-mountain plateau. Here, flocks of sheared sheep came into occasional view. As we struck further south-southeast, the sheep gave way to the cow maternity farms—calves of all sizes, mostly Hereford with some Black Angus, and anxious mammas all over the place.

In general, these were on open range, but the further we went, land was fenced in, especially in Vernal Valley between Steamboat Springs and Rabbit Ears Pass. Here the land was one big spring: I never saw anything like it—water everywhere—running from melting snow into Silver Dollar Creek, which was trying to imitate a ferocious river and succeeding nicely. Incidentally, you hit three water divides in this 515 miles—each of the passes splitting water into those running east and those running west.

Then we started to leave Vernal Valley climbing up to 11,000 feet at Rabbit Ears Pass, named after a rock split down the middle making a presentable pair of ears. Every hairpin turn gave us a different and higher view of the valley with the creek, the water, the farms a mile below.

The rest of the trip was one long hairpin turn after another—up to Berthoud Pass at 13,000 feet and down to 5,280 at Denver—mostly at night. We were in constant snow—over the roofs of the ski and hunting lodges and snowstorms. The towns were winter-dirty and built to withstand cold.

Today down to Trinidad, Colorado and never out of sight of mountains. An excellent chicken dinner, but no good shows in town, so I'm listening to the radio, writing, and have much time to kill before due out at 3:45 p.m. tomorrow.

By the time I hit Chicago, I will have piled up close to 10,000 miles —and then, probably, right back to Denver for another 5,000.

Am still pondering over Mr. Hensel's remarks—also over what he could want me to do as I thoroughly covered his territory last month! Love, Margean

May 17, 1948
From The Riverside, Reno, Nevada

Dear Ones: Am at last started on the homeward stretch—also back into the skeptical Texas territory.

Got into Reno yesterday afternoon. After I got my second wind and after writing reports, I saw "April Showers" starring Jack Carson and Ann Southern. After that, lots of good radio programs came on while I embroidered, washed my hair, soaked in the tub, and went to bed.

Between Denver and Salt Lake City, I had an interesting seat mate. Hailing from Liverpool, England, she was here for a four-month stay with her sister in Vernal, Colorado. She was full of news about British conditions —mostly queues and ration books. She ordered a steak for her first meal here, hadn't seen so much meat in one piece for years, and couldn't get it all down.

Yesterday I had a woman musician to talk to, an unbelieving Mormon. She showed me a picture and clipping of her with Lawrence Welk's band, so she was the real McCoy!

Am anxiously waiting for a letter to catch up with me and am apprehensive that I have passed up some. Am expecting both a letter and my pills at Bakersfield. Love, Margean

May 22, 1948
From Hotel Paso del Norte, El Paso, Texas

Dear Ones: My ticket number is notorious from here to there. Out of San Diego they were so nice as to give me a free deadhead pillow, just to be on my right side, if….! Then yesterday came the old, old dodge of putting a deadhead driver next to me. I just embroidered away, getting down notes under their very noses. Can't catch me that way! This is proving to be quite a contest of wits!

What a hot ride from Tucson yesterday—mountains and desert shimmered. The mountains looked dead and haunted—such flat shadows. Outside of that, only miles of road with the nastiest sudden dips. No appetite with the 100 degree temperature. Am thankful that my next assignment will be in the mountains.

206

I paced around El Paso in search of a sleep shade that I had heard about for sleeping days (will get two, Dad, to help with your daytime sleeping). Will have scads of little things to tell when I get home. Also one of the cutest stories I've ever heard—if I can remember it that long. Remind me. Love, Margean

———

May 25, 1948
From Colonial Hotel, Springfield, Missouri

Dear Ones: Did I leave you gasping by my telegrams? Here's the lowdown.

Rode all night. My first man was a holy terror. We were almost killed in a cloudburst. When passengers are so scared they go up to ask the driver to slow down, that's too much. I got the names and addresses of four witnesses and wrote a scathing report. I told Mr. Morrow about it and he sent a telegram to Dallas to pull the driver out of service until the reports arrive. What I can't understand is <u>why</u> he drove the way he did—he knew I was on!

Anyway, got here at 7:30 a.m. At 8:00 Mr. Morrow rang my room asking me to breakfast with him and Mr. Hinkleman. Mr. Hinkleman is the traveling sales representative of the entire East and was with me on Greyhound. Have known him by reputation for years. Had a wonderful, gossipy breakfast hour and Mr. Morrow said that Pete wanted me to call.

After finishing my reports, I called Chicago and Pete told me to hotfoot it up to Rapid City, South Dakota, part of the way by Greyhound so no one would know I was in the territory. Arriving there, the superintendent and I have an unscheduled date. He's spending too much time skipping out on work and they want to know what he does. It's as simple as that!

After that, back into Chicago where assignments have piled up: Mr. Morrow has a man and our new Chattanooga-Nashville line to look over; Mr. Hensel has work; and more work in the East —probably on the Express that Mr. Tigrett told me about last winter.

Yesterday morning spent four hours writing up a huge ten page general report on company operations. Pete got it today and congratulated me. Got a lot of driver gripes into it without that being obvious plus tips on getting more sales—better trips, etc.

Haven't had enough sleep for two days, but don't have to work until Rapid City—getting there quickly being the important thing. Love, Margean

May 27, 1948
From New Castle, South Dakota

Dear Ones: Between buses. Just before arriving, we ran into one humdinger of an electric storm—complete with downpour, thunder and lightning. Storms here are very complete affairs!

Arriving in Rapid City near 6:00 p.m. will give me time to reconnoiter and plan my strategy. How I hate this assignment! All I have to do, however, is keep track of his terminal activities during working hours, nothing distasteful.

That long ride from Springfield to Cheyenne nearly killed me—on the road steady for 24 hours and me with very little sleep before leaving. The hotel switchboard called me three times before I roused up enough to answer the phone. Love, Margean

May 28, 1948
From Alex Johnson Hotel, Rapid City, South Dakota

Dear Ones: As luck would have it, we picked up the superintendent in Deadwood. He sat with me telling that today he went to Hill City and did a lot of floating around in the company car.

My room overlooks the station a block away—had to change rooms to get this one. I have binoculars and a good view of activities—very boring. Got some oranges and am eating them while perched on the windowsill.

Got a western slack suit that's in the mail. My account must be taking a beating: however, there will be oodles of money at Chicago when I get there. Love, Margean

May 30, 1948
From Alex Johnson Hotel, Rapid City, South Dakota

Dear Ones: Another day of peering out of my ninth-story window. Another day of raw, dreary weather with drippy intervals. Another day of being bored. Only one more day, thank goodness—and thank goodness for the radio!

Did I tell you that I found my sleeping-shade in Dallas? It's wonderful for sleeping in the daytime or in light rooms. Dad, they only had one or

I would have gotten another for you. And, Dad, one of the books I'm sending home is "Darkness at Noon," a story of the Russian treason trials, which I'm sure you will find interesting.

May 31: The last of my boring days. As near as I can find out, he went fishing.

By the time you receive this, I'll be miles closer, even in Chicago, maybe. So happy to head back towards civilization. Love, Margean

—•—

June 1, 1948
From Plains Hotel, Cheyenne, Wyoming

Dear Ones: Had an interesting ride between midnight and 9:15 a.m. We ran into one of the four free-roaming herds of buffalo in Wind Cave National Park that I had read about just the other day. They were lying down on both sides of the road. The driver put the spotlight on them and there must have been near 100, maybe more. Would hate to hit one. Besides these, we saw assorted deer and antelope, the latter like a small deer but light in color with a pronged horn something like an L upside down.

When I got into Cheyenne, I called Mr. Weber to find out whether he wished me to take the 9:30 p.m. or the 10:45 out, and he chose the latter because a new man would be operating it. After business, we gabbed— never do you find two bus people without something to talk about. Love, Margean

—•—

June 8, 1948
From Hotel Henry, Pittsburgh, Pennsylvania
Dear Ones: After sleeping this afternoon, I went to see "Berlin Express", getting out in the middle of a rousing thunderstorm.

Had one hell of a trip, couldn't relax a muscle. A big, fat woman sat next to me, sitting in her seat and half of mine. She had red hair and dime store earrings. She carried: a cosmetic bag which she placed under my feet —"You won't mind, dearie"; a knitting bag with oranges and a thermos bottle; a shopping bag crammed over on the other side of her knees so her feet were on my side; a pillow, which she placed between herself and the window making her stick further over on my side; a sweater, which she laid up on the rack and whose sleeves kept plopping down on my head; and a great big coat which she laid over herself and which, naturally, went half over me. Then three or four times she made me get up while she got out to see that no one had their feet on her bag and twice while she padded in her stocking feet to the lavatory. All night, I was either popping up, getting flopped on the head, or having to grab the safety guard to keep from falling out of my seat.

I fumed and fumed: people were giving me pitying looks. Couldn't move because of seat reservations. Finally, I could stand it no longer: "Lady," I said, "Do you see this cord?" and I dug under her fanny to the seat line. "It's the dividing line, and this half is mine. I'd like to sit on all of it!" The cute driver called back "Do you need some assistance, Miss?" But the fellow behind me yelled back, "Don't think so, the situation's well under control!"

So she dug the pillow out, kicked the bags under the seat where they belonged, and got over on her side. There was a 'sotto voce' from the rear – "Hurray for our side." I am so awful! But really this is why I love buses! Love, Margean

---

June 11, 1948
From Hotel Henry, Pittsburgh, Pennsylvania

Dear Ones: Isn't it terrible the way that one cannot sleep in the afternoon when you definitely have to catch a bus at 12:14 a.m. Giving up trying to sleep, I dressed and went out for a belated dinner. After enjoying a stuffed tomato and apple pie, I bought a Post, turned on the radio and went to sleep.

When I got into New York the other day, there was an airmail, special delivery from Pete asking me where I was and why I hadn't stayed at the Keystone per itinerary. The Keystone had switched me because of some conference or other and it didn't get registered for possible phone calls.

So, next morning I called to find out what in Hell they wanted me for! Merely some extra time to be spent on the limited service which means another trip into New York. For some reason, business is mighty slow here in the East (as Mr. Hinkleman had told me), and I'm to think up ways and means of getting more people to ride. Have thought of several improvements, all of which mean work for someone but, more important, they are not getting the name "American/Burlington" out there enough, if you ask me. That Greyhound hound dog is so easy to picture.

Incidentally, these limited runs are mighty boring with little or no opportunity to stretch one's legs except by walking back to the lavatory (an exercise everyone engages in) and forgetting to turn the "occupied" knob.

This morning I called Mr. Watson who is confined at home with a heart attack. I had hoped to see him as he had created quite a flurry of ill feeling when he was transferred a couple of months ago, and I wanted to hear his side. He had driven with Mr. Merrill at Reno and with lots of others out West that I know, consequently we had lots to gab about. Trotted up to his office to get a copy of the new schedule and to pick up my copy of the "American Way." He has a blond secretary.

Pretty soon will be used to sleeping days, I hope! Lord knows when I'll get home again—probably more work on that Bay City-Louisville franchise; then the Salem, Missouri, deal; and Mr. Hensel's work. Poor Mr. Hensel had expected me in Denver on June 1. Love, Margean

---

June 13, 1948
From Hotel York, St. Louis, Missouri

Dear Ones: Just waiting around until bus time, my usual occupation! But what a day to wait in—a day made for picnics and ball games.

Did I ever tell you that this hotel is in a crummy neighborhood, a part of old St. Louis near the river? The rest of the town has moved west a few blocks, but around here all the bums and down-and-outers collect. It's absolutely not safe to walk down the street so I always take a cab. The hotel, however, is OK and located on the edge of a park. My room overlooks bum-street with its collection of greasy spoons (the menus lettered on the window), burlesque houses (closed for the season), and flop houses.

Last night I sat in my third story window watching the characters ebb and flow. The dyed blondes, satin dresses, the old drunk throwing up on the corner, a fight quickly squelched, people sitting on steps drinking beer—Saturday night in St. Louis. This morning there was no one in sight —deserted and dead. St. Louis is dry on Sunday!

Made up part of my report on the Express Service. Have one real good advertising angle to let them know I'm not sleeping while riding. Love, Margean

---

June 25, 1948
From Hotel Vendome, Evansville, Indiana

Dear Ones: Am in permanent quarters for the next two weeks—a beautiful room with wine colored lavatory, toilet, and bath. A nice, quiet room.

The last time I was here, Ted Frye was along. We covered the waterfront, went through the museum and ate at a wonderful restaurant. I wonder where he is now.

What a nice little town. It has a Chrysler assembly plant; Briggs-Indiana; Inglehart Brothers; Mead-Johnson; Bucyrus-Erie; and an International Harvester, plus others. About 125,000 in population, it's like Flint, only with personality and a nice-sized shopping district. It fronts on the Ohio River whose banks have been converted into a park with a swanky hotel.

I was spirited in and out of Mr. Burleigh's office between conferences and didn't have an opportunity to do anything but take notes on my assignment. After this is finished, I have another one waiting in the East —he didn't elaborate but it seemed to be a foreign line—Southeastern?

I'm here to make a general report on the city bus operations that Mr. Burleigh has just purchased. A fleet of 105 Twin Coaches, some equipped with music, cover fourteen separate runs with ten to fifteen minute service. I had to scout about to find a map of the lines and learn background. Shall start in earnest tomorrow. Today it's 97 and my slack suit sticks like a second skin; my face is covered, like everyone's, with sweat; the streets quiver in the sun. Hope for thundershowers.

Have recovered from my blues about my life on the long, lonesome road, deciding that the more I work the more I save, and the sooner I'll be able to retire. If that grandchild arrives, I'll be here until about July 11. Love, Margean

———

June 26, 1948
From Hotel Vendome, Evansville, Indiana

Dear Ones: It has to be pretty hot to sweat so much that your mascara runs. So hot that sweat from the back of your knees runs down to your ankles after sitting down. But a thunderstorm fixed everything. Four of us stayed on a bus two and a half trips before we could get off! It's now 6:30 p.m. and raining again. I'm going to don coat and plastic scarf for a three-block trip to the library. Love, Margean

June 27, 1948
From Hotel Vendome, Evansville, Indiana

Dear Ones: Another hot, muggy day with showers brewing. People loafed around, went down to the riverside to take speedboat and pontoon plane rides, and eat popcorn. I took my embroidery and meandered down to the hotel veranda overlooking the river. Here I could listen to chatter and watch new styles. That palled after the sun began inching onto the veranda and I meandered back to my hotel.

Think I will finish next week, but am not positive yet. Have about eight books to read. Raining again with thunder and lightning from the southeast. Love, Margean

———

June 28, 1948
From Hotel Vendome, Evansville, Indiana

Dear Ones: My new winter coat is in the mail. It has a removable lining and I'm hoping that the fur lining of my old winter coat will fit it also. It's gabardine with a modified full back and a removable hood. I'm hoping the wool gabardine stands up as well as the wool of my old coat. Coats get a workout on the road.

Got drenched in the daily storm this afternoon while waiting for a bus. Washed my hair last night. However, the daily perspiration does more to keep it curly, it's been a mass of ringlets since I've arrived. Love, Margean

———

July 1, 1948
From Vendome Hotel, Evansville, Indiana

Dear Ones: Got a telegram from Pete telling me my Chicago reservation is ready. I leave here July 5 for Chicago's Congress Hotel—send mail.

It poured again yesterday afternoon and me out in it! I constantly carry a headscarf because the first appearance of those black clouds means rain in a half-hour—rain by the buckets. After an hour and a half everything is clear, the sun is out and steam again rises from the concrete.

Evansville is easier to work than Flint because a regular driver works two routes instead of four as in Flint. In Flint the same man may catch you at three places besides where you caught him, therefore, you can work only one route a day which considerably hinders your timing and effectiveness. Here, where you have to work only one end, no such difficulty presents itself.

What have you planned for the glorious Fourth? I shall prepare my general report on Evansville City Lines. Of course, I wonder what the other assignment of Mr. Burleigh's can be. When they run out of things for me to do, I have a sixteen day trip West just in case things get dull. Love, Margean

———

July 3, 1948
From Vendome Hotel, Evansville, Indiana

Dear Ones: Too bad your first grandchild couldn't have waited until the Fourth to make his appearance—Independence Day, you know.

Tomorrow, Sunday, will be a day of "rest"; at least, I shall work only on my reports. At present the driver reports need only be copied. The initial draft of my general report is roughed and needs only to be enlarged upon before inking up the final copy.

Today's temperature is 93. There is a sign downtown, "It's a Sure Sign of Summer if the Chair Gets up When You Do!" which describes me after an hour of bus riding. Only six more men remain this afternoon. I have ridden with 102: of these, twenty were doubles: making 82 reports altogether. They employ 96 so I consider my coverage pretty thorough. I have worked from 7:15 to 10:30 and 2:15 to 5:30, the peak hours when all the men are out.

Am speculating on my next assignment—"in the East," he said. I hope it will be Southeastern—I should protect my interests as a stockholder! If it is that, a thorough coverage should take two or three weeks. Love, Margean

———

July 11, 1948
From Hotel Marion, Knoxville, Iowa

Dear Ones: What a day spent in a small town hotel with all the permanent guests seated in the lobby reading Sunday papers. But a big muscled, pipeline construction crew has pretty well filled the hotel.

This morning I got up and walked out to the Veterans Hospital where I intend to board the bus. It takes twenty minutes to walk it. After walking back, I roamed around the big Courthouse Square that contains two movie theaters. All the old men were comfortably propped along curbs and on benches.

Then back to the hotel for a chicken dinner and for partially working out my route from Chicago south. After listening to a political roundtable, I decided to come down to the hotel lobby and write this. Love, Margean

---

July 13, 1948
From Congress Hotel, Chicago, Illinois

Dear Ones: Well, at last it's happened. Mr. Burleigh called me in today to talk about the Evansville City Lines. He was very pleased with my general report on men, equipment, lines and passengers. Then I got in the request that I'd like to be transferred—to my surprise, there was no hem and haw and he readily agreed. I said there was no hurry, and that I was willing to go anywhere on the lines, but preferably West. I mentioned TPA (traveling passenger agent) work and the tour department. So—the initial request is made, and things are favorable. How I would like a permanent home!

The Rapid City, South Dakota, superintendent has been fired. Love, Margean

---

July 15, 1948
From Wm. Len Hotel, Memphis, Tennessee

Dear Ones: Am between buses in Cabool, Missouri, the most woe-be-gone Podunk in the world. Streets aren't paved and there's a railing to tie horses to. Last night in Jefferson City, Missouri, I plugged in my radio, placed it on the windowsill, sat on the radiator, and pulled it on. Picked

215

myself up from the floor and counted damages—one blown radio, blisters on two fingers, one on my forearm, but no visible damage to the part in contact with the radiator! Love, Margean

———

July 17, 1948
From Wm. Len Hotel, Memphis, Tennessee

Dear Ones: Back in Memphis—a hot, sultry trip. The part through the Ozarks was scenic enough, but after leaving the hills there was only Arkansas red dirt to look at.

Into my hotel, wrote reports and then I contacted P. Adams for instructions. We discussed ways and means of getting on the Hound-dog trip up to Hardy, Arkansas: they're carrying passengers against their franchise. They're mighty tight-lipped about giving out information because I've called three times (using all my Southern accents), and received three different answers. Love, Margean

———

July 18, 1948
From Wm. Len Hotel, Memphis, Tennessee

Dear Ones: I miss my radio which in its demise tried to take me with it. The trip up to Hardy yesterday was a killer! The 105 temperature made my girdle torture! 110 passengers to get down! The scenery wasn't even pretty until it got dark and the heat lightning set in.

Tomorrow at 5:55 a.m. will be on my way to Chattanooga and return. The next day I'll be on the road with Mr. Adams doing a spot cash fare check. By then, Mr. Morrow will be here.

Finished my Dixie Greyhound snooping, and could only get the run-around everyone else does. Mr. Adams said I had a good master report on it. Love, Margean

216

July 20, 1948
From Hotel Negley, Florence, Alabama

Dear Ones: This is one of those 36-hour sieges for which I am famous and all because I didn't know the turnaround and the hotels in Florence were full. I got up at 5:00 a.m. yesterday, and there's no prospect of bed before 8:30 p.m.: strangely enough, I'm not tired yet!

My 5:55 a.m. boy yesterday was a honey—perfect ride and handling 143 passengers (46 cash fares) in four and half-hours, a record of some kind! I didn't have an idle moment with someone on and off every two minutes.

Then into Chattanooga. This is TVA country and one can easily see the greater prosperity and better cultivating methods as contrasted with those, say, of Arkansas. Same red dirt, but TVA raises corn and hay, not cotton, cotton, cotton.

Fell into conversation with a farm-woman. She said they were planning to start a dairy herd: but it was so expensive, the best cows costing $150. "What kind of cow is that?" I asked. "Jersey," she replied. "That's kind of a shaky investment, why not Holsteins?" "Lord, honey, that's a rich man's cow down here!" According to her conversation, they build up their own herds but those I've seen look awfully mangy and bony to me.

If a Northerner could stand the climate, it would pay to buy a couple of sections of this cheap land and bring down a herd of those "rich man's cows" because milk brings about the same per hundredweight. There would be little investment for buildings, but you would need fences because I haven't seen a decent one yet. These boys don't invest in coolers and instead separate for cream, consequently, most milk is shipped in, especially for the larger cities.

We came into Chattanooga at just the right time, early twilight: then the lights are on, and you arrive high up on Lookout Mountain with the city spread out below. There's a fiery foundry that lights up the sky. It takes less time to get into the heart of this city than any other I know, five minutes after you hit the limits you're in the station. Love, Margean

———

July 23, 1948
From Hotel Cornelian, Decatur, Alabama

Dear Ones: I'm melting into a grease spot here in Decatur while engaged in checking the local 45 mile run between here and Huntsville,

Alabama. Sunday I meet Mr. Morrow in Florence and we'll probably have dinner together—a saving on my expense account!

I ate in style tonight here at my residential hotel, but I couldn't have eaten elsewhere because of the pouring rain. Apple juice, pear and cottage cheese salad, cheese omelet, corn-on-the-cob, corn muffins, ice cream with a cookie and ice tea—all for $1.10. Don't think me a pig, it was my only meal of the day.

Decatur is located on two backed-up TVA lakes—on them, motor boats and rowboats putter and row around. Semi-hillbilly country from here to Huntsville. It's rained hard twice in my two-day stay.

I got in on the 2:15 train yesterday. I figured out a trip leaving at 6:15 p.m. to Huntsville and had difficulty staying out of sight until the 6:05 left. We finally took off, all seven of us. Thirty-five minutes out, one of the rods broke right in front of a service station/country store—never would this ever happen for one of my breakdowns again! So, there we were with me having an hour turnaround at Huntsville and no other bus back!

The driver called and they said they would send the 6:05 bus back for us when it reached Huntsville—its driver, the man I was to ride back with! We waited and waited, drank up the cokes and waited some more. I found a coke crate to sit on amidst the chickens running in and out the store doorway. There were two mangy, under-fed, bug-ridden, six-week-old kittens underfoot, so I invested a nickel in a "tub" of ice cream and put some nourishment into them. They went crazy, spitting and clawing at each other, but their sides filled out.

This occupied time while I listened to the deep South drawl. Everyone was preparing to attend a revival meeting in a huge tent we had passed.

About 45 minutes later the bus came and we headed into Huntsville. I asked when the next bus was back mentioning that I was now late for my clinic appointment. The driver said he was sorry about the appointment and breakdown and that he would load to return in ten minutes. This left me time to look in the telephone book and ascertain whether there was a clinic. There was: Huntsville Clinic, 315 Franklin, telephone 2900: then I turned to Doctors and under telephone 2900 found Dr. H. Anderson. My alibi, if needed, was complete. All these elaborate precautions were unnecessary—no questions were asked.

This morning all the water birds were out, frogs croaked and the country smelled like country. Honeysuckle was blooming. We enjoyed a pleasant ride. For three hours I wandered about carrying my steaming raincoat and then rode back and went to a movie. Then supper, this letter, pressing, bathing and hair washing. This is the glamorous life on the road! Love, Margean

218

July 27, 1948
From Wm. Len Hotel, Memphis, Tennessee

Dear Ones: Am looking forward eagerly to <u>mail</u> in Denver with all the news of that grandson. Less eagerly, I'm looking forward to the money in Kansas City. Right now I'm not low, but I would have been before I left Denver and would have had to give very short notice. The way things look now, it'll be at least the middle of August before I see Michigan again.

Returned this morning from a round trip to Hardy, Arkansas, the return on Dixie Greyhound who's pulling a dirty deal on us. By law, schedules of competing lines over the same road <u>must</u> be thirty minutes apart. Dixie has <u>scheduled</u> her run thirty minutes ahead of ours, but <u>runs</u> it ten to fifteen minutes late, so it's actually only fifteen to twenty minutes ahead and, consequently, picks up all our cash fares! Something will have to be done.

For the last fifteen days, it's been 90+: everything of mine looks like wilted lettuce, including me. Right now I've the tub running full of cool water in which I intend to soak off the Arkansas mud. Love, Margean

———

July 31, 1948
From Cosmopolitan Hotel, Denver, Colorado

Dear Ones: Received your newsy letter and am most anxious to get home and hear the rest of the gossip. While buying a girdle today, I had a pleasant and unexpected surprise. Measuring up, it came out 24" waist and 34" hip—putting me in the "small" classification. I think back to my pudgy days.

Went to a movie last night, "Street with no Name," a FBI picture which put me on the edge of the seat.

August 4th will find me in Omaha with some work down into Kansas City, the exact nature of which I've not been told. While working out of Denver, I'm concentrating on the loitering boys. Love, Margean

———

August 4, 1948
From Pickwick Hotel, Kansas City, Missouri

Dear Ones: I'm positively dying of "hard" work. Yesterday I put in 18 hours between Denver and Omaha. Today I put in 10, tomorrow 18, the next 14, and the next, only 9. Am in a state of suspended animation. <u>Am counting the days until I can settle down</u>.

I feel as though I'm "hotter" than firecrackers around here, nothing definite only <u>that</u> feeling—I know I've done nothing out of the ordinary. I know the bosses don't care, but I do. Will have scads of money waiting when I hit Chicago. Love Margean

———

August 6, 1948
From Pickwick Hotel, Kansas City, Missouri

Dear Ones: Just happened to think—that grandson will be five weeks old tomorrow. He must have grown inches!

I have a cold—complete with runny eyes, runny nose, headache and aching bones. Especially aching bones—so, maybe, it's the flu. It's no wonder, the hours have been terrible this last week. Maybe it's the terrible weather: I've had rain everyplace—cold rain with cold nights. So, now to bed to sweat out this cold (flu?). Love, Margean

———

August 8, 1948
From Hotel Cornhusker, Lincoln, Nebraska

Dear Ones: Nothing is more boring than to sit and wait for a telephone to ring—especially if you've no idea where you're going until it does—no opportunity to make a hotel reservation, etc. That's my plight right now.

My extra boy took a 5:45 a.m. out of here, has to come back, and then go out on the extra board again (with me along). He'll be driving a second section, and when you want to get on one of these, it can be almost impossible—so I'm having anticipatory worries. On top of that, there's an 11:15 p.m. I have to catch out of here sometime.

My cold is slightly—very slightly—improved, helped by twelve hours sleep last night, but I'm still using Kleenex at an astonishing rate. My voice is a thrillingly modulated sexy whisper (if I could only keep it) caused by jammed up germ bugs in my throat!

Today is the first warm day in about two weeks. A nice day for traveling. Yesterday was fine, but the numerous muddy detours and unpaved roads probably spoiled the trip for everyone but me. Corn, pigs, etc. are doing well. Love, Margean

220

August 31, 1948
From Hotel Vendome, Evansville, Indiana

Dear Ones: I had troubles, as you will see as you read on. I almost missed my connection at Hammond, Indiana, and got the last seat, a corner one on the bleacher [*back seat*]. Gradually working up, I finally got a front seat.

I got here, had a nice supper, wrote up reports on two bad drivers and went to bed. I awoke this morning "raring" to go, switched on the radio, and discovered—there is a bus strike! How can I work if there is a bus strike?

So I roamed around listening to comments and trying to discover pickets. This caught Evansville unprepared. Last night the Governor appointed a board for compulsory arbitration that would stave off the strike for thirty days. But the drivers went out anyway—hence the strike is illegal. I haven't been able to uncover the various ramifications but the dominant issue seems to be more pay.

I called Chicago. They went into a huddle to see what to do with me. But at 6:30 p.m. the drivers went back to work and I start working in the morning. Love, Margean

September 1, 1948
From Hotel Vendome, Evansville, Indiana

Dear Ones: This town is in the midst of serious labor difficulties, the least of which is the bus situation. The International Harvester plant and the Bucyrus-Erie plant are both out, plus one other company that I can't recall.

State troopers have been called in to keep order and they are camped all over this hotel. I'm lucky to have a room between them and the racetrack devotees. Love, Margean

September 2, 1948
From Hotel Vendome, Evansville, Indiana

Dear Ones: Today was much like yesterday with me standing on street corners and carrying a crossword puzzle book to occupy my in between times. In one pocket I carry my little 2x3 notebook and streetcar tokens, in the other a big pencil to work puzzles.

Incidentally, yesterday I met Colonel Stilwell. He looks just like a typical British MP. About six-feet tall with pure white mustache and hair, he looks very military and precise. He told me that the job I did before we took over the Evansville City Lines was the best and most complete inspection report on city lines he had ever seen. While I was talking to him, Mr. Hooper of Flint Trolley Coach called and gave me his "love." I guess we three are the Burleigh Team.

State troopers, in their lovely two-toned blue uniforms (complete with guns), are still roaming the city. Eight picketers were arrested yesterday and the union has set up a line around the jail where they were taken.

Horace Hite, his band and radio program have moved into the hotel. Add that to the troopers, and I am lucky to have a room! Love, Margean

---

September 3, 1948
From Hotel Vendome, Evansville, Indiana

Dear Ones: Your one and only daughter must look terribly depraved. I was riding up in the elevator and the operator invited me to attend the Youth Rescue Mission. I thanked her for asking me but can think of better ways of being rescued.

I'm really disappointed in the weather—this afternoon I was going out to Mesker Park Zoo. It's supposed to be a very big one with lots of animals and smells, and the Council is arguing about putting in an air-conditioning system.

At noon I went downstairs for dinner, splurging in the hotel dining room because it was pouring. While I was eating, a man sat down in the booth across from me. After drinking some tomato juice and coffee he left, leaving a whisky bottle on the cushion. Is spiked tomato juice any good—or does the tomato juice and coffee repair the effects of the whisky? My education is lacking.

I went to the zoo, rain and all. Had lots of fun. There were lots of baby monkeys, their mammas clambering around the bars with the little ones holding on for dear life. There were two big chimpanzees whose cage held a big rubber tire on a chain: the male would get in and swing in a big circle around the cage, tiring of this, he would hang on the bars, shake them, and show his teeth. After assorted other monkeys, there were two mandrills. These are also monkeys, but what monkeys! The male's nose is violet and red—real bright—while his rear is red, violet, and blue—real bright! Monkeys have no inhibitions! Also, no sense of modesty! A fine place to show children the facts of life!

There were a boa constrictor, a Gila monster, turtles and alligators. Also two cute lion cubs playing like kittens—very affectionate—very deceptive. Plus a big lion, a new tiger they got this week, a black leopard, a regular leopard, two pumas, a wart hog, an elephant, a kangaroo, a zebra, and assorted camels, buffalo and deer: a worthwhile exhibit and a wonderful afternoon. Love, Margean

---

September 8, 1948
From Vendome Hotel, Evansville, Indiana

Dear Ones: For two afternoons now the forecast has been thunderstorms and, sure enough, black, frayed clouds would fill the sky —but no rain. I have lugged around a very heavy, black raincoat to prevent it—saving dozens of people the trouble.

You should have been with me today—standing by a drugstore on Heidelback, by a grocery on Bellemeade, by a tavern on Weinback. Very exciting! It gives me lots to write about!

Like always when I'm bored, I buy something. Another dress. A beautiful steel gray dress! A lovely business dress! But not for Evansville streetcorners.

Tonight I went to see the excellent "The Bishop's Wife." Love, Margean

---

September 27, 1948
From Congress Hotel, Chicago, Illinois

Dear Ones: Still in Chicago and, for all I accomplished, I might just have well stayed home. Mr. Burleigh was tied up all day with purchase negotiations and I was unable to see him. Tomorrow will be a different story: he has some assignment for me—nature unknown.

I had only one thing to do—sign some affidavits swearing that I had taken such and such a ride, and that my statements were true. They're going to dock the driver $42 for smoking.

This evening I went to see a double feature: "A Foreign Affair," that you must see, about occupation forces in Berlin; plus "The Velvet Touch," starring Ros Russell, an excellent show in itself.

September 28: In two hours on the road to Sacramento. When I arrive, I am to contact Mr. Burleigh who will be on his way to Hawaii. Love, Margean

---

September 29, 1948
From Commercial Hotel, Sidney, Nebraska

Dear Ones: We engaged in a mad turtle race, in other words, a slow moving night. It was a nice, congenial bunch of people who rode—there were sailors, marines, tourists, me and a bottle. After the portable gin mill was set up in the rear, all the military suits became gay. Singing, risqué stories, and general good will (and fumes) filled the bus. The drivers were good conductors for this band of 37 souls. I often think about this but wonder how many drivers do.

Across Nebraska today. Did you ever see anything more forlorn than cornfields waiting to be picked? Or those just picked? Around Cozad, the World's Alfalfa Dehydrating Center, they're making third cutting of their beautiful green alfalfa with its beautiful green smell.

Do train rails get hot when a long train go over? Love, Margean

---

October 1, 1948
From Commercial Hotel, Sidney, Nebraska

Dear Ones: Another month finished. It doesn't seem possible that another year is almost done. What with "gunnery practice" over Berlin plus all the other "cold war" items, one almost wishes that the New Year wouldn't come. I've just finished my *Newsweek* and am most depressed!

This town is filled with railroad noises. The transom windowpane over my door ceaselessly rattles with reverberations from the yards where a large roundhouse and terminal point for men is maintained. Every restaurant has its railroad overall jacket by some booth. Outside of this, it's just a town to go through—five blocks wide and twenty-five long.

I hate these days when I don't start work until evening—in this case 6:10. This day's even worse because there's no electric plug in my room for the radio—and no heat. I've really wished, especially with all this night travel, that I'd brought the fur lining for my coat. Speaking of coats, fall has arrived—very obviously around here. All the hills are withered and sere with that look of neglect that only dead grass can give.

At present, I'm having gooseflesh about getting past Cheyenne tonight. If I'd been smart, I'd have purchased a stopover fare—but I so seldom am smart! I shall have to pussyfoot about with my hood on! I know I am not supposed to be concerned about this, but I always am—shades of Greyhound and JP's FBI training!

I have one consolation to compensate for the horrors of Cheyenne. From 5:00 a.m. until 10:10 when I reach Salt Lake City, I shall have daylight for some beautiful scenery. The hundred miles before reaching Provo, Utah, are marvelous—much of it in canyon beds infested with cute antelope.

Cattle are surprisingly few since the fall sale. In Omaha, I talked to a Wyoming woman who had brought her herd in and bemoaned the fact that beef went down $2 while she was negotiating. She grossed $52,000, but I don't know what her year's expenses would be to figure the net.

Another way of telling when the West arrives is to spot cowboy boots. I nearly fell over yesterday when I spotted a pair on the second section driver.

It seems nice to be back on the road, bumps included. There's something about the feel of wheels that no amount of other kind of work can compensate for. Then, too, there isn't a care in the world outside of your job.

There goes another train. Will close this rambling letter. Love, Margean

---

October 6, 1948
From Hotel Sacramento, Sacramento, California

Dear Ones: The letters have been few and far between, nothing occurring worth a .03 cent stamp.

Today was a Chico round trip where, for the first time, I saw rice farms. It looks like marsh grass, or stubby oats, growing in level, irrigated fields of thirty to forty acres. It must cost oodles to fit up a field—the leveling machines look like road builders' equipment.

Mr. Burleigh will be here either Saturday or Sunday. My reports are done, all beautifully typed by the public stenographer, and today I called Mr. Samuelson so that Mr. Burleigh would know where to locate me.

I purchased two pounds of "finger grapes" which I don't believe you've ever seen – they don't travel well. Anyway, they're green with brown spots and about two inches long. Love, Margean

---

October 7, 1948
From Hotel Sacramento, Sacramento, California

Dear Ones: Today Gibson starts running some of our big, new ACFs. To tell the truth, I wouldn't care to ride in one of them. The roads and bridges are too narrow. The present Clippers were plenty large enough, but the company will wait until a couple of sides are dented in, or a bridge knocked down and the poor drivers blamed, to reconsider. Love, Margean

---

October 8, 1948
From Hotel Sacramento, Sacramento, California

Dear Ones: Went to Chico today seeing pear, walnut and almond orchards and spending time feeding pigeons —ugly birds!

The men are good and I have little work pending arrival of Mr. Burleigh. I envy him his Hawaii trip. Will try to wrangle some agreeable assignments—preferably someplace I've never been. Love, Margean

---

October 11, 1948
From Hotel Sacramento, Sacramento, California

Dear Ones: Mr. Burleigh arrived last night and this morning we are breakfasting. I'm nicely dressed and anticipating toast and tea.

9:30 a.m. Breakfasted. He insisted on some vitamin A for my cold.

3:00 p.m. Waiting for Reno instructions, while my expense account goes on and on! It has rained all day.

5:00 p.m. To Winnemucca, Nevada. Love, Margean

226

October 12, 1948
From Hotel Humboldt, Winnemucca, Nevada

Dear Ones: After staying up all last night, I have a day and a half to recuperate. I have found a nice, young dentist to fix my two cavities. After my dental trials, I shall take a walk and my camera into the hills. On the mountainside above this town, there's a huge "W" waiting to be snapped.

This backtracking to Winnemucca is to catch some of Mr. Samuelson's bad boys. I really had one last night, taking me an hour to sketch out what he did wrong and put it into language he could understand. It all boiled down to "squaring" curves, which puts a terrific strain on wheels, tires, and steering rods—especially the latter. Someday he's going to "square" a curve in Reno Canyon, break the rods, float off, and sprout wings—along with 37 passengers. I don't intend to be one! I will probably have to sign statements on that report.

Today is nice here in Nevada. Nights are sharp though and we hit light snow on Donner Pass last night. Am feeling much better, only an explosive sneeze every now and then. Have some beautiful peaches for my "supper." Love, Margean

October 14, 1948
From Hotel Sacramento, Sacramento, California

Dear Ones: Hell is popping. I have four very bad reports with the prospect of another tonight. After talking them over with Mr. Samuelson, we decided that hearings were in order so I called Mr. Burleigh. He said that they would send the first hearing through with my affidavited reports and, if the dismissals were contested, I would personally appear at the second hearings. I am confidently looking forward to appearing but nothing will happen before the month's end. Shades of the St. Ignace affair, but no drinking involved this time.

Nearly died from fatigue today after last night's work and the strain of trying to find Mr. Burleigh. And now that everything's taken care of —reports written and requests off—with evening here I am unable to sleep. A heck of a state of affairs, as I have to rise at 3:00 a.m. to catch a 4:00 bus!

Met Mr. Samuelson today. One swell fellow. He's an ex-driver who once sued the union for trying to get rid of him and is now a superintendent of some stature with title of Assistant to the President. Before coming here he had charge of our Muscatine, Davenport, and Clinton Line. Not over 35, he's sharp as a tack and has a reputation for toughness and not taking any nonsense from his men. This is the main reason he was given charge of this bunch of hoodlums who boast of chasing off eight superintendents before him. He doesn't intend to run. Married, a six-year-old and a new baby. Knows most of the people I do. I was sent out here to help him.

Received the welcome news that Mr. Kaiser, former assistant to Mr. Watson at Pittsburgh, has been fired. I detested the man—smart aleck! Love, Margean.

October 16, 1948
From Hotel Hayward, Los Angeles, California

Dear Ones: Recuperating again from a night's work—however, it was undertaken with a full quota of sleep. Drivers smoked like mad and drove like hell—of course, it was at night and we met just trucks.

Incidentally, my Friday morning run netted me a beautiful hearing plus an additional witness if we can trace him. It took me three hours to write that report. This driver beat me before on a hearing but he won't wiggle out of this.

In all, we're gunning for five dismissals. Two are top union men, one this driver—and two are the boys that make such a drunken, immoral place out of our Battle Mountain driver terminal. After writing the reports, I ran up a $4.90 telephone bill to Mr. Samuelson during which we laid down our campaign and strategy. I've got my fingers crossed that I might appear at the hearings—just to see the looks on their faces In four of the reports I sat in back of the drivers, and in one report beside the driver in the "co-pilot" seat.

Can't describe much of the scenery, riding at night as I have. This morning, however, we came over the coastal range between Bakersfield and Los Angeles. Last spring the "hills" were carpeted with flowers— today they were brown and dead waiting for fall rains. Everywhere there are signs "Smoking Prohibited on This Road." Love, Margean.

October 22, 1948
From Cosmopolitan Hotel, Denver, Colorado

Dear Ones: Had a nice trip in on the 20th even if I had to stay awake all night. We had a nice load. I made friends with a devoted elderly couple and listened to her operations and cure from cancer. Then, there was the little four-year-old boy that didn't like me. In the Salt Lake City station he fell off his mother's suitcase and I offended his dignity by smiling—after that, every time we looked at each other, he scowled.

Saw one deer on the run (as the season is in full swing), two skunks, a porcupine and innumerable rabbits. There's something awe-inspiring about coming over these mountains at night. They cast shadows in the moonlight and remind me of evil spirits, brooding and so permanent.

The 20th my affidavits were here but I had to have photostats made, a job that took almost all day. Mr. Hensel got back in town about 5:30 and we bribed a notary to wait until we got there. Mr. Hensel's very enthusiastic about the reports and thinks we can get four dismissals out of the five. We gabbed quite a while. One driver I'd inspected four times (and signed affidavits for) has been fired out of Davenport, Iowa—also one other driver from there that I can't place.

Called Mr. Neil today and planned out five days' work that will take me over the pass four more times. Then, from the way Mr. Hensel spoke, there's work north of Cheyenne for me—anything up there will take a week because of the distances involved! It will be way past the middle of November before I'll be home—maybe Thanksgiving. Love, Margean.

———•———

October 26, 1948
From Hotel Harbor, Steamboat Springs, Colorado.

Dear Ones: Received your letter about the wedding (how I wish I could have been there), and that hair-raising clipping about Flint Trolley Coach!

FTC went out, I believe, on September 18, anyway while I was home on vacation. Due to newspaper publication of Kearn's background (the red-headed Red sent from N.Y. headquarters to lead the strike), we have public opinion on our side – the big thing in a public utilities strike. The company refused to negotiate the strike (which is illegal because public utilities are not supposed to strike in Michigan) until the union sends Kearns back to New York. This I learned from Mr. Burleigh when we were in Sacramento.

This damn fire is just the thing this union and Kearns, who refused to go back, would pull. They may fire the bunch—that's what Southern Trailways did. The clipping you sent said 48 FTC buses were damaged

—that's more than half because I think we were running 121 schedules with about 85 buses. Counting up, it's been seven weeks since the strike started and none of those men can afford that. I'm afraid they've cut their throats because nothing could make Mr. Burleigh angrier than this kind of retaliation. Anyway, it was too timely and damaging to be accidental.

As yet no news of a hearing. I'll find out how much has been done when I talk to Mr. Hensel on the 28th. Mr. Samuelson described the procedure for me. The driver is called in. Mr. Samuelson is present plus miscellaneous company people, a union representative and a notary public to make a transcript of the proceedings. The driver is given the trip data from the report and sign-in records so that he can satisfy himself that he actually drove the run. He is asked to give his version of the run and whether he has any witnesses to bring forth: here, he usually says "no," and when he has, he can't back out. Then my version of the run is read. The driver usually denies everything, especially any speed, loitering or smoking.

Anyway, the transcript and discipline are forwarded to Mr. James at Chicago. He can increase or decrease the punishment or discipline imposed: if the union protests, he can order a second hearing, especially if he considers my report airtight. That's where I come in. After that second hearing, at which I would appear, if all action is upheld the only recourse the driver has is to get the union to strike. This requires a vote of the entire line and, in the case of these men with their past records, I don't think they would get it. Interesting ramifications.

The reason I'm rambling on is because midnight is here and I must stay awake to catch a bus back into Denver—I have forty minutes to wait. The trip up here, even over the pass, was boring because there was no moon and I couldn't see anything. The trip back will be even harder unless the man is reckless or if he smokes. They usually are excellent on this mountainous run.

Am reading a highly recommended book: *Economics in One Lesson*. I find it ultra-conservative, interesting and hope to retain its wealth of information.

Did I ever tell you about the cartoon one of our drivers drew? He was called in on a report of mine in which he had smoked: he "fessed" up and took his $42 fine like a man. Anyway, he drew this cartoon of the hearing: Mr. Watson (now at Pittsburgh, but then of Chicago), about four other company representatives, and the notary were accurately portrayed lounging in their seats, all surrounded by heaping ashtrays. The driver was very small and on a three-legged stool in the middle. Everyone is pointing accusing fingers at him while puffing like mad. $42 for one cigarette. I don't know! Love, Margean.

November 1, 1948
From Hotel Dale, Holdrege, Nebraska

Dear Ones: All I hear over the radio is election. There's a basic fight going on all through the West—"wet" vs. "dry." Kansas and Nebraska are facing the same thing. As far as bars are concerned, Utah is remodeling in anticipation of prohibition repeal. Another thing I've noticed about campaigns out here is the stress on reclamation and irrigation not found at home. Lumping the comments and conversations I've heard, I'd predict an overwhelming Republican victory, but who isn't predicting that!

Do you know I made $567 in October with not a single day off—although to be fair, there were a few days I worked only three hours.

Expect to be in Evansville near the 10th. I should be finished there near the 20th, although I may stretch it nearer to Thanksgiving in order to have that day at home, then on the 28th head for Flint. That is, if the strike is settled, and I don't think they can hold out much longer.

Shall close to catch my bus—perennial occupation. Love, Margean.

November 3, 1948
From Hotel Castle, Omaha, Nebraska

Dear Ones: Yesterday I went up to Sioux City through Indian country. Had a terrible driver from the company's viewpoint. Most of the road was unpaved, but he drove 60 mph most of the way and took two unscheduled rest stops to listen to election returns. He wore his cap cocked on the back of his head, a no-no.

Wasn't that election hell? I got in at 12:00 a.m. and stayed up until 2:00 listening to returns, and then went to bed conceding the country to asses for four more years—well, conceding to elephants conjures up a whole other picture. Love, Margean.

November 4, 1948
From Hotel Castle, Omaha, Nebraska

Dear Ones: I believe all this night work lately has crabbed my disposition, particularly as far as my reports are concerned. Maybe it's not the night work but the drivers because I've been assigned the worst recently. Most have been examples of how not to drive and how not to be a driver. Sometimes I long for the hound dog days when there was a rotten apple now and then, but usually you could write a glowing "atta-boy" report that reflected the overall picture of what was going on.

I've devoured election results as reported here in Omaha. And, incidentally, who is this handsome, dark-horse Democrat, now governor of Michigan? There was a picture of him and his little bow-tie in the Omaha paper: he looks incongruous among all the white-haired doddering politicians on the page.

I got in at 7:30 a.m., wrote reports until 10:00, developed a case of writer's cramp and went to bed. When I awoke, it was pouring outside and had been all day and will probably continue all night—if it doesn't turn to snow. Maybe it's the gloom that is also affecting me. Love, Margean.

November 7, 1948
From Hotel Castle, Omaha, Nebraska

Dear Ones: Am recuperating from my trips and scare of yesterday. Leaving Omaha at 7:45 a.m., we picked up a driver about an hour later who was bound for Lincoln, his home terminal. He sat across from me behind the driver, and talked to the driver for most of the 25-mile trip. Because my hair was dirty, I had it braided into a knot at the back of my head, and, with my pearl earrings, probably looked very 1890-ish. At Holdredge I had a four hour layover, so I found a beauty shop, had my hair washed and emerged with a curly, teenish hairdo, quite unlike my former self. At 7:00 p.m. I caught my Omaha bus and got the seat right behind the driver. Imagine my horror, when at 11:00 in Lincoln, we picked up the self-same driver—and he sat with me! I promptly curled up and "went to sleep", hoping he wouldn't wake to the fact that he'd seen me only that morning. He didn't.

My morning trip went off nicely. My driver had had difficulties his previous trip and was avoiding it this time by paying close attention to his mail. It seems he had forgotten to take off a bundle of newspapers which a newsboy at McCook usually received and sold. The boy showed up just as the bus with our driver's relief driver left. Our driver ran around the block hoping to stop it, but missed by a traffic light. Conscience stricken, he telephoned ahead to the next town 45 miles away and had the driver kick them off there. It was hunting season, so he had little difficulty in finding a ride over and he got the papers. It was about 8:00 p.m. when he called the boy's mother and told her he'd finally got the papers back and that he would buy any the boy couldn't sell. "Oh, that's all right," the boy's mother said, "The papers only cost him 20 cents." This is the heart-warming thing you like to hear about. Love, Margean.

November 12, 1948
From Vendome Hotel, Evansville, Indiana

Dear Ones: The end of a boring day. After a supper of cheesecake and coffee, I wrote up my reports and am now loafing. Last night I typed a four-page letter to the Glatzs and promised to drop down to Detroit to see them the next time I got to Flint.

Evansville, having been chosen as a representative city, is in the midst of a national traffic survey. You're liable to be buttonholed on any corner and asked what you think of the traffic situation—shades of my work in Flint. Here in Evansville, we are having difficulties—an outside outfit is trying to muscle in on Mr. Burleigh's city franchise and there are hearings and lawsuits in the air.

After dinner I saw "Julia Misbehaves," a frothy comedy that passed the time, then I listened to mysteries over the radio and embroidered. Love, Margean.

November 17, 1948
From Hotel Vendome, Evansville, Indiana

Dear Ones: Received your letter and the coat lining. Naturally, now prepared for icy blasts, it has turned off warm and my lining hangs unused —really if I had a sweater, the coat would be unnecessary too. Yesterday, however, it poured always seeming to rain harder whenever I got off a bus.

I haven't been into Pete's office for over two months. He sometimes blows a fuse when I am ordered somewhere without his knowledge—I hasten to add that he doesn't blow a fuse _at_ me just _to_ me! From which I have concluded that he likes to know where I'll be. Love, Margean.

November 18, 1948
From Vendome Hotel, Evansville, Indiana

Dear Ones: Received the cookies today, each a treasure from home, and have been rationing them out to myself when what I really want to do is just sit and pig-out. I have a sneaking suspicion that the chambermaid sampled them.

She and I are mortal foes circling at arms' length, but she has me at her mercy. It all started the day I moved in. I told her that I would be out by 8:00 each morning and could she please make up my room before I returned at 10:30. She begrudgingly agreed Most chambermaids would be tickled pink to have one sure room to begin on because they usually have to wait for checkouts in order to begin. But my maid must have another routine. Anyway, when I get back at 10:30 the room is either unmade or in the process of being made up. Then I either have to sit in an unmade room or wait to type my reports after she has leisurely finished my room. In both cases, I glower and steam.

What weather. Yesterday it started nice and stayed nice until 2:00 when it began to pour. That was just the time I started back out to work. I tied my plastic scarf around my head and pulled my coat hood over that—a real weird effect. My last trip was out to Heidelback Road where I usually wait in a drugstore and sip coffee until the next bus comes around twenty minutes later. Yesterday there was a tobacco salesman in the grocery adjoining the drugstore. He came in to check supplies and hand out sample packs of Camels—handed them out, that is, to everyone but me. He started out, then came back and gave me one—"Thought you were a Nun," he said.

This morning the temperature dropped 25 degrees between 8:00 and 10:30, bringing a horrible burst of wind. We all walked at angles against, or with the wind, or else chased hats. I never saw hats rolling down the streets before!

According to the radio and newspapers, I got out of the west just in time. Bus schedules were cancelled out of Denver. Buses were marooned on the highway between there and Omaha.

Reminisced this morning about the wonderful run I had last month between Eli and Salt Lake City, the one where the driver's wife was on and we had a wonderful songfest. Love, Margean.

December 8, 1948
From MaCaskill Hotel, Shreveport, Louisiana

Dear Ones: You get a phone call and it begins. This will be the "Saga of Margean" that brought me from Flint to here.

There was no difficulty getting my ticket. The girl at the Durant Hotel quickly fixed me up and confirmed my reservation out of Chicago. This was done on my way back from the bus station where I'd send you the incidentals I couldn't carry. After puttering around, packing and finishing up Flint Trolley Coach operations, I had supper and, to celebrate, I had a glass of Port wine with my meal—I felt very cosmopolitan!

After supper, I was moping around my room—digesting and listening to the radio—when Mr. Giese, manager at Flint Trolley Coach, called. He had a new and novel way his boys had thought up to steal money but I had to tell him that my checking on it would have to be postponed until next time. Then, like always, we launched into the bus business. He was particularly anxious to hear my comparison of Evansville and Flint lines and, after a fifteen-minute dissertation on this, we switched to unions.

This week the Transport Workers of America, of which our FTC union is a member, kicked out the communist element and we are hoping for a slight reprieve in union aggressiveness. From that, we compared the differences of the two cities regarding faction unions laying down the line that bus drivers should follow. That is, Flint, the radical CIO town, supporting and/or dictating the bus union's policy towards the company, contrasted to Evansville, a town that, to the accompaniment of physical and verbal bloodshed, is switching from CIO to AFL, and hence hasn't time to meddle with the Amalgamated Union to which our boys belong. The chief visible difference is that FTC drivers pull some kind of strike every year and ECL drivers pulled their first (lasting one day) in fifteen years last September, surprising even the drivers. But enough of our rambling chat with two crying children and his wife doing dishes in the background.

By then it was 9:00 p.m., and I had to get to the Durand Hotel to catch the transport service to the airport, six long, cold miles out. The plane, a DC 3, was OT ("on time" to you non-transportation people) but there was lots of express and luggage and we were ten minutes late out. I was the only one on at Flint and there were seven of us in all, not counting the hostess, the handsome co-pilot or the fat captain. We took off amidst ragged clouds, intermittent snow and gusty winds. These winds lasted into Chicago making us all half-ill from the constant drops into air pockets. At Lansing, Grand Rapids and Muskegon, we got rid of all but three passengers.

Hitting Chicago, everything went like clockwork and I soon found myself aboard a Chicago & Southern DC 3. The rest of the ride was the smoothest thing I've ever encountered, only the motors' sound reminded you that you were in motion. Both times I sat in the second seat behind the right wing. I could see the sparks stream by, the blink of the light at the wing's end, the wing-flaps, the propeller. Seats were comfortable but no more so than our bus seats. The seatbelt was no bother but there was no need for it after leaving Chicago: out of Flint, though, sometimes the seat would sink out from under you, a most eerie sensation! At 1:30 a.m. and 3:30, I had hot chocolate; then about 6:45, I had tomato juice, milk and a nut roll. They gave out gum, matches, and some airline labels that I might stick on my luggage. The planes were only about 55 degrees so I had a blanket wrapped around me. The lavatory was even smaller than the one on our deluxe bus. Our second and third captains and co-pilots were very handsome, but no better than my beloved bus drivers. They loitered too.

After leaving Chicago, we cruised at 176 mph, landing at St. Louis, Memphis (where we changed crew), and at Little Rock before hitting Shrieveport. We were nine minutes sharp into my destination.

When I checked into the hotel a convention had displaced me, but I made arrangements about my money order and mail. I'm staying at the McCaskill Hotel next to the station—much handier, but a dump.

Everyone was shivering in the 60 temperature, but I detached the lining of my coat. It got up to 80 in the afternoon.

Worked nineteen and a half hours. Dead! Love, Margean.

December 11, 1948
From Bentley Hotel, Alexandria, Louisiana

Dear Ones: Have been terribly busy trying to do a good job—and I guess I have because Mr. Burleigh didn't say there was anything omitted or wrong with the reports when he called. It's meant working fifteen-hour days, but I have a humdinger of a report each day. I will be on this line another week, leaving tomorrow for New Orleans, from there to Jackson, Mississippi, and winding up in Memphis on the 17th when I contact Mr. Burleigh again.

After the amount of swaddling I underwent in Flint, the change to light topcoat has been most pleasant and, at times, even unnecessary. Today, however, the wind blew—a mild wind with promises of rain tomorrow.

Am having difficulties getting my Christmas cards addressed and the remainder of my shopping done. Incidentally, in the letter from Harry Glatz I learned that he had applied to Mr. Burleigh for inspection or investigative work—he was told that there was no opening. Pretty sure of me, aren't they? Love, Margean.

———

December 13, 1948
From Hotel Heidelberg, Jackson, Mississippi

Dear Ones: I read the following: "Place your stamp of individuality on everything you do; use your own distinctive seal which cannot be imitated; make your every action a part of your personality. Avoid imitation as if it were the plague; avoid pretense as if it were a deadly sin. In this way you will satisfy yourself, the most important person in the world for you to please. The person who fails to do work which gives him satisfaction, fails." Pretty profound, huh?

Yesterday was a long, long, long day with twelve hours on the road between Shreveport and New Orleans: not that the distance was so great—300 miles, plus—but that there were so many highway stops. To top off the general fatigue, the weather was blistering and I sweated from every pore. Today was even worse: a temperature near 85 and a fine mist—humidity pouring all over the place.

And what did I see? Shacks, shacks, shacks—with mangy hound dogs peppering the yards. At every crossroad a family got on or off. Poorly spaced teeth—scabby kids—dirty big toes—odors! I tell you, <u>there will be a revolution someday</u>. People will not continue to live like this!

With no fences, poor, skinny, wide-horned scrub-cattle, razorback hogs and mules run at large along the roadside. When I tell people that cows are $250-plus up North, they laugh down here, they range between $35 and $75.

Lumber yards and sawmills; lots of slash pine. No fields: just cleared patches averaging eight acres-maybe cotton. Further south, some sugarcane. Mere subsistence.

Came across Lake Pontchartrain this morning on a bridge miles long with fishermen and crabbers alongside. Ditto cranes and ducks Miles and miles of marsh. Water all over the place. Mist in the air. I'm all wet. Love, Margean.

———

December 17, 1948
From Hotel Heidelberg, Jackson, Mississippi

Dear Ones: I called Mr. Burleigh today and this is the setup I got. I shall arrive in Flint on the 20th and will make out my summary report that day. I shall be home the night of the 23rd from Flint and will be home until the 27th; then another week in Flint and then California, here I come.

Have been super-humanly busy doing a super-human good job! Anyway, one that has kept me busy about twelve hours a day. Worth a bonus.

Have finished the last of my Christmas shopping and my Christmas cards. I splurged 35 cents on ones for Mr. Burleigh and Pete.

Have been enjoying unseasonable weather of 80 degrees plus for the last five days. A humid, misty, constant rain has accompanied this— everything steams. I hear you're having freezing, icy weather and I shall probably run into it out of St. Louis: until then, I'll leave the lining out of my coat. Mr. Burleigh's vitamin A pills have been doing wonders in keeping the cold bug away (fingers crossed).

Spent five hours of the 15th in a one-horse town of 2,000 with dirt streets. Stores thoughtfully provide planks for loafers to use and one has to sidestep globs of tobacco and spit. I created quite a sensation and I'm afraid the driver wondered just what on earth I was doing there. Love, Margean.

1949

The Cold, Cold Winter of '49

I Turn 21

Downsizing in Chicago

Of Drunks and Cheesecake

Slot Machine King

I Dress in Shifts

I Quit

January 4, 1949
From Hotel York, St. Louis, Missouri

Dear Ones: At last I'm on my way for that long-planned southern trip to the West coast with permission to stay away as long as I like. I was due out of Chicago at 1:30 a.m. last night, but it was raining so and the temperature was steadily dropping by the hour, that it scared me into leaving at 9:00. It was a good thing for the 1:30 run was cancelled.

There was an old bum on my first driver's run. He got out to get a glass of water and when he came back with it the driver jumped him for a bottle of whiskey. He got it, and was going to close the incident when he noticed that the seal was unbroken. Back he went and hoisted an open bottle. It was really funny to see him go over that man—practiced.

It's raining badly, which disappoints me no end because I've things to buy. We're rearranging my reporting so I have to purchase carbon paper and an indelible Eversharp.

Mr. Burleigh is in Lansing so I didn't see him, but heard all about Betty's wedding and bout with strep. Heard all about Ilo's new home. Pete was in a jovial mood, even though he gave a man <u>hell</u> over the phone. If he ever talked to me like that I'd quit—but then I do my work. Joked, grilled me about Greyhound in Flint (and I wasn't even working on that, luckily I'd been observant), and sent me on my way.

I was sick yesterday with what felt like intestinal flu with high temperature but without nose or throat complications. As soon as I hit Chicago, I stuffed with vitamin A and aspirin and went to bed. When the fever suddenly lifted, I got to thinking about the road conditions, got up and left. Love, Margean.

January 6, 1949
From Hotel Texas, Fort Worth, Texas

Dear Ones: Have been enjoying a dull, routine trip thus far. It gets warmer and warmer as I get south, today a real scorcher of 60 degrees. I expect El Paso to sizzle. One woman, heading for Los Angeles, was laden with two coats, a blanket and a pillow—it made me sweat to look at her.

My seat partner boarded at Oklahoma City. There to see her off were a man, his wife and her grandchild. The man, her son-in-law, was in a uniform and all the servicemen on board were stymied trying to think what he was: because she sat with me, I found out. He is the son of Equador's president and is a military attaché in this country. When he was a boy, he

240

was sent to Oklahoma A&M for his education. There her daughter met and married him. He was a handsome, severe-looking man, who I thought was near 37 but was actually 51.

Anyway, this woman lives on a rocket research station in California's Mojave Desert. This has grown from nothing—absolutely nothing—into a city of 28,000. It has all housing, air conditioning, stove, refrigerator, heat and electricity furnished. Free camp transportation, swimming pool, riding academy, schools, hospital, movies (12 cents), stores, all furnished by our tax dollar. All this, not to mention two $14,000,000 laboratories. Now these people deserve the best of everything. They are living in a VERY DANGEROUS AREA. Love, Margean.

January 10, 1949
From Luhrs Hotel, Phoenix, Arizona

Dear Ones: Went to the trailer park to see Mary yesterday; Lawrence was on the road. We had dinner with the Staffords and gossiped about home for five hours. Had chop suey, salad and ice cream and, later, Mary made fudge. They were real glad to see someone from home.

Am having terrifically good luck with the men and have successfully kept out of the handsome Casanova's way. One driver got a ticket, and will have worse trouble when my report comes through—I got witnesses' names. Love, Margean

---

January 11, 1949
From Hotel Hayward, Los Angeles, California

Dear Ones: I wouldn't believe it if it hadn't happened to me. I was snowbound for two hours yesterday evening going over Redland Pass. There was about eighteen inches of snow and a slick ice coating. We inched our way to the top where we were stalled while they untangled a tanker and a trailer-truck wreck to make a one-lane exit. It was six miles from the top where we were, to the wreck and we were backed up two lanes deep: you can imagine how long it took to get that lineup through the one lane. Oil was spilled all over at the wreck site and it was a wonder that there was no fire. It was the first time since 1922 that this pass had had snow.

It's a wonder that I haven't caught a cold, everyone coughing and sneezing in my area. Bless Mr. B. and his vitamin A. Love, Margean.

January 12, 1949
From Hotel Lenhart, Sacramento, California

Dear Ones: Last night was hell. If I hadn't seen it, I would never have believed it—snow, tons of wet, sticky snow impeded our progress all night. Leaving Los Angeles for San Francisco at 7:30 p.m., we had a blinding blizzard until 3:00 a.m. Only buses were allowed over Route 101, the Ridge highway, and our run was the last out of Los Angeles. We inched along.

When I got here, I ran into another storm! The Sacramento Hotel, filled with legislative members, plunked me into this hotel. I was walking in to register when a flock of drivers descended and walked out—the bunch my reports were going to fire. You guessed it—it was "hearing day." After settling in, I located Mr. Samuelson down on the third floor: "I'll be right up," he said. Then I got the lowdown.

After I left last fall, Mr. Burleigh and Mr. James decided they didn't want me to appear and they hired the Swanwick outfit, a large inspection company, to get some more information. Sammy said the company spent close to $3,500 for two and a half months' work. After piddlin' around all that time, they found exactly the same things wrong that I did—furthermore, Sammy said, their reports were trash compared to mine.

Swanwick's headman is here and Sammy showed him my reports. "How I'd like to have that fellow working for me!" he said. "Fellow, hell," Sammy said, "That's a young girl that's ridden hundreds of thousands of miles." "Wait till I see her," the guy said, "I'll offer her a job as supervisor." "Like hell, you will," Sammy said, "she's too good for you." Anyway, Sammy said the guy grabs my reports and went back into the room where his operators sat: "Here, look at this. This is what a girl who'd already ridden fifteen hours can do. Why can't you guys do the same for fifty minutes' work?" And on and on. Anyway, after the hearings this afternoon we're getting together so we can run over the wire recording of the hearing. Love, Margean.

January 14, 1949
From Hotel Lenhart, Sacramento, California

Dear Ones: Tomorrow I start on another jaunt with my Reno-San Francisco boys. You will remember that it was my previous trip with them that precipitated all the hustle and bustle with photostats. One driver is definitely getting the sack for a clear-cut case of cash-fare stealing—the

242

four others will have drastic action taken. Chicago seems to be backing Mr. Samuelson well, at least as well as they usually do—Mr. James, not Mr. Burleigh, seems to be calling these cards.

Evidently that Salt Lake accident is the start of much more of the same in every division. I've been telling them for eighteen months just who they should get rid of but they had to spend thousands of dollars to find out the truth of what I've been telling. This is mostly Mr. James fault —Mr. Burleigh, at least, trusts my judgment.

Since arriving here on the 12th I've done little work except for planning. It's a good thing, as I've been fighting a cold that tried to get started: thus far it hasn't secured a toehold except in the morning. Aspirin, vitamin A and plenty of rest have helped. Actually, I get more rest than I need: there have been so many drivers floating around the hotel that I've been apprehensive about meandering out. Never stare a bull in the face!

Twice when I've gone to the other hotel for my mail, my picture has been snapped by one of those sidewalk candid cameras. After developing, they are pretty good. Typically me—laden with luggage! Love, Margean

—·—

January 16, 1949
To Mr. Samuelson in Sacramento

Sammy, I'm writing the following on the driver's run in a personal letter. No copy will be sent to Chicago. Naturally, the material herein is for your background information and is not to be passed on to the drivers concerned.

My report is started at Oakland to throw the driver off-track but I actually boarded at the San Francisco American Buslines station and had the seat behind him. There was a probable garage employee on riding down to the Trailways depot. The driver's comments were: "There's a big change coming and I hope it's for the better. One side has to crack: I'm going to sit back, watch, keep my mouth shut and not stick my neck out. It's made a Christian out of me."

A deadhead [*a non-driving driver riding the bus*] boarded at the San Francisco Trailways depot bound for Reno. At Oakland a woman employed by the Capitol Touring Service (may be inaccurate) boarded, sitting with the deadhead in the co-pilot seat. She is well known to the drivers—not the usual "girlfriend" type—and had been on several of the Swanwick checked runs, especially those around New Years. She was on the pass-up ride. That driver is going to get a statement from her and if he is given any time off, the hearing will be appealed and this woman will be produced as his surprise witness. She holds that he would not pick up these cash fares in front of a station when the station was open and the agent had refused them tickets (possible source of trouble or drunk). You stated that the driver threw this in your face: his comment was "I think we stuck him there."

With the driver doing most of the talking, the following were mentioned. That it was a slovenly-handled, unfair, "childish" hearing. He specified that the charge was given on the hearing notice but the date of the occurrence causing the charge was not—thus drivers were unable to secure material witnesses: "that's why the whole thing was unfair and partial to the company." He objected to the holdups and delays in the hearings. Stressed the minor nature of the charges. (In the brief mention of another driver's case, they did not seem to support him and apparently assumed that he would be fired.)

Pertaining to Swanwick: the driver said "there were ten men and two women, a seedy bunch of characters—stool pigeons. I know every one of them, and if I ever catch one I'll bash his head in, male or female. They could tell right down to my rings how I was dressed, even that I wore brown shoes – how could they see that in the dark? But, they couldn't tell how I lit that cigarette. It's cost the company fifteen thousand to get them in here." He gloated over the length of time at company expense he had spent in Sacramento.

Rather ridiculed your handling of the hearing—especially the pass-up and the Greyhound business. Mention of you with a little yellow book in one hand—"I can make his face red every time."

The deadhead did not say much. He mentioned some caution-light incident and the driver advised him to run into you for following closely.

Aside from this bravado and bluster, I think you have them thoroughly worried. From the comments about pickups, I don't think they'll ever miss any again. There was a huddle of personnel at San Francisco, Oakland, Vallejo and Sacramento stations. There's hope that contract negotiations will prevent much drastic action: the attitude seemed to be, though, that this would settle things once and for all. They also believe this signals the start of similar "inquisitions" all over the system, with Salt Lake City and Los Angeles next.   Best, Margean

January 18, 1949
From Riverside Hotel, Reno, Nevada

Dear Ones: Excuse the long delay between letters, I was having one of those terrible adventures that give me ulcers and gray hair.

It all began on the 15th. That day I rode from San Francisco to Reno. A deadhead driver was on and sitting right behind the driver. I got my ears full of the hearing and the union's plans which will prove useful to Mr. Samuelson.

Sunday night I rode out to Lovelock to insure getting on the first section (I had it figured out that the deadhead driver would double). But, at Reno, my deadhead got on and deadheaded back into Sacramento. I went to "sleep" but fast and he never saw me, although I was right behind the driver. To top it off, that night (Monday) when we got into Sacramento, there he was again and rode back into Reno. This time I was three seats back and I don't think he saw me unless when I got off. Anyway, no one acted as though they knew I was on. I'll die if he's on again when I go back Wednesday night.

Sunday, I had Everett Merrill and his wife Agnes as my dinner guests here at the Riverside. You will remember he used to be superintendent at Reno before the office was abolished. Afterwards they drove me around Reno pointing out the ritzy houses and points of interest. Tonight Agnes is going to take me on a tour of the Clubs, as Everett will be out on his run. Love, Margean

---

January 20, 1949
From Riverside Hotel, Reno, Nevada

Dear Ones: Tuesday was such a wonderful day. About 12:30 p.m. Agnes Merrill called and asked me over for dinner. Naturally, I was delighted. They live in a nice duplex in the southwest part of town, the newer section, and the house was neat as a pin. It is guarded by a Pekinese that wears a bib! We, that is, Everett and I, gabbed bus business while he cut up the salad and Agnes did the important things. This done, we retired to the living room and gabbed some more over a drink. About 6:30, the delicious dinner was ready: venison in wine, mashed potatoes and gravy, corn, Everett's salad, mint pudding and cake. Then my job—dishes, at which I am an expert.

I do believe I found out their whole lives' history. They're your ages, Everett 46 and Agnes 40. Born and raised around Peoria, Illinois, where they have two farms her father left and half interest in one from Everett's family. Naturally, we talked farming, but they wouldn't go back to live unless desperate. They're completely sold on Reno after five years here.

Then came the war. At that time they lived in Salt Lake City and had built their own home. Everett was drafted at 38, they sold the house, he caught some strep infection and was discharged within ninety days. That's when the company sent them to Reno. They're planning to build again now. Something they can rent, for you can get all the divorcees you want at $35 a week.

Personally, I've never seen such a change in a man since they abolished the office and he went back to driving. He was one of those terribly conscientious persons and everyone took advantage of him. Now, Agnes says, he doesn't have a worry and can sleep and eat again. He has fifteen years' seniority and, with his record as a company man, has a job for as long as he wants. I've ridden with him twice and he's the only driver I've ever been with that can run a schedule in scheduled running time—does a beautiful job, too.

No kids, just the dog, which has quite a history having been out on the desert for two days after a wreck.

About 9:00, Agnes and I let Everett go to bed while we set out to show me the sights—the bar with 2,140 silver dollars at Harrolds Club—the simulated thunder storm—the floor show at the Mapes Hotel. We got 50 cents worth of nickels and played the slot machines: I won $2.00. Then we watched them shoot craps and play faro. Next, we played Bingo. On Agnes' first card she won $10. She split with me and we didn't win another thing. I got home at 1:30 after a wonderful evening. In the morning I went to the florist, ordered some carnations sent and left town at 10:30 that night.

All day it had snowed and I was more than a little ill at ease about Donner Pass, but with chains it was easy and beautiful. The snow had been wet and all the firs in the pass were weighted down, telephone wires were wreathed and cars were buried in the four and a half feet of snow there.

A drunk woman on the bus got mad at the driver, cussing him up one side and down the other and, when her boyfriend tried to shut her up, she started in on him and, when I snickered, she started in on me. The driver put her off at Baxters after getting all our signatures that she was drunk. Love, Margean

———

246

January 22, 1949
From Hotel Hayward, Los Angeles, California

Dear Ones: The company could have saved $3,600 if they had let me appear at the hearings based on my reports. Now this time I get two reports with dismissal material in them: the question is what action will they take. One report is a dead give-away as to my identity, as I was the only one who could have possibly secured the information. Spent all morning drinking coffee with Mr. Samuelson and plotting strategy.

I've been fighting a cold for two weeks now, but Kleenex and I have it licked. All my night-work has taken my appetite away but the scales still report 115 pounds and I have five nights' work staring me in the face.

From all the weather reports I hear, you folks must be having a terrible winter. Love, Margean

---

January 25, 1949
From Hotel Roberts, Provo, Utah

Dear Ones: Have just finished a long (20-hour), cold (-20), snowy ride from Los Angeles to Provo. It was a boring trip, especially when the supper stop didn't have any supper and we had to dine on soup and crackers. I was thankful for a package of cough drops to eat. My cold is practically over.

My ears were numb from walking three and a half blocks to breakfast. Your breath freezes, falls to the ground and breaks in chunks. Really, though, frost is flying all over and everything snaps under foot. One's hairline actually freezes!

Drifts! Cars buried deep! Parking meters covered! But I hear this is nothing compared to conditions further east. Salt Lake City is still shut off from eastern bus travel. Love, Margean

---

January 28, 1949
From Hotel San Diego, San Diego, California

Dear Ones: After surviving the official temperature of -25 on the night of the 25th, I was ready for anything. But on the 26th, I left below zero and rode into spring. In fact, grass is turning green, especially in San Diego.

I'm running short of funds: those unplanned five-day Reno trips depleted my funds drastically. I shall arrive at the Wm. Len Hotel, Memphis, on February 4th. Please telegraph $200 to arrive there on that date. Also, please airmail any mail that may have accumulated. Incidentally, I'll have $1000-plus waiting for me when I get home. Love, Margean

---

February 1, 1949
From Sanger Hotel, Dallas, Texas

Dear Ones: I wish I hadn't missed those two letters—I wanted so badly to hear about the weather you'd been having, for weather was one thing I had plenty of on this trip (all the way from coatless to -25). I can imagine that you were snowed in at least once.

I will be meandering up through Memphis, Kansas City, Galesburg, Illinois, and then home to Galesburg, Michigan. Greyhound is shut down completely, as is Continental-Santa Fe, and they are sending all their passengers to us—we evidently get through somehow. Tonight I find out how! Love, Margean

---

February 4, 1949
From Twickenham Hotel, Huntsville, Alabama

Dear Ones: Yesterday I had a wild and wooly ride. Leaving Joplin after midnight, the rain turned to ice on the road and we slipped, slid and crawled into St. Louis. And cold! I froze more with that 33 degrees than in the –25 at Provo. Right in front, with the heater blowing on me, I couldn't feel my feet!

It's now 9:00 a.m. and I'm in Hoxie, Arkansas, waiting for the 10:30 into Memphis. Leaving St. Louis at 2:00 a.m. I was glad to see just plain old rain.

It's a good thing the houses are built on stilts and the roads on levees for whole stretches of the country are inundated. Lord knows what the cattle do.

I pray the money order is in Memphis: I'm so flat broke I can't get out until it comes. As I said, this has been a very expensive trip. Owing to the number of night runs, my food bill has been higher than ordinary because I'd usually snatch something at rest stops to keep awake. Just two more weeks on the road. When all my trip checks come through I'll be rich. I'm $200 to the good in January. Didn't have time for anything but

248

trip expenses. Then there's that backlog of checks back to November 16th, so I'll be able to replenish my sagging bank account.

I'm thoroughly tired of my two dresses, besides which, they're dirty. When I get to Huntsville I'll have them cleaned again. My fur coat has taken a beating but it has kept me warm.

American contract negotiations are on. They're asking 6.5 cents a mile but I doubt if they'll get more than 6.35 cents, especially with times what they are. Our business has slumped and I hope they ask me why— well, they usually do. I have a few answers from this last jaunt. Last week the winter furloughs started. My buses were filled with deadheads and their gripes—a bad time, in my estimation, for contract talks on the men's part. Burlington settled for 6 cents, their old rate with some company concessions.

Hoxie, Arkansas, is a one-side of the highway town of about 500 people. I'm in the town's combination café taxi-stand bus station, the object of avid curiosity and speculation which I'm doing my best to ignore. Had some bacon and eggs, terrible, also some coffee, terrible.

I'm getting north and home through a lot of transfer shenanigans in Iowa and Galesburg, Illinois. If I get "hot" anywhere, I'll just shift onto Santa Fe. Thank heavens Chicago lets me figure how, and when, and with whom to get where, if you know what I mean. Love, Margean

———

February 7, 1949
From Twickenham Hotel, Huntsville, Alabama

Dear Ones: I got here on Saturday, coming in with an audit of 67, including kids, on the bus. Talk about hick towns: everybody was in town and meeting everyone else. One could hardly maneuver on the sidewalks or in the stores. The men lounged against storefronts and spit tobacco juice while the women gossiped and got in my way. Cars were racing up and down under my window until almost dawn. Sunday morning calm brought church chimes and bells.

All Alabama and a good share of Arkansas is under water – cornstalks and cotton float, houses are isolated by wide moats, there's mud, mud, mud everywhere—but yellow daffodils are out.

I don't know what's to happen to this area's economy. Last year's '48 cotton crop, the most extensive in the South's history, brought almost depression prices. Prospects for this year are even lower. You ought to hear and read the wails about Truman's 75-cent minimum wage promise. Will put the South's lumber industry in the red, they say.

Lucky to get out of the West when I did. Yesterday there was only one road, from the south, open into Reno. I bet Donner Pass is full. I hope the roads stay clear north and east of Kansas so I can get home as planned. Love, Margean

<hr>

February 9, 1949
From Wm. Len Hotel, Memphis, Tennessee

Dear Ones: It's a good thing I haven't had to work much for the last four or five days. Tuesday, out of the blue, I came down with a tough cold. I double-dosed all my pills and went to bed, hoping I would improve. I sneezed, gasped and hacked from Huntsville to Memphis last night keeping everyone awake. This morning I have laryngitis, usually the last stage before getting better. As soon as this is posted, me, my book and my radio go to bed to spend a quiet day.

It rained coming up last night. I have hit all kinds of weather in this six-week jaunt, from -25 to +60; from sunshine to rain, snow, ice and suspended frost. These drastic changes probably had lots to do with my cold. Love, Margean

<hr>

February 9, 1949
To me from P.C. Johnson, Chicago, Illinois

Miss Worst: We have your schedule for the week of February 9-16 and would like to have you make a change in same as follows:

When leaving Springfield for Kansas City, arrange to go direct from Kansas City to Davenport, Iowa, without any stops en route. On your arrival at Davenport, we would like to have you ride the local operations of <u>Muscatine, Davenport and Clinton Buslines</u>, which operates between these points and give us a complete check after several days work on this operation. Towards the latter part of your ride on this operation, we would like to have you pick up conversation with the drivers, if possible, and question them as to how they like their work, how things are going. You might also indicate that you are a friend of Mr. Samuelson, who was formerly in charge of that operation, and try to ascertain how the drivers like their new supervisor, Mr. Davis.

I am certain that you will know how to handle this matter as outlined above, but if there is any question in your mind with respect to same, please phone me from Springfield on Friday, February 11, so that I can give you final verbal instructions.

This is an important assignment and I want you to handle same as I have outlined it, so do not hesitate to call me if there is any question in your mind.

In the event you do not feel it necessary to phone me for confirmation of the above instructions, please wire me so that I will be certain you have received these instructions.

P.C. Johnson (*Handwritten*) Suggest you phone me Friday regardless.

———

February 11, 1949
From Colonial Hotel, Springfield, Missouri

Dear Ones: Didn't I write that the only two reasons I wouldn't be home on the 16th would be either weather or God (pardon, the office). Upon arriving here at Springfield, the hotel clerk handed me a big, official-looking envelope, plastered with special deliveries, containing a wonderful "important" assignment.

I am to scoot up to Davenport, Iowa, and find out what the drivers of Muscatine-Davenport-Clinton, a line we own, think of their boss, Mr. Davis. Mr. Samuelson was their former boss. I just love these cozy little assignments that require my talking to the drivers! Anyway it looks like I may be home on the 19th or 20th, but, as I have to stop in Chicago first, there's nothing sure.

As per the letter, I called Chicago and received a reiteration of instructions from Pete and the news that they're sending me an affidavit to sign (probably someone from my Reno trip), and the most welcome news that our franchise went through. Hurray!

My cold, despite dosing and repeated application of bed, remains with me. Last night, I grabbed a front seat by, and on top of, the heaters. I sneezed, coughed and sniffled for three hours and tried to make one small coat cover me. Finally, the compassionate driver lent me his coat. This I put on, wrapped my fur coat about my legs, and finally got warm and my voice back. Love, Margean

———

February 12, 1949
From Delmonico Hotel, Shenandoah, Iowa

Dear Ones: I don't know what made me go to the Pickwick in Kansas City and ask for mail, for I'd changed my itinerary and didn't stop there. Anyway, I received your most welcome letter with all its news of weddings and friends. No, I didn't get the letter containing the Glatz, Jr. announcement and I hope the hotel forwards it home.

Have been looking over the reports of January and this month. So many bad ones—I wish I would be sent on some "atta-boy" runs.

In sixteen days, I'll be 21 – can get a liquor card. Will be a "millionaire" when I hit Chicago! Love, Margean

———

February 14, 1949
From Hotel Blackhawk, Davenport, Iowa

Dear Ones: Gee, it was swell to hear your ever-lovin' voices last night! Do you realize, when I wind up on the 18th, I will have spent 47 days on the road without a day off—almost seven weeks! Had a lot of fun, though, and several days I didn't "work" too hard.

My first ride on MD&C today was fruitful with exactly the sort of information I was looking for. In a not too discreet way they led me to presuppose that Mr. Davis, superintendent, is none too popular. It was really very FBI-ish the way I wormed the conversation around to include what I wanted but I have qualms about pushing the matter further. Shall "commute" with this driver the next few days and try to soften him up through constant association. As I told you, Mr. Samuelson was the former superintendent here—how the drivers liked him.

Safely back in Davenport, thank goodness! There's an inch of sleet on the roads, and we ran from Muscatine here by stopping every mile or so to scrape off the windshield. Great driving. I hope runs are cancelled tomorrow. Love, Margean

———

February 18, 1949
Summary of Muscatine—Davenport—Clinton Assignment

The following summary and impressions were secured from four MD&C drivers. Separate reports were submitted on the individual conversations and on individual operation of the runs.

Drivers unfavorably compare Davis' handling of MDC with that of Samuelson: and, especially, do they unfavorably compare their handling of drivers. Davis, according to one driver, is unsure of himself, inconsistent; his discipline fluctuates and drivers never know what to expect from day to day. He does not have the knack of disciplining without making his drivers angry—as one driver put it, "When he gives you a bawling out, you're mad at him for life." Nor does Davis give any oral appreciation when his men handle extra work. One driver mentioned that bus work takes a lot of cooperation and Davis makes you feel that you work under, not with, him, and, consequently, you are none too willing to go out of your way to help him out. None of the drivers went so far as to say Davis was inefficient, but, as I previously stated, he suffers by comparison with Samuelson.

No complaints were heard relative to their work as such. Those to whom I spoke liked the "commuter" nature of their passenger loads and liked driving. They would like a closer connection with Burlington operations, a connection that would enable them to bid Burlington runs, transfer their seniority onto Burlington or work the Burlington extra board. On the runs I rode, few driving faults were observed and passengers were handled in a friendly manner. Drivers knew most of their passenger load and rendered personal service that made a passenger enjoy riding.

February 22, 1949
From Congress Hotel, Chicago, Illinois

Dear Ones: Oh, what a time I had! They had cut that Chicago run the day before, so I hurriedly called the train station and the Chicago-bound was due in ten minutes. I made it!

Into the office where Pete is out of town and Mr. Burleigh wants me to go to Evansville, so there I go. Am to call him when I finish sometime around March 4th. Shall save some money. Didn't have much time to talk to him, as there was some conference this afternoon.

Next, I went to the tour office and bumped into Mr. Justice, Mr. James' assistant. Found that the three Reno drivers were fired so Mr. Samuelson's worst troubles are over. Incidentally, this makes Mr. Merrill top seniority man there. And, yes it was my report on the Reno driver, with his rehash to the deadhead, that got him. Sammy has only one real bad apple left.

To bed—dead! Love, Margean

February 26, 1949
From Vendome Hotel, Evansville, Indiana

Dear Ones: Has been like spring for the last two days and the lining
is out of my coat. Tomorrow, Sunday, I shall dress up in my suit and furs,
consume an expensive dinner in the hotel dining room, maybe take a few
runs, and go to a show. Everywhere on Main Street couples will be strolling
and window-shopping.

Last night I went to a theater that has all re-runs: "Stagecoach,"
starring John Wayne, was playing. I had always wanted to see it as it ranks
among the top two or three westerns.

While I've been here, I've scurried around in flats with my hair
flying. The hotel has been filled with basketball teams and it's been quite
embarrassing to have these gawky highschoolers whistling. Anyway, I
know the bus drivers never notice me.

Incidentally the day before I arrived, one of my boys was here driving
the Gene Autry charter. We've had it since it left Los Angeles about two
months ago and I've been playing tag with it at various places.

Haven't bought a thing. What with dentist bills and renting this
typewriter it eats up my trip money. Love, Margean

———

March 4, 1949
From Vendome Hotel, Evansville, Indiana

Dear Ones: Received my birthday gift this morning. Thanks so much,
the gloves fit perfectly. Grandma's dollar will buy a stickpin for my scarf
—shall write a thank you letter. Did I tell you I made a scarf? I was in
Sears and spotted a brilliant, light green silk remnant. I was able to get two
scarves from it that I painstakingly stitched by hand. One will be for my
lovely sister-in-law. Love, Margean

———

March 26, 1949
From Hotel Castle, Omaha, Nebraska

Dear Ones: After the staggering amount of riding Thursday and into
the wee hours of Friday, I proceeded to hibernate and sleep soundly for
fifteen hours. Today I'm all set to start again.

We've moved into our new Omaha station with its very attractive interior, however, I don't like the bus-lane setup. It reminds me of Lansing and the mess they have in getting buses out on time.

Back in Chicago the axe has fallen. A drastic purge! Betty is no longer there so Pete has to do his own work, and I don't know what he'll do when my work starts pouring in. Darrel Wilson is out—also H. Panish of the Tour Department. Those cuts are just the people I know personally. I wonder what kind of money problems there are! And really, just what is going on! Thank heavens (I think), I'm still under Mr. Burleigh's protective wing.

It was quite funny. Last night I caught this driver out of Burlington when I'd always ridden with him between Omaha and Des Moines. He asked me if I hadn't ridden with him before. I said "Yes," and told him about it. About a year ago I came through here from California with just a light coat and those thong sandals of mine. It was real cold and everyone was bundled up in fur and overshoes while I was freezing. On top of that, the heater didn't work well and I was starting a cold with sneezes. So he lent me his big sheepskin-lined coat and tucked under it I got my feet and me thawed: now isn't that the perfect kind of thing you like to hear about! Of course, he doesn't remember that I've ridden with him twice since and seen him innumerable times in the Omaha station. So much for memories. Love, Margean

———

March 31, 1949
From Wm. Len Hotel, Memphis, Tennessee

Dear Ones: What a difference 500 miles have made! Trees are all out, fruit trees are blossoming and spirea is in flower.

Yesterday I had to make a round trip to Corinth, about 125 miles southeast of here, and it poured all day. It started off by hailing but ran out of that a few miles south. In Corinth I got soaked. While coming home, there was a beautiful electric storm with horrible thunder. All the little streams were a turbulent, muddy brown and most were over their banks. The country is terribly flooded.

This afternoon I start for Dallas, an all-night jaunt. The Dallas-Texarkana portion of the trip will be entirely new with my first trip into Little Rock. It's been over two years since I've been in this area and I'll cut across three north-south routings I've taken on other assignments.

If everything goes the way I've planned, I'll call Mr. Morrow from here to find out whether there's anything else he wants done. If not, I have a feeling that Pete will telephone that Don Auld of Dallas wants to see me.

This reminds me that this noon I spotted one of our boys who, the last time I rode with him, worked out of Dallas. Then in February, I spotted him in Springfield. If he'd stop to think, he'd wonder why he keeps seeing my face—and I wonder why he wanders the lines. Love, Margean

———

April 4, 1949
From Wm. Len Hotel, Memphis, Tennessee

Dear Ones: Have received your welcome letters plus a special delivery from Pete. All he wanted to know was what to do with my accumulating checks and I replied to hold them. Now that he has no secretary, he has to handle all my affairs too; which, at the rate I've been going, requires a lot of detail work. It really makes me wonder what is going on back in Chicago—about the layoffs and the future of the company.

Have had nothing but horrible quandaries the last few days. First, there was the problem of scheduling myself back and forth between here and Dallas with Texarkana my hot spot. So far, so good.

The big problem has been securing American-issued fares. On the 2nd I deadheaded another company up to Ardmore, Oklahoma, three hours north of Dallas to secure tickets. Instead of giving me two OW-2 tickets, which I wouldn't have had to get reissued until I was in Texarkana, she gave me two OW-1 tickets that I had to have reissued at the American station in Dallas. Well, that was all right until I began to think later about how I was going to get a driver's punch on that second ticket, the one I wasn't riding on. I temporarily settled it by deciding that when he punched the first ticket and returned it, I would pencil the punch design onto the other ticket and snip it out with manicure scissors.

When the bus came in, lo and behold, it was the last American driver I'd ridden with on February 4th between Springfield and St. Louis, when I'd paddled his britches, figuratively speaking, for his handling on ice. But this handsome Casanova didn't know me and very gallantly told me to sit on the bus if I wished while they had dinner.

As I sat in the seat behind his, my mind reverted to my problem, when all the sudden I spied its solution. The driver had left his punch on the bus! I quickly got out my other ticket and punched it. When the driver loaded up, he punched my regular fare and I thought I was set.

256

In Dallas, I whipped myself into the station for my two re-issues that would take two or three minutes to make out, hoping that the unloading would hold my driver until I was through. But the agent was slow, and the driver tapped on the window, yelling for him to be sure to save him the ticket-tear—and here the agent was making out two tickets. The driver didn't see that then, and by the time he got into the station, the tickets were made out, I had them and the agent was getting ready to give him the tears of both tickets! (I hope you understand this complicated, technical transaction). I don't know what happened—if he tumbled right then or at all. But if I'd have been him, I'd have wondered (1) why I had two tickets when I was alone, (2) why they had consecutive numbers, and (3) how in h——— the second ticket got a punch mark!

Next morning, after all this slippery work, I boarded my Dallas bus at 5:20 a.m., all set to find out what happens to an American passenger between Dallas and Memphis. I found out plenty! (1) I had to have that ticket reissued twice more. (2) I got the runaround on my routing and spent two hours bounding over Arkansas' unpaved roads and wooden bridges instead of straight out as my ticket said (Continental thus acquiring about $3 more of my fare by doing this). And (3) I didn't get any time for breakfast, dinner or supper. Anyway, my final report is filling up rapidly and will look good in Chicago.

Tonight I try the same thing again from another angle and finish up here in Memphis on the 7th. I think that if Mr. Morrow doesn't want me back in Springfield, I'll scoot over to Don Auld in Dallas to tackle that assignment I don't want to do. Pete's going to write me later about this. Damn.

When will that grandchild walk! I keep showing people his picture and everyone agrees he's quite some baby! Love, Margean

———

April 12, 1949
From Sanger Hotel, Dallas, Texas

Dear Ones: Hello there! After three days of night work, I spent this evening in bed and slept hours. Have been run ragged to ride with four men and I caught them all by a roundtrip to Sweetwater and a roundtrip to Abilene.

Last night I spent the hours between 12:00 a.m. and 4:00 in the Abilene Greyhound station. It's amazing the number of persons that stay up. Policemen, cab drivers, street cleaners, traveling people, bus passengers —all trooped through the adjoining restaurant, all drank coffee or ate their fill of ham and eggs. After the distraction of drinking and watching people, the bus ride, lacking traffic or distractions, almost made me drop off. All in all, my four boys behaved themselves and drew routine reports with appropriate "atta-boys."

I don't expect to be home for six more weeks. Right now I am waiting for Don Auld to get back from Big Springs to see what else needs doing. I intend to stop over in Phoenix and run out to see Mary and Lawrence again.

Received the money: thanks so much—wasn't running out yet, but thought this would be an opportune time. Have purchased only a red flower, as it is the fashion this spring to load up with artificial posies. Looks exotic on my black!

Dallas is shivering in a cold wave of 70, really a relief after last week's 90. Tonight we have a total eclipse of the moon, within scope of my window, I hope. Love, Margean

---

April 14, 1949
From Hotel Hidalgo, Lordsburg, New Mexico

Dear Ones: Let me see if I can recall all the things that have happened. For instance, after finishing my assignment, I went to Dallas to wait for Mr. Auld's return from Big Springs to find out if there would be anything further he wanted. He got in about 7:30 and took me out for a shrimp dinner: naturally, we gabbed bus business.

Early on the morning of the 16th I plan to leave El Paso for Phoenix, where I have 36 hours off, and intend to get some walnuts so Mary can make another batch of fudge. This will be the first time, since leaving home on March 24th, that I'll have time to relax—and how better, than with old neighbors.

Deadheading into Lordsburg tonight we had a drunk on board. He finally became so obnoxious that the driver put him off with the assistance of two policemen and last seen he was being propelled down the street.

Then there was the gal I met while waiting for a late bus in Sweetwater to return to Fort Worth. She plunked herself into the co-pilot seat and before we reached Fort Worth the driver had her name and address.

I was seated in 2-A back of the driver and to one side of her. "Let me try on your shoe," she said to me: so I obligingly slipped off my pump and handed it to her. She hoisted her skirt above her rolled stocking, put the shoe on and waved the foot around to get the view from all angles. We —myself, the driver, and about six sailors and marines—were in a position to see a more than ample display. The marine sitting with me was quite disgusted: "It looks better on you," he said as she returned my shoe.

On one of these trips the bus was full and, at Weatherford, an old Granny boarded and had to sit on her suitcase. "I like little boys," she said to a cute three-year-old. "Do you suppose you could like me," one of our old Casanovas sighed.

Then a story from the night I got on in Abilene. For three-quarters of an hour before the bus came, the agent and I listened to a pompous bag of wind spin tall tales. The bus came and this pompous old ass elbowed his way past me, dropped his bag on my foot and beat me on the bus. I'd already negotiated with the woman in the front seat to sit with her, but he shoved his bag under the seat and told the lady, who was explaining that the seat was for me, "First come, first served." Everyone on the bus was thoroughly exasperated, especially me! "Are you from Texas?" I asked him. "Yes," he said. "I'd never have known it," I said, "Most Texans are gentlemen." "You tell him," said several voices, and the driver nearly split. We went along about an hour during which he filled the lady's ear with wind about the oil wells he owned. Finally, she could stand it no longer. "Do you mind standing up while I get another seat, I'm tired of listening to you talk," she said. Every one roared. Love, Margean

---

April 17, 1949
From Leurs Hotel, Phoenix, Arizona

Dear Ones: Am all black and blue. Yesterday I got off the Greyhound in Las Cruces, collected my bags and started up the steps to the ladies' room when the ankle I hurt last week turned on me and I went backward down two steps with my suitcases on top of me! About a dozen people hauled me up before I knew whether I was hurt or not: I wasn't, except I now ache all over and my ankle is swollen.

Pain or no pain, I hadn't been in Phoenix 45 minutes before I was out to Mary's. Everyone was home and I'm invited out today for Easter. Last night after hamburgers and strawberry sundaes, we rode around Camelback Mountain and smelled the orange blossoms. Any place, any time, you can smell them. Love, Margean

---

April 18, 1949
From Las Vegas, Nevada

Dear Ones: Was so horribly stiff from my fall that everyone laughed at me. My left shoulder blade, where I first hit, is a delicious concoction of blue, green and purple.

Had baked ham for Easter dinner—also homemade cake with inch-thick seven-minute frosting. Sat around, embroidered, walked over to a pottery lot and got some knickknacks that she'll deliver when they return to Galesburg.

I expect to be home the last week of May with Mary's family returning about a week before me. Let's have them over to hear their adventures and to repay the four meals, fudge and popcorn they stuffed down me. Love, Margean

---

April 18, 1949
To me from P.C. Johnson, Chicago, Illinois

Dear Miss Worst: Referring to your memo of April 16th relative to your proposed itinerary for your return trip to the Eastern territory.

It will be satisfactory for you to complete such work at Sacramento and Reno as Mr. Samuelson may desire and then continue east to Cheyenne and work the Black Hills territory.

In connection with your trip in the Black Hills region, it has been suggested that you check the rest stops between Casper, Wyoming, and Cheyenne, after completing your check in and about Rapid City, Billings, etc. Rumors have been received to the effect that, at some of the rest stops between Casper and Cheyenne, the slot machines in operation at these stops are owned by some of the bus operators. Endeavor to secure any information you can on this matter while in that Region

After your return to Cheyenne, it is suggested that you do not contact either Mr. Neil or Mr. Hensel, but continue east from Cheyenne into Omaha, thence down to Mr. Morrow's territory, and when completing that assignment, work your way back into Chicago.

Please wire me your understanding of the above instructions, so I will be certain that you have received this letter. Yours truly, P.C. Johnson

---

April 21, 1949
From Sacramento Hotel, Sacramento, California

Dear Ones: Had a letter from the office when I got here. When I get into the Black Hills, Pete wants me to find out which of our drivers owns a bunch of slot machines and services them on his runs. I already know, but shall get credit for some original "detecting" work, and maybe find out more.

On the 18th I had a lovely trip from Los Angeles to San Francisco through Taff, Coalinga, Hollister, San Jose—a longitudinal ride through the mountains with hours of beautiful, twisting, hilly trails. Down in the valley farmers were using excavating equipment to level off for irrigation —unique farming.

Mr. Samuelson has lots of work here and I'm scribbling this while waiting for him to call—he's a busy man in the midst of contract negotiations. Do you remember my telling you about the driver that deadheaded four trips with me last winter in Reno? Sammy was telling me how flabbergasted he was when he found I was on all those trips—"I didn't see him."

Was it in the paper about an 83-car train of Santa Fe's derailing near the peak of Cajon pass on April 18th? I saw the smoking wreckage.

My black and blue marks are almost gone but I'm still a little stiff when I get up. Am so thankful I didn't break my back or legs! Love, Margean

————

April 25, 1949
From Hotel Oaks, Chico, California

Dear Ones: I presume you've been tearing your hair because the mailbox has been empty. As usual, busy and nursing a summer cold. Sammy has had me racing back and forth between local and road operations and the way it looks I have a few more days of the same. And such horrible adventures!

For instance: Friday I was to take the 10:00 a.m. bus out of Sacramento and return on the 3:00 out of San Francisco. We had a deadhead who turned out to be the driver of the 3:00 so I couldn't take it. The 5:00 bus was driven by the fellow I came up with, so I had to wait until 7:55 before I finally got out of San Francisco! Expecting to be back early, I had only sunglasses with me so had to ride back blind! Worst of all, expecting to return before the air cooled, I didn't have a coat so I rushed at the last minute to buy a stole. It's a nice investment—black wool jersey with red tassel fringe—making me look like a grandma? Why do such horrible mix-ups happen to me?

And then yesterday I took a roundtrip to Chico during which a curious incident happened. A man boarded the bus at 9:45 and rode into Chico, and then rode all the way back into Sacramento on my return trip—sounds suspiciously like a Markel man or a Swanwick inspector. Worse, the driver with whom I rode into San Francisco a couple of days ago, deadheaded from Yuba City into Sacramento on this trip. I almost got ulcers wondering whether he'd connect my face with that trip. He didn't.

This morning I'm supposed to have breakfast with Mr. Samuelson and figure out more work. When I finally leave for the east, my itinerary calls for seventeen days. It will probably take longer by the time I scout around for information on the "Slot Machine King."

Sylvia Glatz's little note contained a subtle hint about working for Mr. Burleigh again, also that Allen has gone back to inspecting for the outfit handling Great Lakes. You just can't seem to get it out of your blood.

I'll need money when I get to Cheyenne. Ye Gods, this trip is eating money! Fares through yesterday, have been $195. I figure I'll have over $1,136 waiting in Chicago. <u>If I could bank all that, I think I'd retire</u>. Love, Margean

---

April 30, 1949
From Plains Hotel, Cheyenne, Wyoming

Dear Ones: After some long nights, I again have time to write. Have had laryngitis for four days. Three of them I couldn't even whisper and when I picked up the money order, I had to write out the answers to her questions. Thank goodness it doesn't hurt and is an indication that my cold is about over.

All I've seen of <u>THE</u> winter here has been some dirty snow in gulches.

Am anxious to start tonight. It's been over a year since I've been to Billings and seen Thermopolis' Wind River Canyon. For the latter, I've scheduled a day trip—who said this wasn't a vacation. Also hope I can pick up information about the "Slot Machine King."

Must now take a nap to be real chipper when I leave at 10:00 p.m. for that herd of buffalo. Love, Margean

---

May 1, 1949
From Franklin Hotel, Deadwood, South Dakota

Dear Ones: What a thrilling ride last night. We got into the Wind Cave and Custer National Parks about 4:30 a.m. Light at 4:00, we saw countless deer and antelope, all three herds of buffalo, a herd of elk and several mountain sheep. All the deer and elk were without antlers. It was the first time I'd seen these buffalo in daylight: what awfully lean, hairy creatures with cute baby calves.

Lots of snow here in the Black Hills—not deep, but all over. Tomorrow when I hit the peaks there may be more there. Here in Deadwood, the eaves are dripping in the warm-feeling 55.

Deadwood is an old, old town that's one long street between high walls, down in a gorge. A poisonous creek runs through the center, a swift, black, sludgy-looking stream that contains cyanide waste from the plant above here. Food had to be dropped in during this past winter.

We're just four miles from Lead, where the world's largest gold mine is. Have been by it several times in this same narrow gorge. Houses are built on several levels and seem to be zipped to the canyon sides. Love, Margean

May 2, 1949
From Franklin Hotel, Deadwood, South Dakota

Dear Ones: What a hectic day! Last night sometime the pipes of my lavatory broke and by this morning water had run down three stories and spoiled two ceilings. They discovered it, hurriedly checked, and woke me by pounding on the door and wanting to know whether I'd left a faucet on.

Me, sleeping the sleep of the dead after staying awake all night, finally roused to investigate. The half-inch of water on my bathroom floor woke me in a hurry. I yelled back that no faucets were on and that I'd let them in as soon as I dressed. I put on my bra, slip, and dress and, with my hair in pin curls, I let them in.

"Jesus," said the manager when he saw the floor. While they conferred and mopped, I got my hair combed. When they went down to get some tools, I got my girdle and sox on. When they went down to shut off the water, I got my lipstick on. So, all in all, I dressed in shifts while men were running through my room like mad. Love, Margean

May 4, 1949
From Billings, Montana

Dear Ones: Had a long, rough ride from Deadwood here through lots of road construction. Icebox Canyon in the Black Hills was all torn up. Today I start my long and devious way home. I hope I remember what home looks like.

Have been in very bad mood, at least the boys will think so when they get the results—lots of sloppy operation and very little supervision. Love, Margean

---

Report: Slot—machines, Cheyenne Area

I received the driver's name from Mr. Samuelson who had been told by a visiting driver about the "Slot—Machine King." On 5-5-49, I rode with said driver from Casper to Cheyenne. There were no slot machines visible in either the Douglas hotel station or the Wheatland drugstore station where we had rest stops: nor were there any undue activities by the driver at these stops.

The only slot machine in operation in our stations was seen in the garage station at Shoshoni, Wyoming, north of Casper. On 5-4-49, run 106, which I was riding, made an unscheduled rest stop at this station. Several passengers got out for cokes and the driver jokingly suggested that we try our luck on the quarter machine. Comments were made by male passengers relative to this being a lucrative stop for someone. The driver made no statement relative to the ownership of this particular machine but he did say that it brought in $580 a month of which the house got half.

May 7, 1949
From Hotel Cornhusker, Lincoln, Nebraska

Dear Ones: Have had nothing but snow and rain since leaving Billings. A horrible amount of wet, sticky snow that stuck to windshields and broke windshield wipers and tied up three hundred cars between Rawlins and Wamsutter, Wyoming, as you probably read. When I left Denver they were advising all travelers to check their wipers before leaving.

Can hardly wait to get home and see the grandchild. Also recuperate. I'm tired of traveling and bet I covered over 25,000 miles since leaving in March.

Tracked down one suspicious, questionable slot machine in Shoshoni, Wyoming. Thank goodness I ran across something—another time I haven't failed them. Love, Margean

———

May 19, 1949
From Dixie Hotel, New York, New York

Dear Ones: When I got into town last night at midnight I went in search of a Western Union office—never again, too many bums and drunks. I got scared and went back to the hotel. Today the bums and characters were out in force on 42nd Street where the second-rate movie houses are. Spent time looking at Times Square and Broadway. Never saw so many well-dressed women in my life.

On this trip I'm supposed to make a general report on the Express Service.

Bought Gene Fowler's "Beau James," the story of Jimmy Walker and his times. Wonderful. Shall ship it home when finished. Love, Margean

———

May 21, 1949
From Hotel York, St. Louis, Missouri

Dear Ones: Have covered lots of territory since my last letter, mostly at night.

Last night we had an accident. We were parked in front of a restaurant where the driver, a deadhead and the steward were loitering. A taxi parked on a service station exit next to the diner and its driver went in. The cab rolled into the right front of the bus, smashing its headlight and fog-light. It happened like a movie—just before, I said to my seat companion, "I don't believe he set the brakes in that cab," and then it started rolling.

I slept 13½ hours last night recuperating from my New York-St. Louis trip. I feel very tired tonight and will probably chase the clock around again. Had just hours of report writing to do, three extra ones on account of that accident.

Everything I saw during daylight looked so green—corn's up about three inches. Love, Margean

Report on American Buslines Express Service

Covered by this report are one round trip from Chicago to New York and one round trip from Pittsburgh to St. Louis on our Express runs. It is supplemented by individual driver reports 130A through 143A, and by a trip report of times involved.

Stewards and Steward Service: No steward was carried from Chicago to Pittsburgh and, because of this, two 'refreshment stops' were made. Stewards were carried on all other runs. Their activities were (1) handling hand luggage, assisting passengers to their assigned seats, distributing pillows and assisting the driver with checked luggage: (2) keeping lavatory and coach clean: (3) selling snack supplies. Those stewards with whom I rode performed these duties efficiently, although without their caps.

Their usefulness to the driver in loading was particularly evident. There was an excellent spirit of cooperation among the drivers and stewards with whom I rode, although this may not prevail with all drivers. Tips were usually tendered to the steward by alighting passengers.

The lavatories were cleaned at frequent intervals en route: the coach was swept at meal stops. There was no passenger abuse of lavatory facilities. However, passengers still neglect to turn the knob locking the door and lighting the "occupied" sign, even when expressly asked to do so at the beginning of a run. A painted or stenciled sign relative to the necessity of turning this knob is needed within the lavatory. No soap was carried. The light fixture or shade was missing in most of the lavatories baring the bulbs and wiring. For hygienic reasons soap must be supplied. The light fixtures are a hazard and must be fixed!

Snack supplies consisted of sandwiches, 25-30 cents, candy, 10 cents, and soft drinks, 10 cents. Stewards also carried fruit, milk and coffee. Coffee was not popular: in hot-to-handle paper cups from which it was difficult to drink on the moving coach, it was a hazard. Milk sold on one coach proved highly popular. Wax-paper wrapped sandwiches were usually purchased in small quantities en route and were, consequently, fresh.

It was noticed that the white jackets worn by the stewards, while clean when starting, became badly soiled before completing a trip. Most did not wear their caps.

Runs: Delays were caused at run origins (New York, Pittsburgh and St. Louis) by the listing of the driver's board, overseeing the proper seat selection, loading luggage, issuing reserved seat tickets (passengers were prone to forget that an additional ticket was required) and distributing pillows. Delays en route were caused by changing drivers, loading passengers at intermediate points, loitering (see attached trip report and drivers' individual reports) and road construction.

Seat mix-ups still occur where two stations sell the same seat. In one instance, both Chicago and St. Louis sold the same space on the New York-bound bus and the two passengers involved were at dagger's point as to who would get the seat. Another annoying point is the selling statement by agents that passengers will not have to change buses en route from or to the East when, as a matter of fact, passengers to and from St. Louis must change at Pittsburgh. Some passengers create quite a disturbance when told they must change.

At East St. Louis on 5-22-49, the agent was complaining to the driver that the east-bound Express of the previous night could not carry his passengers and he was forced by irate would-be passengers to refund several tickets. From his comments and attitude I gathered that this was a frequent occurrence.

Run D-2, due in St. Louis from the west at 6:15 p.m. and due out as the Express at 6:45, has a meal stop scheduled at St. Louis. To pull out on schedule, an Express run must begin loading at least fifteen minutes before scheduled out: passengers are unable to check their tickets, buy their reserved seat fares, board the Express and eat their evening meal also. This lack of time for a meal is an annoying item with through passengers. Schedule adjustment is needed.

—---—

May 25, 1949
From Hotel Vendome, Evansville, Indiana

Dear Ones: After half a week of hard and steady riding, I am about to settle down in a rut for ten days, a comfortable rut of ham sandwiches and cafeteria food. Have affection for Evansville after all these years.

Passed through the tornado devastated town of Shellburn, Illinois, (about Galesburg's size, or smaller) where twelve were killed and fifty—three hospitalized. It was horrible: trees stripped or down, poles and wires down, homes and buildings down and the gym section of the brick school collapsed. Repair and cleanup crews were working in the rubble. One car with four people in it was blown through a house (saw the terribly battered, twisted car and demolished house); the four were killed. Thirty yards away, a home with a picture window stood untouched. Every vehicle going through is stopped for contributions. It looked as though a bomb had struck. Love, Margean

June 3, 1949
From Hotel Vendome, Evansville, Indiana

Dear Ones: I've been melting for the last three days. It's been over 90 and none of my clothes are cool. Because it's so hot, I've difficulty working up enough ambition to ride buses. I start very early, skip the hottest part of the day and then work the late afternoon and early evening. In between, I rest in my room with the fan on full blast and a pitcher of ice water handy. At night it doesn't get much cooler. Love, Margean

———

Lying there in that sweltering heat, I thought about the past three years and the 138,000+ miles I had traveled. I thought about all my friends, now married with homes while I lived out of a suitcase. I thought about the future of my company and rumors of its impending bankruptcy. I thought about my future in what was a male-only business. I came to a decision. I didn't want to be talked out of it.

I went home, telephoned Chicago, and resigned. I had grown up and was ready to live.

———

Afterword

Trying to discover what happened to people and companies after fifty-four years was fun.

Of the original 1946 Great Lakes Greyhound inspectors, I was friends with Thurston and Edith Allen all of their lives. For a couple of years they remained with the independent company that inspected for Great Lakes Greyhound after 1947, but then they made a drastic move. They bought a food concession trailer and hit the carnival and fair circuit. With two German shepherds and a good firearm they lived this life for thirty-five years before retiring to Florida. Each year when they came to southwest Michigan we would get together, relive our bus days, and hear the adventures and operations of the world of Carnies.

John Burton Tigrett was an easy trace. On line, an obituary gave me his life history and the fact that he'd written an autobiography. This book, "Fair & Square: A Lifetime Among Friends", was a revelation. When he returned from World War II in 1945, three Chicago financiers (formerly associated with Greyhound) had purchased American Buslines and made a four-year agreement with Mr. Tigrett for him to acquire local bus companies to enlarge this into a national bus line with intrastate rights. He spent a lot of time before state transportation commissions securing or being rebuffed in his attempts and was assisted for a time by fledgling lawyer, Adlai Stevenson. He also told of spending $150,000 for inspection services (which I didn't hear about in my two years with American Busline/ Burlington Trailways and, perhaps, occurred before Mr. Burleigh and I were on-board). He was a man of entrepreneurial spirit owning the patents for the "drinking duck" also known as "Dippy Bird." He sold 28 million of these, making millions of dollars. I can remember this perpetual bobbing bird on his desk before he went public with it. When his four-year contract with American Buslines/Burlington Trailways ended in 1949, changes occurred rapidly and I left. In later years he assisted Armand Hammer, Paul Getty and others in business ventures. According to his book, he knew everybody of note both here and in Europe.

Manferd Burleigh rated a photograph and long entry in the "National Cyclopedia of American Biography." He was involved with interstate buses from 1927 and presided at the birth of Great Lakes Greyhound in 1937. In 1940 he was one of the authors of "Modern Bus Terminals and Post

Houses" which shaped bus facilities in the whole country – this book now fetches $300 on the rare book market. In 1950, shortly after I left, he started divesting his interstate bus interests and left to focus on city lines. By his 1964 death, he controlled city lines of Flint, Grand Rapids and Muskegon, Michigan; Evansville, Indiana; Charlotte, Raleigh and Winston-Salem, North Carolina; Greenville, South Carolina; and Jacksonville, Florida. Truly, he was a major mover in all aspects of the bus industry.

Me? I came home to find my friends and relatives married and raising families. I worked with handicapped veterans and in VA Hospital social work before friends saw to it that I met an energetic, ambitious young man (an excellent driver) who became an Engineer. We married, had two children and, when our youngest was eight, I went back to Western Michigan University. Securing a school librarian degree, I worked for the Kalamazoo Public Schools for twelve years. That was followed by eighteen years at the Kalamazoo Public Library as a Reference Librarian and Community Information Librarian. I still work there as a substitute. Edward, my husband of 57 years, and I travel extensively and love the back roads. We always drive. We drive a stick shift.

What did I learn in my three years of growing up on the road from ages eighteen to twenty-one?

1. To always be on time, preferably early

2. To always have something to read with me

3. To know that it will always rain—I have about ten umbrellas

4. To always wear black—it doesn't show the dirt and scarves are lovely

5. To always have my clothes cleaned and pressed, ready to go

6. To pack a suitcase in a half hour for six weeks out

7. To talk to people—everyone has a story

8. To take a chance with people—John Prater who hired me at eighteen was before his time

9. The most important thing I learned in my almost 100% male world of those three years, was to have a passion for my work and the world within which it operates. Bus men had a passion for their work and loved a listening ear that knew what they were talking about. No matter what level—driver to administrator—they endlessly discussed the nitty-gritty of their work, their frustration points, their buses, other companies, passengers, and—especially—gossip.

Fifty-six years later, those bus men that I contacted relative to this book were incredibly helpful, supportive and mentoring...even if I had been that hated creature, a Company Inspector, a Company Checker, a Company RAT.

270

Bibliography

Adams, John W. *A Million Miles or More*. Xlibris, 200l. Experiences from 1952 through 1985 as a driver and supervisor in the bus industry Much on the constant changes in ownership and equipment, levels of management, ridership, plus poignant tales from the road.

Beard, Robert J. *Square Wheels on the Interstate: The Hits and Misses of an Over-the-Road Bus Driver*. 2002. Reminiscences of driving from the '60s through the '90s. Great information on training, life while waiting on the "extra board", changing character of the work and ridership. And, of course, stories from the road.

Byrd, Russell A. *Russ's Bus: Adventures of an American Bus Driver*. New Jersey: Motor Bus Society, 1987. Reprint of the 1945 original. Byrd started in 1927 when there were sleeper buses, when roads were still unpaved, when there were no weather reports, before Interstates, motels, and automatic shift. He retired in 1982!

Lehrer, Jim. *A Bus of My Own*. New York: G.P. Putnam, 1992. A memoir with much on the family struggle to make a success of a mom-and-pop interurban bus line. Lehrer eventually became a bus memorabilia collector and owner of his own bus. One gains an appreciation for the passion bus people have for their profession.

Lehrer, Jim. *We were Dreamers*. Scribner, 1975. A 1945 look at the Lehrer family obsessed with owning and operating a mom-and-pop interurban bus company in rural Kansas. Conveys the picture of the bus industry in a state of flux, mergers and buy-outs where money meant success.

Lehrer, Jim. *White Widow*. Random House, 1999. A novel of bus driving in the '50s. The camaraderie, temptations and details of a bus life are there.

Simon, Rachel. *Riding the Bus With my Sister*. Houghton Mifflin, 2002 This saga of Simon's mentally impaired sister relates the community that develops between city riders and city drivers.

Suttle, Howard. B*ehind the Wheel on Route 66*. Data Plus! 1993. 90 rides from 28 years cover the people, the weather, the equipment, and the roads—all illustrated by the author.

References

Crandall, Burton B. *The Growth of the Intercity Bus Industry*. Syracuse: Syracuse University, 1954.

Jackson, Carlton. Hounds of the Road: *A History of the Greyhound Bus Company*. Bowling Green, OH: Bowling Green University Popular Press, 1984.

Meier, Albert E. and John P. Hoschek. *Over the Road. A History of Intercity Bus Transportation in the United States*. Upper Montclair, NJ: Motor Bus Society, 1975.

Schisgall, Oscar. *The Greyhound Story. From Hibbing to Everywhere*. Chicago: J.C. Ferguson, 1985.

Taff, Charles A. *Commercial Motor Transportation*. Homewood, IL: Richard D. Irving Inc., 1951; 7th edition, Centreville, MD: Cornell Maritime Press, 1986.

Thompson, Gregory L. *The Passenger Train in the Motor Age*. California's Rail and Bus Industries, 1910-1941. Columbus: Ohio State University Press, 1993.

Walsh, Margaret. Making Connections. *The Long-Distance Bus Industry in the USA* . Aldershot, UK: Ashgate Publishing,

About the Author

Margean Gladysz still works as a substitute Librarian in the History Room of the Kalamazoo Public Library. She lives in a retirement community and still writes many, many letters and e-mails, the latter usually saved to paper, reflecting her concern that history is being lost to the Internet. The unedited letters of this book have been requested by the Labor and Urban Affairs Archives of the Walter P. Reuther Library at Wayne State University.